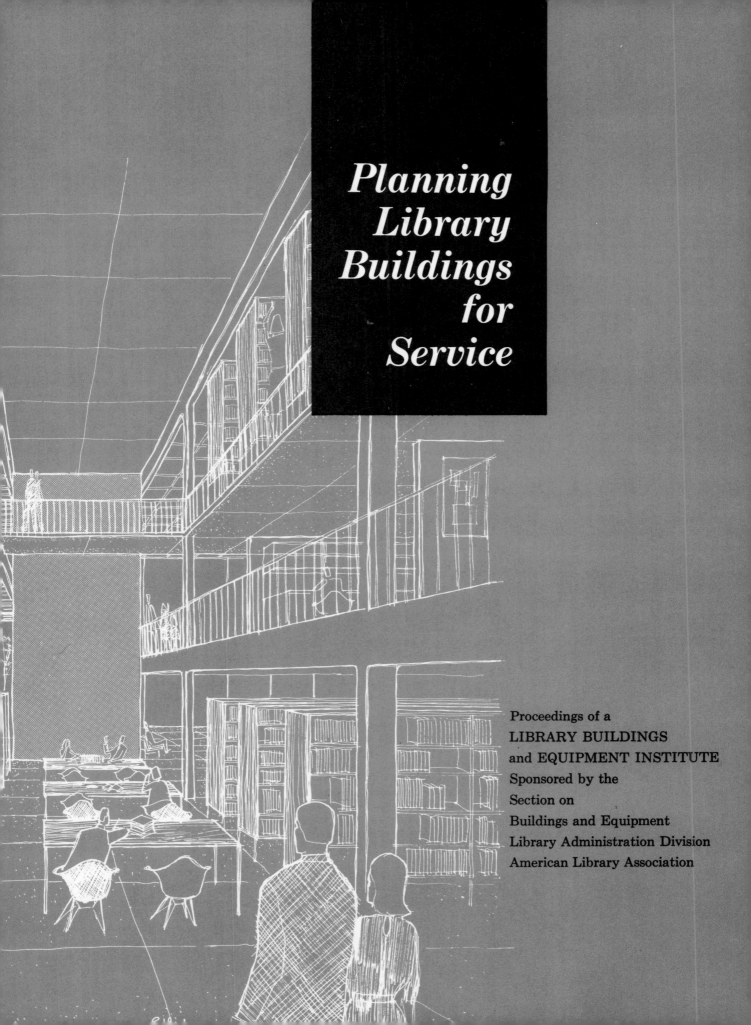

Planning Library Buildings for Service

Proceedings of a
LIBRARY BUILDINGS
and EQUIPMENT INSTITUTE
Sponsored by the
Section on
Buildings and Equipment
Library Administration Division
American Library Association

Planning Library Buildings for Service

Planning Library Buildings for Service

Proceedings of a

LIBRARY BUILDINGS

and EQUIPMENT INSTITUTE

Sponsored by the Section on Buildings and Equipment

Library Administration Division

American Library Association

July 6-8, 1961

Kent State University

Kent, Ohio

Edited by HAROLD L. ROTH

American Library Association

Chicago 1964

Foreword

The second major Institute organized and operated by the Section on Buildings and Equipment of the American Library Association Library Administration Division, held July 6-8, 1961, at Kent State University, Kent, Ohio, emphasized the service aspects of planning library buildings. The text of these Proceedings is made up of a number of general papers followed by the presentations of specific plans of college and university, public, and school libraries. The sequence of papers in the present volume differs from the order in which they were presented at the Institute in the interest of better continuity.

The Institute was attended by more than 400 librarians, architects, consultants, trustees, and other interested participants — the largest group ever assembled for the purpose of gaining information on the planning of library buildings.

General sessions were again devoted to areas of common interest to anyone contemplating a library building program. They included general papers and panel discussions, and the presentation of specific solutions — usually in a preliminary stage — to library building problems of college, university, public, and school libraries. Opportunity was afforded all participants for free time to discuss individual problems and plans between sessions.

Committees that helped to plan the program and conduct meetings included: Architecture Committee for Public Libraries, Robert H. Rohlf, Chairman; Buildings Committee for College and University Libraries, John B. Nicholson, Jr., Chairman; Equipment Committee, William S. Geller, Chairman; Planning School Library Quarters Committee, Mildred S. Nickel, Chairman. Thelma Reid, Vice-Chairman of the Section, and Ralph T. Esterquest, Secretary-Treasurer, also served as members of the Planning Group.

The success of any Institute depends a great deal on the facilities and services of the host institution. The housing arrangements provided by Kent State University through the efforts of John B. Nicholson, Jr., Librarian, were superb. Mr. Nicholson, who served as local arrangements chairman, was ably assisted in his task by Mary C. Amner, Dorothy M. Green, Helen P. Kaltenborn, and Dean H. Keller, all of his staff.

Much credit must be given to Alphonse F. Trezza, Executive Secretary, Library Administration Division, for his cooperation in the handling of all fiscal matters and for making the excellent registration arrangements. Mrs. Marlene Traudt, a member of Mr. Trezza's staff, must also be credited with her share in arranging for the collection of publications, pictures, and other building materials on display at the Institute.

> *HAROLD L. ROTH, Chairman*
> *Section on Buildings and Equipment*
> *Library Administration Division*

American Library Association

Library Administration Division
Section on Buildings and Equipment

    CHAIRMAN
        Harold L. Roth
        Director, Public Library
        East Orange, New Jersey
    VICE-CHAIRMAN AND CHAIRMAN ELECT
        Thelma Reid
        Chief Librarian, City Schools Library
        San Diego, California
    SECRETARY-TREASURER
        Ralph T. Esterquest
        Librarian, Harvard Medical Library
        Boston, Massachusetts

Committees

    ARCHITECTURE COMMITTEE FOR PUBLIC LIBRARIES
        Robert H. Rohlf, Chairman
        Director, Dakota-Scott Regional Library
        West St. Paul, Minnesota
    BUILDINGS COMMITTEE FOR COLLEGE AND UNIVERSITY LIBRARIES
        John B. Nicholson, Jr., Chairman
        Librarian, Kent State University Library
        Kent, Ohio
    BUILDINGS COMMITTEE FOR HOSPITAL AND INSTITUTION LIBRARIES
        Mrs. Juanita Z. Wiles, Chairman
        Librarian, Bronson Methodist Hospital
        Kalamazoo, Michigan
    EQUIPMENT COMMITTEE
        William S. Geller, Chairman
        Assistant Librarian, Los Angeles County Public Library
        Los Angeles, California
    PLANNING SCHOOL LIBRARY QUARTERS COMMITTEE
        Mildred S. Nickel, Chairman
        Director, School Libraries
        Lansing, Michigan

Committee on Local Arrangements

    John B. Nicholson, Jr., Chairman
        Librarian, Kent State University
    Mary C. Amner
        Associate Librarian, Kent State University Library
    Dorothy M. Green
        Associate Librarian, Kent State University Library
    Helen P. Kaltenborn
        Order Librarian, Kent State University Library
    Dean H. Keller
        Assistant Humanities Librarian, Kent State University Library

Contents

Presentation of Plans

General Papers and Panel Discussions

Elements in Planning a Library Building Program

RALPH E. ELLSWORTH
Director of Libraries
University of Colorado
Boulder, Colorado

One would suppose it to be easy to isolate, describe, and define the basic elements in library building planning, but I find it impossible to do this so long as one thinks of library buildings as of a single type. On the other hand, as soon as one realizes the futility of trying to think about the planning of all types of libraries at once, the problem becomes capable of solution.

Let us remember the fundamental fact that a library is not simply a library, but a particular kind of a library, of a specific size and character, serving a specific and unique community, in a specific climate and geographical setting. Libraries, like people, do have elements in common, but their differences are more significant than their similarities. Of course, with respect to furniture, equipment, color, and decorations, there are factors common to all types of libraries, but these things do not make a library building.

Let there be no mistake about this: a library building is a serious work of art, and as a work of art, it is unique and precious and not to be thought of in the collective sense. Architects know this. We librarians once did, but we have forgotten and we need to be brought back to this truth.

In my discussion of the elements of planning, I shall confine myself to the one kind of library of which my ignorance is the least noticeable—academic libraries in higher education. To be sure, even this category covers a wide variety of libraries: junior college and senior liberal arts college libraries, both within and outside a university; technical libraries; and various kinds of university libraries. Among these I shall concentrate on university and liberal arts college libraries.

What, then, are the main elements in planning such libraries?

The first element is knowledge of the college or university for which the planning is being done. To the layman, one liberal arts college is much like another and one university like all the others, but this is not so.

How do you get to know an institution? First, by reading everything the institution has written about itself, particularly the alumni magazines. Second, by talking to the chief administrative officers and as many members of the faculty as one can. Third, by visiting with students in the coffee shop of the student union. I might even suggest seeking out a wise old Catholic priest who has listened to countless confessions from college students. Fourth, I would test the academic atmosphere of the college by learning its rank in the various national testing services as well as the percentage of its students that go on to graduate work. I would look for special traditions and curricula that emphasize excellence and individual study activities. Then I would examine the curricula. Fifth, I would try to find out, if possible, how and in what direction the institution may be moving, even though it may not be conscious of these trends itself.

The sixth step in getting to know an institution is to interview the campus planning officer or committee to learn what they have in mind for the physical evolution of the campus and for its future growth patterns. Seventh, I would look up some of the senior or retired members of the faculty in the hope that they could tell me how the fundamental traditions of the college are changing. Eighth, I would meet with the librarians and the library planning committee to find out what they know about the college's or university's needs and character.

The second element is architecture. During the past twenty years, I have worked in varying degrees of intimacy with more than fifty different architectural firms. Naturally, architects differ in their tastes, working habits, and degrees of sensitivity and ability, but I will say that their level of ability is uniformly higher than that in the library or teaching professions. Architects are all well trained and many are well educated. Some can produce buildings of great beauty; others can produce buildings that may not be outstandingly beautiful, but that do serve their purpose well.

Architects have two other qualities in common: first, they expect the client to give them a written program stating exactly what is wanted; second, very few follow the old stereotyped notion that a building is planned from the outside in. Most architects have taken it for granted that their job is to design a building in which certain activities are to be carried on and that the exterior shape and design will be an expression of those activities. In my experience, only two architects started with an exterior design and then expected the librarian to make a library of the structure if he could.

Of course, the recent trend toward total planning of the campus may at times result in dogmas and Procrustean beds based on unproved assumptions. If, for example, the campus planning architects have proposed a formal pattern of campus buildings, along classical lines, it may turn out that, to fit the pattern, the library style would be wrong so far as its shape and fenestration are concerned. Again, it has happened that a library was located at a certain place to meet the needs of an over-all campus design pattern without regard to the fact that the particular site would require multiple entrances. However, these situations are rare and generally a violation of the principles of good campus planning. The best architects are concerned with deeper and more subtle harmonies among buildings than with mere surface similarities.

Architects do differ in their ability to get the most out of a building dollar, but one should be wary of quick generalizations. You may be getting exactly what you are paying for, but on the other hand, you may not, even if you know what you're getting. The economies of design and construction cannot be measured by the square-foot costs announced in the library journals when the building is new. Perhaps, as with automobiles, it isn't the miles per gallon you get, but the size of your garage bills that determines true economy. Moreover, at the end of the normal twenty-five-year life span of an academic library building, the question of how useful the building will be for other functions may be worth

considering. Nevertheless, when all things have been considered, it still remains true that architects differ in their ability to stretch the dollar.

If I were to be critical of architects—and I am under no mandate to be critical—it would be for their habit of following fashions and fads and for confusing their ability, in a technical sense, to *do* certain things with the *appropriateness* of doing them. I refer to such things as glass walls. Personally, I am particularly conscious of glass walls because in Colorado the sun shines brightly and the winds sometimes blow hard from the west. Most Colorado people live on the eastern slopes, which means that the best views of the mountains are on the western side of our buildings. So there is, you see, a conflict. If, for example, you have seen the Air Force Academy Library at Colorado Springs, you will recall the worst possible example of the use of glass walls. Recently, I visited a campus where the faculty had pasted wrapping paper and aluminum foil sheets on their windows so they could avoid being parboiled and blinded.

So what do architects do? They cover up their glass walls with screens of one kind or another. I believe it was Charles Stone who started this idea. By analogy, I have read that in the Middle Ages people either didn't want to or couldn't take baths and so they doused themselves with perfume.

In a recent discussion, a friend in the East defended his east wall, in spite of glare and heat, on the grounds that it opened up the one remaining nice view on the campus. I argued that a landscape view is like that of a woman. A full view of a nude female has much less sex appeal than a view in which she is artfully revealed and concealed.

The third element is the librarian's level of planning knowledge. Frankly, in planning, I am less happy about librarians than I am about architects. It is not that we are so stupid or badly educated and trained, but that we happen to be practicing librarianship at a time when we must make our decisions on the basis of information we don't have and can't get.

Those of us who are experienced in library building planning know that a great deal of knowledge and experience is required. Yet most librarians will probably never have to *repeat* the experience of planning a library building. To pose a rhetorical question, is it wise for the librarian to devote a couple of years to learning something he may never use again? Wouldn't it be better for us to spend this time on other things, such as reading books or learning about computers?

What really worries me about librarians as an element in planning is our inability to write programs that tell the architect in words and figures everything he needs to know about the building. It is really quite difficult for anyone to know an institution fully, as was made clear in the discussion on page 9. It takes time and effort. One of the reasons is simply that no one, literally no one, can guess correctly about future developments. For example, in the 1930's, no one could predict how rapidly the birth rate would rise; no one realized that world events would cause us to focus attention on the Near East, the Far East, and Africa.

What are the future implications of our current excitement about the quality of education? Will we send two thirds of our students home? What will television teaching do to study habits? Will universities stop teaching introductory remedial courses in all basic subjects? What is happening to professional schools? And so on. No one knows the answers to these and many other questions, and yet they should be anticipated in the planning program for the library building.

Of course, although we don't like to admit it, we really don't know much about the basic problem of book storage. One has only to read the study, *Patterns in the Use of Books in Large Research Libraries*,[1] by Herman H. Fussler and Julian L. Simon, to know that if we had the time and money to make the preliminary studies, it would be possible to send many of our books to dead (and therefore cheaper) storage without causing too much annoyance to scholars. But then one could argue that such disposition would destroy the concept of the research library.

A still more critical question is that of knowing how to evaluate the influence of miniaturization and electronic transmission systems. In a news story in the March 27, 1961, issue of the *New York Times*, Professor John G. Kemeny, of the mathematics department of Dartmouth, proposed the creation of a huge national research library that scholars would consult by an automatic long-distance dial system. Professor Kemeny said that such a library could be assembled in twenty years at a cost of less than a billion dollars. The material would be stored on tapes on which one ordinary book page would occupy about one square millimeter. Thus, more than 265 pages could be stored on a square inch of tape. Instead of using the traditional card catalog, a scholar would find the volume or article he sought by using a device equivalent to a telephone dial system. Library users would not borrow books in the present-day sense, but would receive copies of the appropriate taped information through the cable system to the display and recording equipment at their own institutions.

Who is to say that this cannot or will not be done? And if it did happen, would there not be an effect on the kind of library a large university would plan? However, when we face this question, all we librarians can say is, "Well, it could, and probably will happen, but we don't dare count on it."

The fourth element is the political position of the client. In theory, the client is the codification of the first element, but that is not what I have in mind here. I refer to the desires and idiosyncrasies of the key person with whom you have to deal. In a university, it is usually the president, or someone on the board of trustees, or, in the case of private institutions, it may be the donor. I know of one university in which the donor's wishes were such that the resulting building left much to be desired.

In a paper of this kind, it will be sufficient to say that, whenever you encounter a situation in which the client's wishes run counter to logic and good sense, you do the best you can and that's that.

The fifth element is the budget of the client. If, after the program has been completed and quantified, it turns out that sufficient funds are available, there is no problem. But when the opposite is true, obviously something must be done. It is not the purpose of this paper to prescribe remedies, but typical solutions to this problem might be mentioned: (1) ask an outside expert to review the building plans to see if different solutions can be found; (2) lower the quality of the building, i.e., substitute cheaper materials; (3) reduce the size of the building; (4) postpone some of the costs by reducing the areas to be constructed to the bare necessities; (5) postpone the purchase of some of the equipment and furniture; (6) temporarily house some nonlibrary function in the library and thus transfer some of the costs to another project; and (7) raise more money. The last solution will be the most satisfactory, from the point of view of the architects and the planners, although the client may be expected to feel otherwise.

The sixth element is the geography of the campus, which has a bearing on the question of the proper site. Good over-all campus planning is quite new, although there are examples to be found of good early work. On my own campus, as an instance, Charles Z. Clauder in 1919 developed a complete campus plan with scaled models. The entire University of Chicago campus was deliberately planned. In contrast, some universities—Michigan, Harvard, Iowa, Columbia, and Illinois—appear to have just grown that way.

Today, there are expert firms of campus planners who know how to find the kind of information outlined in the first element of planning and who know how to utilize space so that the proper relationships among buildings will exist; so that future planning needs are foreseen; so that beauty is present; and so that communication and transportation needs are met.

I have had personal experience with several such firms—Sasaki, Walter and Associates; Murphy and Mackey; Mackey; Martin, Stuart and Noble; and Baxter, Hodell and Donelly—and have found them to be very helpful. These firms seem to know where a library should be put, how to orient it in relation to

1. Herman H. Fussler and Julian L. Simon, *Patterns in the Use of Books in Large Research Libraries* (preliminary ed., privately distributed for review and criticism; Chicago: Univ. of Chicago Library, 1961).

other buildings, and how to allocate space for future growth. By extension, I would guess that all well-trained architects know quite a lot about this subject.

The essential point is that each campus problem is unique; you cannot explore around the country and simply adopt other people's ideas and solutions for your own problems. Nor should you be critical of what might seem to be unusual solutions until you fully understand what the real problem was.

For example, the April 15, 1961, issue of the *Cornell University Alumni* carried a series of articles on the new Cornell Library and a photograph which shows a formidable outside stairway leading to the library. Anyone who knows Upper New York weather must shudder when he contemplates the problems this stairway will cause but, nevertheless, I feel sure that it was not placed there without a great deal of thought and that, in the end, it was found to be necessary.

At the same time, you should not be overly impressed by campus planners. They are rather new at the game and they certainly are not infallible. There are times when it is wise to sacrifice a space principle in order to gain an academic value. However, the better planners know this and the better they are, the less rigid and dogmatic they will be in approaching a given problem.

The seventh, and last, element is the program. There has been quite a bit said about programs in recent years. I would point out first that, in the past, many libraries have been built that were full of mistakes; we tend to blame the architects for these errors, and rightly so, but I would suggest that more blame be put on the client than we have in the past. This is because you will find in most cases that the client did not have a clearly expressed statement of his desires and needs to provide for the architect.

For this is what the program is: It is a complete written statement of what the client wants and does not want. It should be written by the client before the architect appears on the scene. The architect should study the program and then, if he thinks there are statements in the program with which he disagrees or that he cannot accept, he should put his views in writing, and these should then be discussed with the client's representatives. The final decisions can then be put in writing and signed by the client and the architect.

No important points should be omitted from the written document and left simply in the form of oral statements. Some clients and some architects may dislike this rule, but experience demonstrates that it pays to be careful. This is particularly true if the architect is a large, diversified firm located at some distance from the client.

One of the major problems of program writing for college and universities today is that the technology of learning is changing so rapidly (and is threatening to change even more radically) that we no longer can feel certain about any aspect of planning.

Those of you who have seen the Trump Report,[2] or who have read the reports of the Educational Facilities Laboratories, Inc., will realize the magnitude of the ideas that are fermenting in elementary and secondary school building planning. To be sure, the schools are at least two decades behind the thinking on educational methods to be found in colleges and universities; but that is to be expected, because schools have been run by trained experts and colleges and universities by educated amateurs. The point is that if the lower schools ever do put into practice some of the new ideas, the graduates of these schools will come to college with learning equipment that will force us to raise our library sights many notches.

Fortunately, many of us have been wrestling with these ideas for years, and we are not afraid of them. We have even gone a long way toward planning libraries that can absorb the new ideas, for, in reality, they are quite simple. They boil down to the themes some of us have been preaching all along: more emphasis on individual study; more emphasis on physical facilities that give the individual learner more privacy; more freedom of access to all learning media; and better ordering of the tools and media of learning. The modular method of planning was developed for these purposes, and after fifteen years of experience we are learning now how to use it.

We have learned in college and university library planning that fixed-function planning is no longer possible. We have not yet learned enough about the right kind of furniture and equipment, nor do we know very much about how to make so-called audio-visual materials properly available for individual use. The audio-visual people tend to think almost exclusively of group use, which means that we must learn more about individual use.

There are other program problems that worry us: for example, the nature and scope of the special facilities for general education. Is the Yale theory better than Harvard's? And if so, why and in what ways? Since few institutions are able to find enough money to build enough buildings to house the 1970 enrollments or enough teachers to teach them, will all the gains made in the direction of individualization be erased? Will teaching by television really make any difference? What will the mushroom growth of the junior college movement do to our senior colleges? These are just a few of the uncertainties.

I have attempted to state and examine briefly the main elements of planning academic libraries, the elements that seem important to me. You may not agree that they are the key factors of concern, but I am certain that a great deal is yet to be learned about all of them.

2. J. L. Trump, *Guide to Better Schools: Focus on Change* (Chicago: Rand McNally, 1960).

Judging Values When Purchasing Wood Library Equipment

RUDOLPH WILLARD
Visiting Professor of Furniture Manufacturing
North Carolina State College
Raleigh, North Carolina

In judging wood library equipment, you must decide on what specific values you want. *Appearance* is a legitimate value to be sought. This is especially true where an addition to a building is to be furnished and you want the appearance of the new furnishings to harmonize with the old.

Appearance entails the following characteristics, each of which is or can be regarded as separate:

Style of design
Species of wood (oak, maple, walnut, and so on)
Color of finish
Depth of body of finish
Smoothness of surface of finish
Degree of sheen of finish (high gloss, dull
    rub, and so on)
Cover materials for upholstery or cushions

Fortunately, of course—because beauty is subjective—these appearance factors can be judged from a sample of new merchandise. There is no simple right and wrong in appearance. What you like is right for you even if wrong for someone else.

Durability is another important value. Durability depends upon the following characteristics: strength, rigidity, resistance to dents and scratches, and surface resistance to wear.

With adequate strength, the furniture will not fall apart or break while in service. Even though a chair or table does not fall apart, it may become wobbly; a shelf may sag too much because of lack of rigidity; or the joints may become loosened. Resistance to dents depends chiefly on how hard the wood is. Maple is harder than mahogany. Resistance to scratches depends primarily on the quality of finish coats, not the color of the finish. Resistance to surface wear depends largely on the finish coats, but it is also affected by shape—a sharp corner on a table top will show wear more quickly than a rounded corner. Unfortunately, the durability characteristics of new furniture cannot be judged simply by looking at samples.

Ease of maintenance may be an important factor. Maintenance includes routine dusting, cleaning, and polishing. It also entails repairs in case of accidents which cause breakage, dents, and scratches.

Ease of maintenance cannot be evaluated by looking at new samples except in minor respects: for example, dark colors generally show dust more than light colors.

Convenience in the arrangement of space is probably important, especially with regard to charging desks, card files, and shelving. Space convenience can be estimated for new furniture, but the question should be treated in considerable detail—a problem in which experience will be especially helpful.

Comfort is very important, especially with respect to the design of chairs. A chair that would be comfortable for reading alone would probably not be comfortable for reading and taking notes at a table. Table height also affects relative comfort. However, the comfort factor can readily be evaluated in new furniture.

There are a number of fallacies which seem to be rather widespread among people who are not acquainted with working in wood:

Fallacy No. 1: *"It is poor quality; it is made out of cheap wood like pine."* While it is true that various kinds of wood have different characteristics, it is also true that a good furniture manufacturer knows how to process any of them so that the resulting furniture produced will have more than the necessary durability. This statement does not apply to relative surface hardness. Poplar is an excellent wood but it is soft and will dent more easily than oak or hard maple. However, poplar furniture, if properly manufactured, will last for generations. Thus, the choice of wood should be governed primarily by reasons of appearance. If you like the appearance of walnut better than birch, then buy it if it is worth the extra cost to you; but don't expect it to be necessarily more durable or of a better general quality. Again, a word of caution about maple: Just because it is maple, it is not necessarily hard. There are true maples that are softer than poplar; the so-called soft maple is harder than some mahogany; true hard maple is very hard.

Fallacy No. 2: *"It is poor quality; it is veneered rather than solid."* Some years ago there might have been some justification for this idea because much veneer was applied with vegetable glue which had poor resistance to moisture. However, during World War II, great advances were made in the manufacture of glues from synthetic resins. These adhesives have high resistance to moisture and strong holding power. With large-volume use such glues are now inexpensive enough so that practically all furniture veneer is applied with them. If properly manufactured, veneered panels are now as durable as solid wood, if not more so. We know how to make veneer construction so that it will stand forty-eight hours' soaking in cold water followed by two hours in boiling water, but who boils furniture? There is apt to be less trouble with shrinkage, swelling, and warpage of veneered panels than with

solid woods. Many matched-grain effects are possible with veneer that are impossible with solid
wood. Thus, if you like the appearance of a matched
veneered table top, do not be concerned about durability simply because the piece is veneer rather
than solid.

Fallacy No. 3: *"I want good quality."* When you
say this, you really have not said anything meaning-
ful. "Quality" is a very complex thing. To get what
you want, it is necessary to break down this complex concept of "quality" along the lines already
discussed under "What specific values do you
want?"

In this connection, there naturally arises the
question of the relationships between price, cost,
and quality. For most durability factors, it is not
so much a question of extra cost to the manufacturer
as it is a question of whether he knows the proper
techniques of construction and processing and
whether he rigidly polices his factory operations
to ensure uniform adherence to the proper techniques. It is know-how and will-to-do, rather than
extra cost, that will achieve satisfactory durability.

Most of the quality factors that do increase costs
to the manufacturer affect *appearance* rather than
durability. Table tops as flat, smooth, and free from
surface defects as plate-glass mirrors do involve a
lot of extra work and hence extra cost. The same is
true, in general, of ultra-smooth surfaces and of
extra-fine workmanship, such as matching mitered
moldings at the corners. High-priced species of
wood cost more than cheaper ones even though they
may be structurally no better. Excessive resistance of a surface finish to heat, alcohol, and so on,
costs considerably more.

Prices quoted by manufacturers do not necessarily reflect their true cost. Sometimes a manufacturer will bid to get the contract; sometimes he
does not want the contract and will bid so as not to
get it, but such procedures are no different in the
supplying of furniture than for other goods.

Not all manufacturers would incur the same cost
in the production of identical items. Some factories
have higher production costs than others. Thus,
while it is natural to assume that a higher-priced
item is of better "quality" than a lower-priced one,
this is not necessarily the case. There is also the
possibility that the higher price covers certain aspects of quality which are not important to the purchaser.

To be on safe ground, you must break down the
general concept of "quality" into its components and
then decide whether each of these is worth what you
will have to pay for it. For this reason, it is best to
write out detailed quality specifications.

Some of the value factors in furniture can be
judged by inspection of a piece before buying, but
these present only minor problems in evaluating
furniture. Examples are:

General appearance
Color
Smoothness of surface
Degree of sheen or polish
Space convenience
Comfort (sitting posture, height, and so on)
Arrangement for shelf adjustment

The major problems in judging furniture arise
out of the things you cannot see, such as:

Suitable construction for durability
        and freedom from trouble
Proper processing
    Drying of lumber
    Application and drying of glue
    Application and drying of finishes
Durability of the film of finish

The American Library Association is actively
endorsing and sponsoring work to develop specifications and simple performance tests so that the manufacturer can tell in advance what service requirements his furniture will have to fulfill. He can then
control his construction and processing to meet
these requirements. The purchaser can also carry
out these performance tests to determine whether
furniture offered to him meets the requirements.
As an alternative, the purchaser could write the
contract so that the supplier would guarantee that
his furniture will pass the tests. Such certification
by the supplier would be helpful in controlling the
unseen aspects of quality in a small-lot purchase in
which the purchaser did not have facilities for making the tests. It is too soon to know for sure, but it
is my opinion that such specifications and tests will
be available for general use within the next few
years.

Tables

The table top is the most important part of a table. Veneered construction is as good as solid and
permits some appearance effects not possible with
solid. Color does not affect durability. It is hoped
that the specifications and tests referred to above
will make it possible to judge how well the finish
will stand up in use. Where durability of surface is
worth the extra cost, plastic laminates make an excellent top surface for a table. They withstand heat,
water or alcohol, and abrasion very well. Formica
is a trade name which may be more familiar to you
than the generic name "plastic laminate." Several
other manufacturers produce materials comparable
to Formica.

Rigidity is generally satisfactory on designs in
which the legs are braced by side aprons. Some
modern designs omit the apron for reasons of appearance or to get more leg room for sitting. In
such cases, the legs can be attached in such a way

as to be rigid and stay rigid in use; but this calls for some special precautions in construction. Splayed legs are more of a problem than vertical legs. One probably cannot judge whether a certain construction is adequate; but if the table is without aprons, the purchaser should have his supplier convince him that the legs will stay rigid in service.

Stretchers between the legs near the floor are generally not necessary for rigidity. They interfere with sitting close to the table, and they show wear quickly because people tend to rest their feet on the stretchers.

Chairs

Chairs constructed like ordinary dining chairs tend to have one prevalent defect, whether they have padded seats like dining chairs or wood seats like library chairs. The rigidity of the chair depends largely on the joint between the side seat rail and the back post. Usually this joint is made with two glued dowels. When a person tilts back in such a chair, an excessive leverage stress is set up which tends to pull the dowels out of the holes, with the result that sooner or later many chairs of this kind become loose and wobbly.

There are two general approaches to a solution of this problem. One is to design the chair so that it is either impossible or at least uncomfortable to tilt back in it. The other is to arrange the construction of this critical joint so that the whole stress is not thrown onto two dowels. The two dowels can be adequate if properly glued, but who can tell whether a given chair was in fact properly glued? Some sort of reinforcement is desirable as a safety factor.

There is a chair construction, frequently used in college snack bars, that negates this difficulty, although the appearance might not be suitable in a library. The construction calls for a round, bent wood stretcher. One end of the stretcher attaches to the back post near the floor, curves up and attaches under the seat about halfway front to back, curves down and attaches to the front post, and continues around to the other back post in the same way. This gives the effect of a triangle: one side is the back post; the second side is the seat; the third side (slightly bent instead of straight) is the stretcher.

The triangle is an inherently rigid structural shape. If, for example, you were to take an ordinary wooden box and remove the top and bottom, you would be left with a four-sided structure consisting of two sides and two ends nailed at the corners. If you sat on it, it would be wobbly. But if a diagonal brace is nailed from one corner to the opposite corner, two trianges are created, and the box becomes rigid instead of wobbly. The same principle is applied in open-back steel shelving, where two diagonal rods with turnbuckles are applied to the back corners forming an X (four triangles). This device

alone converts a wobbly stack of shelves into a rigid stack.

Wood chair seats are more durable than fabric-covered seats, but one point should be watched—when wood absorbs moisture from the air, it swells across the grain. An ordinary chair seat can swell as much as 1/8 inch to 3/16 inch in width. In some chairs the back of the wood seat is confined between the two back posts. When the seat swells, it is likely to force the back posts apart, pulling out the dowels which fasten the back seat rail to the back posts; then the chair becomes wobbly. Wood seats should be applied in such a way that nothing in the chair construction confines the seat widthway across the grain.

Shelving

Either veneered or solid wood can be satisfactory. For adjustable, loose shelves, veneer on a lumber core would stay flatter than solid wood, but warpage need not be a serious problem with solid wood shelves if they are properly made.

Sag of shelves can be checked by loading the shelf and measuring the deflection. If the shelf is veneered on a particle-board core instead of on a lumber core, sag develops slowly, and it might take as much as a month or so to develop the maximum sag. This construction currently is little used for shelves but may come in the future because of cost considerations.

Rigidity of the stack is no special problem if the stacks are to be fastened to the building. But if not, lack of rigidity can be a serious problem. Solid plywood-back shelving, glued and nailed all around, will provide adequate rigidity even though the plywood is very thin. This, of course, gives closed-back shelving.

Discussion

Question: What kind of finish can be used on library tables so surfaces will not be damaged by cigarettes or soft-drink stains?

Answer: Probably the surest course is to have the top faced with a plastic laminate such as Formica. Good photographic reproductions of many wood grains and colors are available as well as surfaces in solid colors, fabric effects, marble, and so on. The plastic laminates have good resistance to cigarette burns, Coca Cola stains, and even alcohol, though I doubt if this is much of a problem in your library.

Plastic laminate applied to wood costs more than solid wood or veneered tops, but offers advantages. In addition to burn and stain resistance, the surface is very hard and smooth. You need not worry about a heavy-handed writer with a hard pencil marring the surface. The surface resists abrasion better than ordinary finish on wood. It may eventually show wear, as can be seen at lunch counters where in time the edge wears enough to destroy the pattern and color of the surface, but in library usage this would take many years. A plastic laminate surface resists dents and scratches better than wood. It is not, however, adapted to going around sharp curves. Tops with plastic laminate faces almost always have straight, sharp-cornered edges. If these sharp edges are objectionable, a molding with easy curves can be applied to the edges of the top. This molding can be metal, plastic (of a kind different from the laminate), or hard wood.

Question: Will a chip-board (particle-board) core hold a wood screw as well as a lumber or veneer core? Which core will do the best job in this respect?

Answer: The holding power for wood screws varies in the following order—best first: veneer core, lumber core, particle-board core. There is a big difference in particle boards with regard to the capability of holding screws. It depends on the method of manufacture of the particle board.

While particle-board holding power is not as good as that of lumber, it is often more than adequate for the job to be done. If it is adequate for the purpose, there is not much point in requiring more, even if it is not the best. That is, if you want to haul a wheelbarrow load of coal, there is no point in using a five-ton truck simply because it is stronger than a man and a wheelbarrow. Incidentally, special threaded screws are available with considerably more holding power than standard wood screws, and the cost is not excessive.

Question: Is there a *real* shortage in certain woods, such as oak, which makes it so difficult to match existing equipment?

Answer: No. Shortages may raise prices on a scarce item, but no wood is so scarce that it cannot be bought.

Question: Is there any *one best* kind of a joint construction for rigidity and durability?·

Answer: No. Parts of different kinds of furniture come together in such a wide variety of ways that no one joint construction is best for all situations.

Question: Are furniture manufacturers using Epoxy glues? Do they work?

Answer: Furniture manufacturers are using very little of the Epoxy glues. The glues have excellent strength but are expensive, and the process of using them is a bit messy and hard to control. For most furniture gluing, there are other resin glues which provide adequate strength and moisture and are easier to use and cheaper. Epoxy glues are relatively new, and it is quite likely that many of them will be developed, improved, and their prices reduced so that they will be more widely used in the future.

Question: Our maintenance men will not repair a broken chair because they say it's cheaper to throw it away and buy a new one. Does this sound like a correct cost analysis?

Answer: No. In the first place, that is an opinion, not an analysis. It might be true if the chair were almost completely wrecked, but this is not likely. Perhaps the men lack the skills or the equipment to do the job. Surely many broken chairs can be repaired more cheaply than buying a new chair.

Question: Should a local cabinetmaker ever be considered in preference to a library furniture manufacturer?

Answer: Yes. You may not decide to give him the business, but you have nothing to lose by considering him. Presumably, the manufacturer would have had more experience in what sort of construction and processing is required in library use, but some local cabinetmakers have excellent skills and experience. Of course, some are not so good. As with auto mechanics, some are good, some bad, some terrible. On an order for a single item for very few items, the local man would be apt to have more advantage than on an order for a large quantity of identical items.

Question: Some manufacturers offer maple, some birch. Please compare characteristics, similarities, and differences, if any.

Answer: Hard maple and birch are very similar. Both are excellent cabinet woods. Theoretically, hard maple is slightly harder; birch is a little less apt to shrink, swell, and warp. But, practically speaking, there is little to recommend one over the other.

Question: What is the best way to clean furniture?

Answer: This depends on what was used for the finishing materials, and nobody but the manufacturer knows what was used. Some cleaners, waxes, and the like are not compatible with certain finish materials, while they are satisfactory or better with others. The best way would be to direct your question to the particular manufacturers who made your furniture.

Question: How can different suppliers bid on the same things—the same specifications, and so on—at very different prices? How should the buyer judge the merits of the bids?

Answer: Different suppliers have different costs. For example, a manufacturer on the West Coast, bidding on hard-maple furniture, would have to pay freight on his lumber all the way from the northeast. If he were bidding the same item in alder, he could get lumber in his immediate vicinity.

Sometimes a difference in bid price is the result of how badly the manufacturer wants that business at that time. Maybe he's desperate for an order to keep operating; perhaps the competitor is swamped with business and really does not want any more right now. Sometimes people make mistakes in their figures, either high or low. Often, the specifications are loosely written and permit wide latitude in interpretation. One man may be proud of quality and interpret high; another may interpret low. The two products may differ considerably in quality, but both may meet the specifications if the latter are presented vaguely.

In the case of a great difference in the bids, it seems to me that it is the responsibility of the higher bidders to convince you why (if at all) they are offering a better value than that represented by the low bid. This, of course, assumes that the low bidder is a responsible company that can be expected to fulfill the terms of the contract.

Question: Please comment on rubbed oil finish.

Answer: I presume you mean the old-fashioned linseed-oil finish. It is an excellent finish but very slow, tedious, and expensive to apply. Very few manufacturers use it these days. Some manufacturers do offer production finishes which simulate the appearance of the old-fashioned oil finish. These are generally thin-bodied variations of lacquer finish. They are satisfactorily durable, reasonably low in cost, and require less routine maintenance than a pure oil finish.

Question: How about impact-resistance treatment for such items as table edges? Is this feasible?

Answer: Yes, if it is important enough to justify the extra cost. Edge moldings of metal or plastic applied to table tops would provide sufficient impact resistance. There is also a densified-wood process which was developed at Little Falls, New York. I believe the producer's name is Lindstrom. This material was used successfully on bases for swivel chairs to resist foot scuffing, and on posts of desks in the kneehole where a chair would scar the posts. I should think that edge moldings could be made from strips of densified wood, have high resistance, and still look like wood.

Question: Can a lightweight chair be as durable as a heavy one?

Answer: Yes. There are only a few spots on a chair that are apt to break or become loose. Proper construction at these places is worth much more for durability than extra total weight. The snack-bar chair I discussed under "Chairs" is an extreme example. It is very *light* in weight. It is flexible, not rigid. It is inexpensive, but it stands up under snack-bar roughhouse conditions.

Question: Is not the integrity of the manufacturer the most important form of certification you can have?

Answer: Yes, with emphasis. But, how can you judge the integrity of the manufacturer? Maybe you have done business with one for a long time and know from experience that his integrity is high. This still does not prove that another manufacturer, unknown to you, has any lower integrity; it only proves you do not know about the second fellow. It is very much like moving to a new town with a family of children. You want a family doctor, and you want a good one. You know it is important to have a good doctor, but there is the problem of determining which of them is best for you.

Wood, Metal, or Plastic Equipment

DONALD E. BEAN
Library Building Consultants, Inc.
Glenview, Illinois

By way of preliminary remarks, I want to talk to you about equipment layout and designing, because these factors have a strong influence on the materials to be used.

First, if you are contemplating a new building, I suggest that you make your equipment layout before the preliminary building sketches are approved. Do not wait until the final plans are completed. You will probably find that several changes will be made in the building plans because of what is revealed by the equipment layout. As time goes on, you will find it increasingly difficult to make these changes, and, after all of the working drawings are finished, impossible to make some of them. This is a point I believe to be very important and one which might seem to be obvious. Yet it is a fact that many errors in building planning are the result of failure to go through the painstaking process of a detailed furniture and equipment layout early in the preliminary planning of the building.

Now, admittedly, this will take a lot of time. And, of course, this is just the point at which the architect and the library board or the college administration are pressing for approval of the sketches. I have known many cases in which the librarian or the library committee has been handed the preliminary sketches with the request for a report or approval within the next few days. Refuse to agree to this. Insist, if at all possible, on a reasonable interval in which to study the sketches and prepare an equipment plan. This may very easily require three weeks or a month or even more. It is worth it, because this is perhaps the most important time in the entire period of your library planning.

Second, when I use the term "equipment layout," I hope this will not be taken to mean merely tables, chairs, shelving, and perhaps a charging desk. I would expect you to make your equipment layout complete with all of the technical items that will be needed to operate the library when it is in use to its fullest extent, not merely when the building is new. Many changes will thus be found to be advisable which otherwise might be missed. It may be argued that nobody can predict exactly what equipment will be needed fifteen or twenty years from now, but this is true of the whole building plan. Somebody has to try.

Third, you should have the equipment arrangement drawn to a scale. I have seen many cases in which the arrangements shown on a rough drawing could not be accommodated. Measure the aisle spaces and the equipment sizes carefully and make certain, for instance, that chairs are not shown in a 2-foot space when that aisle requires 4 or 5 feet or more. I mention this because it is exactly what happened recently in the case of a drawing prepared, as a matter of fact, by a very prominent architectural firm. This is no disparagement of architects, but they are human beings and not infallible.

When calculating book capacity, always increase the full capacity figures by 20 or 25 per cent to provide for 7 to 9 inches of each shelf to be left vacant for expansion. Every librarian knows that a library in which the shelves are completely filled is extremely costly to operate—if indeed it can be operated at all.

Now let us consider the furniture itself. In the remainder of this discussion, I would suggest that the key word is "suitability." No matter how well constructed, or how good-looking, or how much of a bargain a piece of equipment may seem to be, it is anything but a bargain if it cannot do the job for which it is intended. "Suitability" in equipment is the most important specification of all. As a side remark, I know of one very capable librarian in a college library who was successful in controlling the purchase of equipment she deemed best by causing this statement to be inserted into the specifications: "The librarian shall be the sole judge of the suitability of the equipment offered by the bidder."

What is "suitability" in various items of furniture? Let us consider just one example: A chair is no good as a chair unless one can sit *in* it, not merely on it. This does not mean that a chair should be entirely form-fitting, because then it may assume some of the characteristics of a strait jacket. The chair should allow the occupant freedom of movement. However, if one can sit only on the chair and not in it, he might as well purchase a bench or a stool and save a lot of money. "Suitability" as applied to chair comfort requires a certain relationship of the seat to the back if the chair is to be used for reading alone, away from the table; and a different relationship if the chair is to be used at the table. In the latter case, the back support should be at the small of the back and the chair posture should be upright enough so that the back may be given some support, even when the user is writing. Few chair backs will do this. Yet this support is the most important criterion of "suitability" in a chair for a reading table, regardless of whether the chair is made of wood, metal, or plastic.

This discussion of suitability in library equipment materials will cover those three materials: wood, metal, and plastic.

As we all know, wood that is suitable for library furniture—the so-called furniture hardwoods—is becoming increasingly scarce. For instance, in the past ten years, white oak has been used hardly at all. One can still now and then obtain enough white oak to equip a library building, but not enough to assure continuity of operation of a factory. The supply of white oak was practically exhausted during World War II. I am amused when I remember that immediately after that war, the library equipment company with which I was associated was scouring the country for tracts of white oak trees. Our representatives found a choice tract and thought they had a verbal agreement to purchase those trees for a price of $38,000. However, a whisky manufacturer suddenly entered the picture and bought those trees for $70,000. Only then did I learn a very important fact: good bourbon cannot be properly aged in red oak barrels; they must be of white oak—so exit white oak for library furniture!

At any rate, the library equipment manufacturers standardized largely on birch and maple. However, these woods, too, and all hardwoods, are now becoming quite scarce. Within the next few years we shall see an acceleration of the trend which has already started—that of substituting metal and plastic for many parts of library furniture for which they have not been used before.

What are the comparative characteristics of these three materials—wood, metal, and plastic—as applied to library equipment? First, with respect to wood:

1. Wood is good insulation against heat and cold. What this means in furniture is that wood is warm to the touch.
2. Wood is the most easily "worked" of the three. By the term "worked" we mean that wood can be readily cut to shape, and it can be readily bent to shape after it has been subjected to a steam bath.
3. Wood is subject to swelling and shrinkage with changes in atmospheric conditions. This can be controlled by proper seasoning, by certain construction devices, and by adequate finishing. However, we have all seen a chair stretcher or rung which has separated from a chair leg for no apparent reason.
4. With wood furniture it is possible to repair the finish in spots without giving a patchy appearance. This is much more difficult in the case of metal. A wood finish can be changed in color without covering up the beautiful grain, and if you are partial to a beautiful wood finish, as I am, this is an important point.

What about metal in equipment manufacture? Aside from the increasing scarcity of good wood, there are certain other reasons why the use of metal for equipment is increasing—metal used either alone or, as is often the case, in combination with wood or other materials.

Metal can be fabricated into shapes having much more structural strength than a piece of wood of the same size. We all know of the use of steel in multistory bookstack columns. We also know that even a single-story steel shelving upright can be made $7\frac{1}{2}$ feet or more in height, whereas a wood shelving upright cannot be made more than about 7 feet in height without bowing, unless it is made excessively thick. What is the significance of this? It means that your steel shelving can actually be seven shelves in height, whereas wood shelving in more than half the cases is limited to six shelves in height, even though seven shelves may be furnished with the order. The difference is about 17 per cent in book capacity.

We have all seen steel shelving trimmed with wood panels on the range ends for better appearance, and sometimes trimmed with wooden bases and tops. In addition, most manufacturers can supply a variety of colors—an advantage which has not been practicable until recent years.

What some of us do not know are the reasons why metal is actually becoming more suitable for parts and certain items of library equipment than heretofore. These reasons stem largely from the tremendous advances made in the manufacturing processes.

The automobile industry is to be thanked for some of this progress. Some of us are old enough to remember that automobile bodies used to be made almost entirely of wood. Later, the uprights were of wood, but sheets of metal were fastened to these wooden uprights. Then came a major advance: a machine or press that could form pieces of steel into a frame to which were then fastened steel sheets for the enclosures. This provided an all-steel body. Finally, there came a revolutionary change—a huge awe-inspiring press which can take a single sheet of steel and cut it and bend it in such a way that it performs the double function of both frame and enclosure.

Now, this oversimplified explanation describes the same thing that happened, for instance, to steel filing cabinets and some other equipment such as drawer bodies and desk bodies. The increased ability to design machines for complicated metal fabrication is coupled with an increased knowledge of how to handle stresses and strains in the design of metal furniture. In addition, of course, metal will not warp or shrink or swell, as will wood.

In the immediate future, we may expect to see a great deal more metal used in combination with wood. We will see more table and desk tops of wood in combination with metal underbodies. We will see desk drawers in which each side and the bottom consist of two very thick sheets of metal with foam plastic in between them, so that one sheet forms the outside and the other sheet forms the inside liner of the drawer. This will reduce the weight of the drawer a great deal and also make it relatively noiseless in operation. We will see a great deal more of what we already have seen before in metal combinations, but greatly improved, and with an increased lightness and heightened delicacy of design which may be worthy of the adjective "exquisite." This very lightness and delicacy of design are what many metal products have lacked heretofore, because of the lack of the kind of production machinery now available.

When we discuss our third class of materials— that of plastics—we may be certain of one thing: some of what we say here today is certain to be out of date tomorrow; the changes are coming that fast. Only the other day I saw an advertisement of a new plastic material of great tensile strength, with the additional property of being able to receive a nail or wood screw just as well as wood. This single property opens up tremendous possibilities for the use of that plastic in all sorts of everyday items, including some parts of library furniture.

What are plastics? Well, they constitute a large and very rapidly increasing group of organic materials—chemical combinations—which may not be synthetic but usually are, and which in some cases can be molded or laminated under pressure to take the place of many more commonly known substances. Sometimes they can even be applied in liquid form. These chemical combinations are increasing in number too fast for me to keep pace, but I shall try to cover a few well-known major uses in the library equipment field.

One of the first such uses was as a top ply for library tables. Formica, of course, is well known for this. This material, which is known technically as a high-pressure plastic laminate, has several excellent characteristics for table tops. It is very hard, very durable. Perspiration does not affect it. It never needs refinishing. It presents an excellent writing surface. It is warmer to the touch than steel.

The patent on Formica has run out, so these high-pressure laminates are being made by others. The increasing competition is bringing additional benefits. The material is now available in 60-inch widths, whereas it was formerly limited to 36 inches. It is available in sheets 12 feet long. There is a rapidly increasing variety of patterns and colors. The price is gradually coming down under the combined pressure of competition and high production. Progress has been made in reducing one of the defects which formerly made it less suitable for table tops, namely its high gloss.

Plastic for table tops still has some serious limitations. The problem of applying it to a compound bend has not been solved. As most of us know, a reading-table top should have a slight rounding of the top and bottom edges. This is important. It is to prevent discomfort to a writer's arm and also to prevent the chair back from being gouged by the sharp edges when pushed against the table tops. But you cannot put this rounded edge on a curved plastic table top or run it around a corner because of the necessary compound bend. The problem can be handled by using a wood binder or edging, but then you relinquish one of the main advantages of plastic. The finish on the wood binder will deteriorate under the heavy abrasion it receives from coat sleeves and books, and in the summer from perspiration from sleeveless arms.

A second serious difficulty in the use of plastic for table tops is that it is sometimes expected to cover up the sins of poor cabinetwork. This it cannot do. Furniture construction that is suitable for a store or a tavern or a cafeteria is generally not suitable for a library. Commercial shops and restaurants expect to redecorate about every seven years or less. A library cannot do that. If you use plastic for your table tops, you will be wise to see to it that the same high standards of workmanship are specified as in the case of all-wood tops. For instance, the one detail that has already been spoken of, the slightly rounded top edge, costs money. It is worth it.

One of the most common furniture uses of plastic during World War II, and again during the Korean War, was in label holders and drawer pulls. Many people have not forgotten the difficulties with these, for they had a tendency to become brittle after a few years. However, a great deal has been learned since then. The Bell Telephone Company has had a plastic dial in use for over fourteen years, and it is practically indestructible. From this same plastic, a leading library furniture house has made a combination label holder and drawer pull that will stand up under the same drop test as metal.

Similarly, plastic upholstery covering is improving rapidly. Its workability is just about as good as leather. Formerly, one of the handicaps to the use of plastic for upholstery was its tendency to disintegrate chemically under abrasion at sharp corners and edges. This tendency has been checked.

Plastic, however, still has some disadvantages in the field of upholstery. (Perhaps we should say "some forms of plastic.") Anybody who has ever put smooth nylon seat covers on his automobile knows how hot this material can become in the summertime. Plastic cannot breathe in the way leather does. There is also some evidence that plastic may be more expensive to maintain than leather. As a practical matter, these two disadvantages are of importance only where upholstered seats are used, and these are not recommended for use at library tables anyway. (It is interesting to note the impact of plastic competition on the leather industry. The leather manufacturers have been forced into making more than 400 colors available today.)

What about the use of solid molded plastic for chair bodies? Most of us have seen such chairs, often with slender metal flared legs. The difficulty here is the difficulty with most plastic items, namely, the necessity to make many thousands of the same item in order to achieve a reasonable price. For instance, the cost of making a mold for a little label holder some years ago was about $900. Two companies are today experimenting with the possibility of a plastic card-catalog tray, and I am informed the mold for such a tray would cost about $8,000. I remember some years ago that, in a conference with a very well-known architect, he showed me a molded plastic chair body, the appearance of which was quite pleasing. I investigated the possibility of taking that chair and altering its posture in order to make it suitable for use at a library reading table. I was shocked to find that this company would need a production run of some 15,000 chairs in order to make the change at a reasonable cost. The library in question was not quite that large.

I mentioned the experimentation with a plastic card-catalog tray. The main reason a successful tray has not been developed is that certain stresses cause warping and distortion of the tray. That, of course, is a vital defect in a card-catalog tray.

Finally, let us consider the use of plastic in finishing materials. Much progress has been made in lacquers. In recent years some of them, applied properly, have competed favorably with the wearing quality of the old-time varnish finish. However, in this discussion of plastics, I have been saving until the last what I think is one of the best pieces of news. There is a new finishing material called "polyester." It can be handled with conventional finishing equipment, which means that it can be brushed on or sprayed on. Moreover, I am informed on good authority that polyester almost equals a high-pressure plastic laminate—that is, it almost equals Formica and similar materials—in its resistance to wearing, scratching, and staining. Polyester seems to be the coming finishing material and will almost inevitably replace lacquers and varnishes. What a happy day it will be when we are able to purchase a piece of library furniture in the confident expectation that it will probably never need to be refinished!

Environmental Control

STANLEY JAMES GOLDSTEIN, A.I.A.
Architect and Engineer
25 Halsted Street
East Orange, New Jersey

There have been remarkable strides, since 1945, in the arts and sciences of designing and constructing buildings. No one of us can be unaware of the postwar proliferation of new products, processes, production techniques, gadgets, materials, and equipment items available for use in buildings at the beginning of the 1960's.

Similarly, there have been propounded comparable and, in some senses, almost revolutionary philosophies and theories of architectural design and planning, reaching to every major building type in our Western civilization. Libraries, and library services, are caught up in the vast changes which are the direct and indirect products of the cold war, of the space race, of James Bryant Conant's studies of the American high school, of our population expansion, of urbanization, of industrialization, and of information retrieval and data processing techniques.

We all know that there are examples of good library buildings today, but across the length and breadth of America these are still too few in number. Public architecture, by and large, still suffers from the sins of a dreadful mediocrity of official and professional thinking, and this extends from initial site selection through planning, design, construction, color selection, lighting, heating, ventilating, furnishing, and landscaping. Far from being visual and organizational delights, most of our public buildings, in the *urbs* or the suburbs, are simply boring or an affront to intelligence, and most are assuredly inflexible to change and expensive to maintain. To achieve that level of design which produces a work of art, we must *first* properly organize all the elements of the building and site.

In the largest sense, design begins with both the city and the neighborhood as the environment. Urban renewal, neighborhood preservation, city planning, and urban design are now bywords in all but the remotest corner of this country. Whether in the context of campus planning or of city planning, our libraries are firmly enmeshed in these problems.

The library site—its size, shape, and character, with its neighboring buildings, trees, streets, and the population to be served—constitutes the social, political, economic, and meteorological microclimate in which we place this creature of the design process—the living library.

To offer but a small example of the effect of our buildings and cities upon the "natural" environment: We are all aware that in most metropolitan areas, there are 10^0 to 15^0 temperature differences between downtown and wooded suburban locations. Remove the trees and grass and other foliage, replace with stone and macadam, and you have a desert waste, thermally speaking, and too often an "asphalt jungle," sociologically speaking.

The exterior envelope of a building is a fabric which must shelter, filter, or control such natural and elemental forces as wind, sun, sky glare, rain, snow, cold, heat (whether by radiation or air temperature), dust, dirt, pollen, odors, noise (whether from other buildings or activities, or just the roar of traffic), and, finally, the visible surroundings, or what we may euphemistically call "the view."

I begin with the microclimate, the building envelope, and the site and the view, to make a point: I am totally against a philosophy of constructing a library building without some public landscaped outdoor space available to users of the library. We should not be building "think tanks" or merely air-conditioned boxes. We are all perfectly aware that we can, if we wish, build a brick or metal box building, and put a fully air-conditioned and artificially lighted library inside that box. Perfect control, yes. But, to paraphrase Norbert Weiner, that is not for the human use of human beings.

The purposes of environmental design and control are simply to provide comfort, pleasure, and a measure of efficiency for our activities. To achieve these, we must select satisfactory temperature conditions, humidity conditions, sound and noise levels, lighting (by daylight with its variable sunlight and glare, or by artificial means), ventilation, air purification, the external view (both beyond the site and on site), and, finally, color in the view—from natural and construction materials, furnishings, and painted surfaces.

With regard to the specific of creature comforts, it may be said that we architects and engineers have available well-nigh unlimited technical means to control every sensory-perception factor in design. Unfortunately, each building is so different from every other one that the application of these technical means to a specific building is far from perfect. Drafts or stagnant air, glare or insufficient light, noisy rooms or noise from adjacent spaces, under- or overheating and cooling, lack of electrical and lighting and air-conditioning flexibility for accommodation of changing space uses—all these are more typical in our buildings than we care to admit.

Now, why such problems in this day and age? The reasons are several. Perhaps the most fundamental one is that each building is a one-of-a-kind situation, a *prototype never fully perfected*, never fully understood by its own builders and creators, and so different from any of the other simpler man-made commodities in our daily lives. Buckminster Fuller, one of the great creative geniuses of our time, said a few years ago that the great tragedy of American architects is that they are putting buildings together today with new parts, yes, but essentially with the same methodology that the Greeks and Romans used some 2,000 years ago. The building process is far from industrialized. Compare, if you will, the gigantic effort necessary to perfect the atom bomb, any single type of airplane, any single missile type, and the nuclear submarine as a naval vessel.

Mr. Fuller is so right. I have watched many clients look out in terror over a field of building materials on the site; they wonder how those odds and ends and bits and pieces can possibly be brought together on time to fit, and, located properly, to serve the myriad of functions in a building. With competitive bidding in today's construction market, the labor specialization, and the "don't give a damn" attitude of both contractors and tradesmen, it is a wonder that anything fits and stays together through the one-year guarantee period. And you know full well it is the rare building, indeed, that is finished on schedule.

Traditional architectural and engineering compartmentalization has established four specialities as the appropriate division of labor and study among the design professions concerned with what I call "environmental control":

1. Plumbing (the sanitary environment)
2. Heating, ventilating, and air conditioning (the thermal environment)
3. Lighting and electrical services (the luminous environment, and this includes color-planning considerations)
4. Acoustics and noise control (the acoustic environment)

In the language of the space age these categories would be called "systems." And it is precisely in this realm of separate and independent systems—applied without sufficient thought to the interdependence and organic relationships of the parts to the whole—that we as building designers begin to fail in our environmental design responsibilities to you the building owners, managers, and users. System analogies are insufficient and too rigid for total-design usage; we must turn to relativity and operations analysis, if you will, for a look at other dimensions of our problems: time, rates, changes, variations, statistics, parameters, and comparisons of variable and fixed items.

An organic and fundamental conception of the study of physical and environmental control, as applied to building design, would take into account the following analyses:

Physiological principles (basic)
Psychological principles (recognized, at last)
Historical development, past and probable future
Physical or scientific principles
System functions
System types
Components
Design standards
Control methods for systems and components
Architectural integration
Relationship of building envelope and use to
       system design and choice and to com-
       ponent selection
Current research (in all of these fields)

To proceed from generalizations to something more concrete, let us take a library reading room and discuss its environmental design for an understanding of the issues at stake for both architects and librarians.

The "new look" in American architecture, for at least the past decade, has been predominantly concerned with exterior walls of glass for most building types. For the library reading room this is not an especially new idea in principle; architects for generations past have always been reasonably generous with glass for daylighting there. However, ceiling-to-floor, wall-to-wall glass, unrelieved by sufficient muntins, mullions, columns, pilasters, or other shade-producing elements in the pane of the glass, can be devastating to environmental control by reason of the indecent exposure to sun and seasonal temperature changes. "Bring the outside in" was the architectural battle cry in favor of more glass. But, without overhangs, awnings, blinds, louvers, drapes, or air conditioning, a glass-walled reading room with the sun streaming in, regardless of latitude, is no more and no less than an unventilated and blinding greenhouse. Further, the excessive use of glass drives up the initial investment in air-conditioning equipment and the operating cost of this equipment. I won't belabor the point, because many of you have such conditions in your libraries.

To return from the specific to the general, let me say that, as in most aspects of life, moderation is a good principle to follow. There is nothing wrong with using a reasonable amount of glass as an appropriate material for the exterior envelope of a building, and a library building at that.

But, we should have specific reasons for desiring to use a particular amount of a particular type of glass in a specific location facing in a definite direction to receive a predetermined amount of skylight and sunlight during different seasons of the year, and to permit views outward to a particular area of the library site and beyond to a selected portion of the neighborhood, with necessary shading devices over the glass to control light and heat, for a particular mood desired, and for a particular size

and scale and type of reading room, in a particular type of library. To be able to live with this glass area, we must calculate the amount of light and heat received from the skydome and from the sun, at different times of the day and year, and we must provide means both to modify the light and heat entering the room and to counteract or supplement the changes from what we select as an optimum range of livable conditions for light and temperature.

There are many, many techniques of bringing heat to a cold glass wall in the wintertime. We can put steam or hot-water pipes or radiators at the sill line, or we can place hot-air outlets there. The choice of heating medium isn't particularly important *until* we begin to think about the erratic behavior of the sun. Then you need a heating system that can stop delivering heat the moment the sun comes out from behind a cloud and can start delivering heat again the moment the sun darts back behind a cloud.

As a matter of fact, you may well need air conditioning—that is, cooling even in the dead of winter—if your glass-walled southerly facing room is comfortably heated on a cloudy winter day and, suddenly, the sun comes out, streaming into the room from the usual low winter angle.

Lighting of the glass-walled reading room is another, and perhaps more poetic, problem. There is nothing particularly poetic about the blinding glare of sunlight on white paper, but the changes in lighting intensity, in a room exposed to daylight, can be enjoyable to humans. Remove the full blast of the sun's rays, leaving a dappled effect, even a moving one, and you have created a marvelous and generally pleasing change in mood in a habitable space. As Frank Lloyd Wright said, "Let the sun be your decorator."

Of course, as the sun sinks slowly in the west, and on cloudy and dark winter days and at night, you should turn up the house lights to maintain a sufficient level of illumination for readers' eyes. Here we can get very technical: how much lighting intensity; what wave lengths or colors of light; what sort of distribution pattern; what kinds of fixtures; what types of sources (incandescent or fluorescent, or both); what spacings of fixtures; what range of permissible reflectances from walls, floors, ceilings; how often to relamp; how often to clean the fixtures; what about economy of operation versus first cost of fixture and lamp; what effect this has on the air-conditioning system; and so on.

Indeed, more light has been the historical trend. Thirty foot-candles were needed for reading purposes not too long ago, then 75, now 100 or more. Both technical research on apparatus and physiological and psychological research on people have been leading inexorably to much higher levels of illumination in all types of buildings.

There is another emerging fact, perhaps astonishing at first glance, but perfectly reasonable upon reflection: The trend to more light gives rise to great amounts of heat given off even by fluorescent lighting, and this heat is of such a magnitude as to require ventilation of the lighting fixtures and of the rooms involved. Even the trend to luminous ceilings leads to air conditioning and incorporation of the lighting and air-delivery systems *in* the ceiling. It is entirely possible to heat in the wintertime from the lights!

So now we not only have integrated lighting and heating, but have provided systems which are beginning to merge functionally in an organic energy-delivery sense. These mutations are now with us for use in building design. (By the way, I make the blanket statement that every library building in America should be fully air conditioned.)

From both old and new system types, and from complaints of the public, we learn that the system control types are of vast importance to the maintenance of human comfort conditions. On-again, off-again heating and cooling should be a thing of the past. The basic faults with most heating and ventilating systems, outside of the usual primary equipment oversizing, are in the control systems, and by these I mean the electrical network of thermostatic sensing devices and gadgets that activate the heating, ventilating, and cooling equipment items automatically to maintain nearly constant temperature and humidity conditions for comfort.

The more open the planning of your libraries, the more flexible the space for rearrangement to suit changing conditions. This flexibility places a considerable burden upon lighting and air-conditioning systems, which must be planned beforehand to accommodate to a wide variety of potential conditions, and control problems then become acute.

Allied with open planning and fluorescent-lighting and air-conditioning considerations are related problems of generated and transmitted noise. Many of the most economical fluorescent lights, for example, are very noisy due to internal ballast vibration, and progress to date on the development of quiet ballasts is far from satisfactory. I am hoping that both General Electric and Westinghouse will push toward a new frontier of quiet for those troublesome ballasts.

Air-delivery noise in air-conditioning ductwork is a commonplace, and is usually caused by whistling of air as it passes over the outlet louvers. This can be avoided only by more precise calculation on the part of the designing engineers of delivered air quantities and of register-size selection.

Then there is a source of noise in or near an occupied space; one wants to blot it up or at least confine it. The best acoustic planning is simple foresight to locate noisy areas away from quiet areas and to use heavy partitions between quiet and noisy areas. Acoustically absorptive materials act

on a time basis, as you may know, to blot up sounds as quickly as they are emitted from a source, be it human or mechanical. The economic and aesthetic disposition of these absorptive materials is both a science and an art. Also, the selection of cleanable materials and surface textures on acoustic materials becomes very important to economical housekeeping in a public building subjected to much traffic and, therefore, airborne dirt. Of particular importance, as air-conditioning equipment types grow in size and complexity, is the confinement of peculiar equipment noises to equipment spaces, a problem which daily becomes more taxing to the ingenuity of both acousticians and architects.

There are more and more new problems evolving in our complicated world. We are beginning to use insulating glass (like Thermopane and Twindow), not only to reduce heat losses and gains, but to keep out heavy urban traffic noises. It becomes necessary to use newer and more complex air filters in air-conditioning systems to eliminate, or at least reduce, the terrible amounts of contaminants in our polluted urban air. And the more complex and numerous the filters, the greater the maintenance and operating costs of air-conditioning systems.

We are finally beginning to realize the effects of size and scale of environment on the human body and psyche. The phenomenon of acoustic scale has long been appreciated—after all, the provision of good hearing conditions in Symphony Hall in Boston is quite a different technical matter from that of providing decent conditions in a small listening booth, even with stereophonic sound! But there are also a luminous scale, a color scale, and a thermal scale of habitable space, and the designers who ignore these do so at their peril.

Let me mention the obvious, but often-neglected, point that the tremendous increase in the use of mechanical and electrical equipment and systems means that there is a proportionate increase in the square feet of floor area and cubic feet of building volume eaten up by these equipment and system items. Don't forget this when programming space needs.

By this time I have given you a cursory glance into some of the interprofessional problems involved in environmental design. Satisfactory solutions depend not only on the inevitable technological research, but on more and better education of both the design groups and their clients: the users and managers of institutional buildings.

The responsibilities of the design professions should lead those groups to more thoroughgoing collaboration, rather than to mere specialization. The responsibilities of building owners and managers should lead to a more systematic programming of their own peculiar use requirements and a systematic cataloging of errors in judgment by architects, librarians, library consultants, and engineers.

Let me mention some user organizations (be-

ides your own) that have begun to organize themselves in meticulous fashion, both because of dis-
satisfaction with past and recent buildings and
because of a large predicted building program over
he country.

First, the American Institute of Physics recently
ublished a book, through Reinhold Publishing Cor-
oration, *Modern Physics Buildings,* as a result of
year-long assignment of a university physics pro-
essor and an experienced architect, together with a
mall staff, to the problem of collecting and screen-
ng information on college and university physics
nstructional and research facilities.

Second, the Institute of Theatre Technology, a
ecently formed and dynamic organization, based at
he Juilliard School in New York, has set in motion
remarkably complete research program to im-
rove the level of theater building in this country.
his is a serious effort, and all sorts of people in-
erested in the theater have been enlisted to work
n various technical aspects. Among the categories
f research now under way are the following, which
y analogy may interest you:

Techniques of programming
Theater categories and types
Examples of theater buildings before and after
    1949, both American and European
Acoustics, both noise and sound control
Orchestra pit requirements
Rehearsal space requirements
Dressing rooms
Space requirements for mechanical, electronic,
    and electrical equipment
Scenery handling requirements
Mechanization and automation of staging
Sprinkler systems
Audience seating
Smoke and exhaust ventilation
New construction materials
Substitutes for the curtain
Building code and safety problems
Control boards
Needs of the theater administrator
Television in the theater
Ideal sight line and viewing angle criteria
TV geometrical aspects
Measurements of the seated human figure
Lighting positions in auditoria
Control booth requirements
Geometric requirements for projection lighting
Storage standards
Rest-room standards
Coat and hat checking facilities
Box office problems
Present theater practices and the reactions of
    playwrights to these facilities
A thorough bibliography

My reason for mentioning this list of thirty-one
items is to underscore what is essentially a cataloging and information retrieval problem. Information
on all these items is in existence, either in written
form or in use as someone's standard operating
procedure. However, the information is not readily
available in proper and suitable form. An effort is
being made to collect this information for everyday
use by all concerned. In addition, an information
newsletter is being published as a clearinghouse for
research and ideas.

Let me mention a little research project of my
own: As we have seen, the plumbing, heating, ventilating, air-conditioning, and electrical trades and
processes constitute the means of artificial control
of the building environment. Architects have generally referred to these items as "mechanical and
electrical equipment of buildings." As an architect
and as an engineer, I have been engaged in teaching
an approach to these very subjects, at the Graduate
School of Architecture at Princeton University, and
have come to certain and somewhat painful conclusions about the present state of these arts, as related
to the practice of architecture, and I want to share
these conclusions with you.

First, these so-called mechanical and electrical
services represent a very large fraction of building
cost—35-50 per cent, and growing!

Second, they represent, understandably, the
largest portion of engineering consultation required
in building design. In many cases, these engineers
have as much or more design work and responsibility
as does the architect for the project.

Third, these mechanical and electrical services
have represented, traditionally, the areas of least
interest and smallest degree of comprehension by
architects and the most difficult to learn out of
school.

Fourth, these mechanical and electrical services represent the major areas of consumer contact,
comfort, and criticism. Having read the publications of your recent Institutes, I know that this is so
for libraries, as for most other building types.

Fifth, these services represent the fields most
susceptible to technological advance, with the largest volume of applicable industrial research.

Sixth, they represent the major areas of what
we call coordination with structure, space requirements, and finish materials. What I mean here is
this: If you want a modular library, the planning
should include regular and sequential spacing of
lighting, air conditioning, electrical outlets, and
noise control elements, as well as the basic structure, windows, and bookshelving or readers' tables.

Seventh, the mechanical and electrical services
represent the principal items of cost of building
maintenance and operation.

Let me digress here for a moment, to remind
you of *some* of these housekeeping chores and

budget items:

> Dirty acoustic tile ceilings due to air delivery from registers; also smudges and stains on walls and ceilings from other types of heating and air-conditioning equipment items
>
> Replacement of incandescent and fluorescent lamps
>
> Cleaning of lighting fixtures, diffusers, registers, grilles, and louvers
>
> Cleaning and replacement of boiler, refrigeration equipment, and cooling-tower parts
>
> Replacement or cleaning of air filters
>
> Maintenance of pumps, valves, burners, and fan motors
>
> Cost of electrical power, fuel, cooling water
>
> The training of janitorial staff in the operation and maintenance of complex operation and control systems, equipment, fixtures, and components

Eighth, these mechanical and electrical services represent the fields most related to the advance of standards of living in all building types: air conditioning, better control of temperature and humidity, and higher levels of lighting intensity.

Ninth, they represent the concepts most seriously affected in scientific and engineering premises by advanced structural, social, industrial, and architectural concepts, such as open planning, future expansion, space flexibility, modular planning, and structural integration.

Tenth, they represent the areas of engineering consultation in relation to building construction most likely to decline in level of relative engineering performance, as space age, nuclear age, and automation age engineers are attracted to more interesting and more lucrative fields; in other words, the mechanical and electrical engineering offices are likely to get the bottom of the man-power barrel.

On the basis of these ten conclusions I feel safe in stating that the technology of environmental control is the most difficult area of building design, construction, and use, and that it will get worse before it gets better. This affects all of us. I mention these points in detail, so that you may view them as we in architecture and engineering view them.

With the encouragement of the director of the Princeton Graduate School of Architecture, I have set out to attempt some reforms in this field on a nationwide scale. There is an inspiring model for this sort of activity, which most of you have heard about, I'm sure. Some five years ago, just before the first Sputnik, a group of 100 dedicated physicists and physics teachers, led by Professor Jerrold R. Zacharias of Massachusetts Institute of Technology, organized what they called the Physics Science Study Committee, and have by this time realized most of

the tangible objectives involved in a complete overhaul of the framework of the teaching of physics in high schools in the United States. New textbooks, workbooks, laboratory apparatus and demonstration equipment, movies, and so forth have had to be produced. Supporting this, an entirely new and creative philosophy of science teaching was formulated. Financial support has come from the National Science Foundation, the Ford Foundation, the Fund for the Advancement of Education, and the Alfred P. Sloan Foundation. The remarkable example in physics is now being repeated, as you may know, in secondary school and collegiate chemistry, biology, and English.

I have been at work for nearly a year enlisting the support of the American Institute of Architects, many of its distinguished members, and several of the fifty-odd schools of architecture in the country. We are attempting to secure sponsorship and encouragement for an Environmental Control Study Committee, which would cut across all the interested industry and user groups and the schools of architecture and engineering; it would be based at Princeton.

Don't think that librarians are alone in the types of mechanical and electrical equipment complaints listed so pungently by Louis Kaplan, Associate Director of the University of Wisconsin Library, at your 1954 Institute. You may remember that Mr. Kaplan polled eighteen of his library colleagues with recent building experience to ascertain the planning pitfalls you should avoid. Most of the disappointments occurred in the field of electrical facilities, such as the location, types, and quantities of light switches; sufficient and properly located specific appliance and general convenience outlets; specialized lighting for exhibit cases, exhibit areas, and specialized activities; lighting for carrels and bookstacks; flexible and expandable lighting and outlet provisions coordinated with furniture and equipment in offices and workrooms (spaces which are very susceptible to change); plus intercommunication, paging and signal systems, emergency lighting, and many others.

You may recall, also, that Mr. Kaplan places no faith whatsoever in the ability of the electrical engineer to read the minds of librarians. I would agree; the only hope would be that the librarian and the architect must be sufficiently energetic and thorough to foresee and program all electrical requirements flowing from the intended use of various spaces in the library building. These requirements can then be translated into electrical engineering plans and specifications.

The same complaints are registered not only by librarians but by school boards and hospital directors, plant managers, and municipal officials. However, your group is different in that you have this Institute—a highly literate, articulate, and organized ntity—which could make its wishes and interests known. I commend to you this thought: that both short-range and long-range improvements in your plant and management can be realized by some sort of effective liaison with and support from the American Institute of Architects, generally, and, in particular, from this proposed Environmental Control Study Committee of which I spoke. You can and should influence the next generation of architects and mechanical and electrical engineers. I would thus encourage your group to experiment further with such fruitful ideas for the organization and dissemination of information.

I have referred to closer collaboration with the American Institute of Architects and the possibility of support by the Environmental Control Study Committee. You might be interested in encouraging research on your design problems in professional schools of architecture and engineering. These would cost you nothing but the effort to frame the problems you want researched.

I should think a very important research task would be the development of suitable criteria for evaluating and comparing library buildings, spaces, systems, and equipment. This has been done for schools and hospitals, as you may know. For more examples of full-fledged attacks on environmental design problems, I would refer you to the excellent publications of Educational Facilities Laboratories, with which you are all familiar.[1]

I make all of these suggestions at my own peril, and if you follow any of them, of course, you risk greater institutionalization. But I think that a more organized and systematic approach to today's complex problems will ultimately yield greater freedom and better results for all concerned. Surely, this is the way to better libraries in America.

1. E.g., *The Cost of a Schoolhouse: Planning, Building and Financing the Schoolhouse* (1960); *Design for ETV: Planning for Schools with Television Facilities Needed To Accommodate Instructional Television* (1960); *Profiles of Significant Schools* (a continuing series); *Case Studies of Educational Facilities* (a continuing series) (Educational Facilities Laboratories, Inc., 477 Madison Ave., New York 22, N.Y.).

Human Mechanics in Relation to Equipment

FRANCIS JOSEPH McCARTHY, F.A.I.A.
Architect
San Francisco, California

Many writers on the subject of library planning have estimated that the life of a library building is about twenty years. Hence, they suggest that planning should be based on a period of twenty years. In assembling materials for the paper to be presented at this meeting, I reviewed certain old notes and literature I have collected over the years, and I came across a 1939 article by Frederick Kiesler of the Columbia University School of Architecture,[1] in which the author expressed concern about the technological inconveniences encountered by architects in the correction of design factors originally built into the building, which later had created difficulties because of changes in library operations. For this and other reasons, Kiesler concluded that planning should be based not on a period of twenty years but on one of thirty years and also that planning should take account of what we now call the factors of "human engineering." Kiesler's central theme—and one with which I would agree—is that progress in design is in part based upon modifications of certain standards, and that the total process of changing standards takes place over a period of about thirty years.

I mentioned the concept of human engineering. It was about twenty years ago that Kiesler made the study which introduced certain ideas that we would now call elements in human engineering. Kiesler developed a model for a home library in which the basic concept of the storage of books rested primarily upon human physical factors; that is, for example, shelves in Kiesler's model library were designed in accordance with the characteristics of the human body. Shelves below 27 inches high were "knee shelves"; those 27 to 29 inches high were "torso shelves"; and "head shelves" were 4 to 6 feet high. Above were "overhead shelves" 6 to 7 feet high, and "step shelves" up to 7 feet high. The result of Kiesler's study was a mobile home library (sections moved in a circular pattern), itself not too far removed from the ordinary public librarian's ideal of the most effective technique for getting books and people together.

With these two general ideas in mind as background—that is, human engineering and the necessity for assuming a much longer period of time to

1. Frederick J. Kiesler, "On Correalism and Biotechnique," *Architectural Record*, September, 1939, p.60-76.

be absorbed in the final adoption of new standards of design—let us consider certain studies I have carried out with a number of colleagues in various places in the country on the most efficient use of space in the library, and some resulting ideas or suggestions on the types of furniture or modifications in furniture that might be introduced to create greater efficiency in library operations.

First, a number of studies we made on the arrangement of bookstack sections produced the following results: for 10-inch shelving, we concluded that the minimum spacing between stacks would be 3 feet 7 inches. To scan books on the shelves requires 2-foot 8-inch aisles, or stack sections 4 feet 5 inches on centers. Two people passing on the aisles would create the requirement for aisles from 3 feet 2 inches to 4 feet wide. The requirement im-

posed by having a book truck standing between the stack sections would be an aisle 2 feet 3 inches wide. If provision were to be made for space between stack sections which would be sufficient for a book truck and one person to move easily, a 4-foot 6-inch aisle would be required. If one were to provide sufficient room for a person to bend over comfortably in the stacks and another person to pass, one would have to have stacks on 6-foot 7-inch centers. The mechanics of these operations are illustrated in Figures 1-5.

Tests of shelving conducted at the Ames Factory at Milpitas, California, and at the University of California, Los Angeles, for loading and scanning showed that we could use 4-foot sections with a loading of 50 pounds per square foot and remain within allowable limits of deflection. We did not

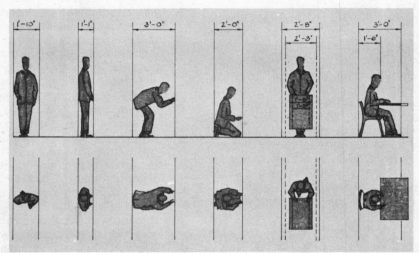

Figure 1
Minimum clearances
for various body positions
in library stack areas

Francis Joseph McCarthy, F.A.I.A.

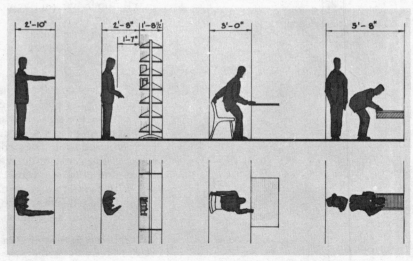

Figure 2
Minimum clearances
for various body positions
in library stack areas

Francis Joseph McCarthy, F.A.I.A.

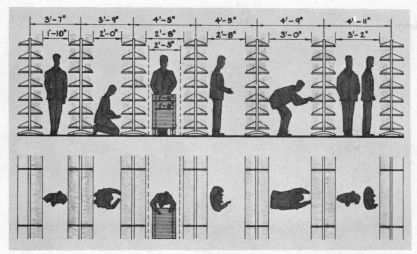

Figure 3
Minimum clearances
for various body positions
in library stack areas

Francis Joseph McCarthy, F.A.I.A.

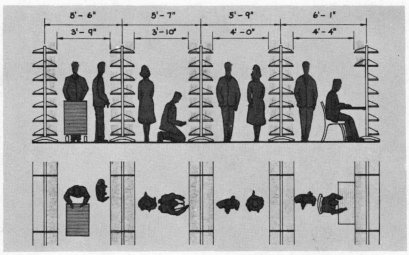

Figure 4
Minimum clearances
for various body positions
in library stack areas

Francis Joseph McCarthy, F.A.I.A.

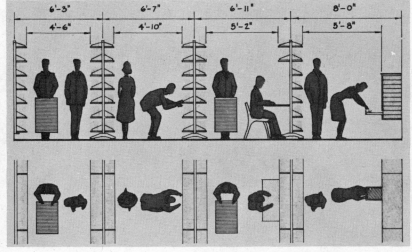

Figure 5
Minimum clearances
for various body positions
in library stack areas

Francis Joseph McCarthy, F.A.I.A.

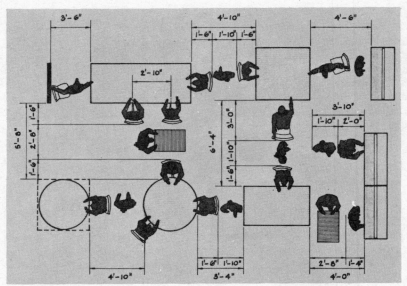

*Figure 6
Minimum clearances
for people and equipment
in reading rooms*

Francis Joseph McCarthy, F.A.I.A.

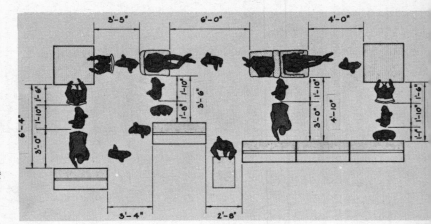

*Figure 7
Minimum clearances
for people and equipment
in reading rooms*

Francis Joseph McCarthy, F.A.I.A

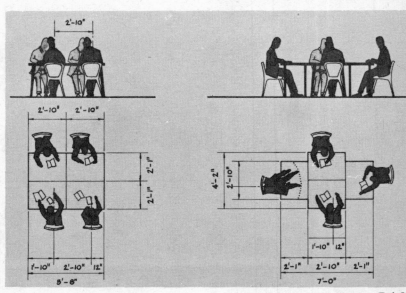

*Figure 8
Table space requirements
for readers*

Francis Joseph McCarthy, F.A.I.A

ave to add more steel or have the channels closed. Such shelving was found over-all to be 30 per cent cheaper than the standard 3-foot style.

We have 45,000 volumes shelved in the San Leandro library. We have shelving for 100,000 volumes, but the building does not look empty. One is not aware that the equipment dominates the scene. This is one of the results of questioning what the person sees. Through raising this kind of question, we developed some other uses for the stack areas at San Leandro. For example, we installed little assignment tables throughout the workroom for pages and others, without taking space away from the regular floor space and desk space.

We have changed the spatial arrangement of cabinets for shelf lists and card catalogs. We had some difficulty with this because we had to estimate on the basis of 3-foot spacing and 15-drawer units, but we did adjust the heights of various units for convenience which gave us much greater flexibility than having fixed cabinets in the center of the floor.

Traditionally, one of the great roadblocks in the library is the catalog card section. We wondered why we build these whole walls of catalog drawers and decided that the sections could be spread out. The catalog drawers were arranged in groups of 120 drawers per section. The tops of the cabinets were used for consultation; the projecting tables were for people working on the drawers. This arrangement worked out quite well; it would be applicable also in college libraries (see Figure 12).

Other studies were made on problems of furniture spacing. Over the years I have accumulated a distaste for the traditional arrangement of library rooms in which the shelves are set back and the library tables are arranged so that the total effect is that of a mess hall. The objective of our study was to produce somewhat less inhuman arrangements of

library furniture (see Figures 6, 7, and 8).

The next set of studies we undertook was directed to the question of the most desirable height for shelving books because, after all, shelves are only useful when their contents can be readily seen and reached. The maximum height for women—a height which will permit a woman to reach easily for a book and remove it—is 72 inches (see Figure 9). However, over the years we have been using stacks 7 feet 6 inches high. This is a carry-over from the traditional construction of library buildings in which the stacks were structural members of the building, that is, the stacks reached from the floor to the ceiling. Again, the lowest shelf we would recommend is 12 inches from the floor—a shelf one might call a kneeling shelf. Twelve inches at the bottom to 72 inches at the top would permit seven shelves, 12 inches apart, or six shelves with more generous spacing.

For young adults or teen-agers, we discovered that 5 feet 6 inches was the maximum height for easy removal of books from the top shelves and, at the bottom, 9 inches from the floor for the lowest shelf. We found that 45 inches was the maximum height for the top shelf and 4 inches from the floor for the lowest shelf for juveniles, that is, six- or seven-year-old children. This will permit four or five shelves in the juvenile section and provide for the most efficient use of the shelves (see Figures 10 and 11).

I have often found myself raising a traditional question about the 3-foot module to which librarians have been committed for so many years. I am not questioning the usefulness of the 3-foot module, but rather the subservience of librarians to the idea that it cannot be changed. The Greeks used the module as a design discipline when it was convenient. When it was inconvenient, they gave it up. In general, we

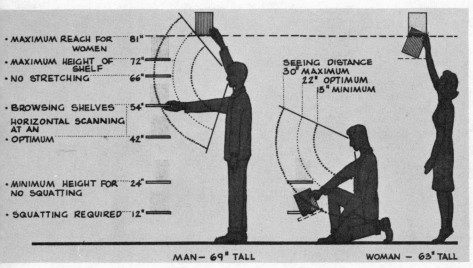

Figure 9
Optimum shelving
conditions for adults

Francis Joseph McCarthy, F.A.I.A.

found that questioning conventional arrangements and practices very often resulted in new, more efficient uses of library space.

I have long had a profound dislike of the conventional vertical files. Such files block vision, they require stooping, and the drawers are difficult to use. A quite different file does exist—one called the "Rock-a-File." The original manufacturer has gone out of business, but the patents have recently been purchased by another manufacturer, Yawman

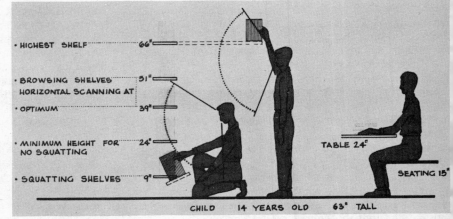

Figure 10
Optimum shelving conditions for teen-agers

Francis Joseph McCarthy, F.A.I.A.

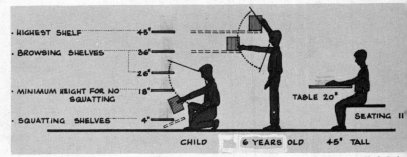

Figure 11
Optimum shelving conditions for children

Francis Joseph McCarthy, F.A.I.A.

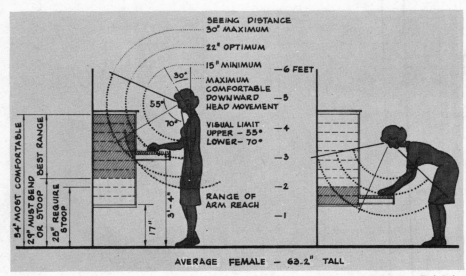

Figure 12
Desirable heights for catalog tray consultation

Francis Joseph McCarthy, F.A.I.A.

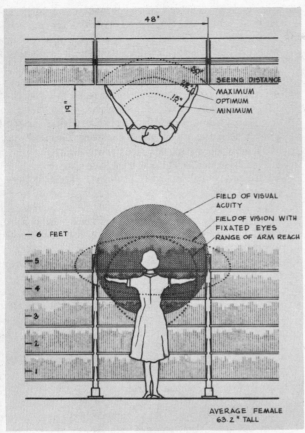

Francis Joseph McCarthy, F.A.I.A.

Figure 13
Study for feasibility of
scanning the 48-inch shelf

& Erbe. In a recent discussion with representatives of the latter company, I found that it is entirely feasible to manufacture individual drawers for pamphlet materials which would be hung individually on the stack sections, permitting complete flexibility in location.

Similarly, there is an advantage in public libraries—particularly with respect to the teen-age users—in arranging seating so that it is spread throughout the library, thus dimming the noise as opposed to having a concentration of seating so that the level of crowd noise is at or beyond the level of reasonable control.

I believe that, ordinarily, the librarian is provided with inadequate specifications for library equipment and supplies by the manufacturers. This is especially true with regard to the size of various types of equipment. We found, for example, that it was extremely difficult to learn the best heights for loading docks, loading doors, and even the best positions for loading doors intended to service bookmobiles. As further examples, there are wide variations in the sizes of vertical files; we found that the differences in tiers of as few as five catalog drawers varied over an inch among three manufacturers.

To sum up: there is need for a central agency or group to assemble a great deal more of this kind of information, based upon recognized principles of human engineering or what might be called "biotechniques," and make such information more readily available to the library profession (see Figures 13 and 14).

Critique

MISS HAMLEN: I am afraid that if I were to choose the type of shelving recommended by Mr. McCarthy—with nothing on the top or bottom—our budget would tend to suffer even more. That is, we would probably spend less and less for books. For this reason, we have gone along with the traditional type of shelving—7 feet 6 inches—so that we could accommodate as much shelving as possible. For the problem of height, we have found very nice, lightweight stepladders which can be moved easily and from which the top shelves are readily accessible.

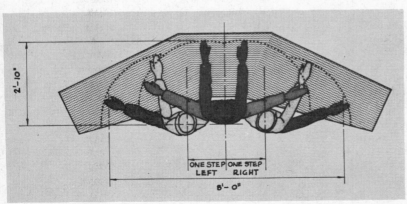

Figure 14
Study for charge desk—
maximum usable space from
one position or station

Francis Joseph McCarthy, F.A.I.A.

Second, I cannot altogether accept Mr. McCarthy's criticism of the traditional concept of shelving—both in height and in aisle width. I would suggest that his opinion is perhaps too revolutionary. At the same time, I would like to see something done with respect to mobility of shelves, not necessarily in a circular pattern but perhaps horizontally, especially at eye level. Is there a method for making the shelves mobile so that a particular shelf could be raised to eye level?

Third, I am interested in 4-foot shelving. In our own situation, we had a lot of old shelving which had to be fitted in with the new and, of course, it is always better if these are interchangeable. However, I would have been very much interested to have known about the 4-foot shelving mentioned by Mr. McCarthy, which apparently reduced the total amount of weight and which could be installed at less cost.

In general, I believe we have made great strides in breaking away from traditional ways of planning our libraries wherever it has been possible. Of course, we need always to have people like Mr. McCarthy to show us how we can be even bolder in this direction.

As an administrator I am, of course, concerned with the budget as all of us are. The thing that impressed me most about Mr. McCarthy's discussion was his novel use of space and this so-called "freeing-up" of the library. This kind of thing is marvelous if one can afford it, but I do feel we are going to be compromising somewhat through, say, the use of space on the lower shelf, or developing a new pattern for shelves—tilting, or curving, or treating them in some other way to make the lower areas more accessible.

The general arrangement, I think, is very good. I am quite intrigued by this new grouping of reading tables—the checkerboard effect which Mr. McCarthy described—and I will predict that public libraries will learn from this, that we will see changes from the present patterns, and that we won't be so traditional from here forward.

What I would like to do is set up a sort of experimental library and bring this equipment into it. Then I would get some people into it and have them actually use it. Then from an unobtrusive place I would observe their behavior during crowded periods to get some idea of the best possible arrangement before arriving at a permanent plan. If some sort of model could be devised, I think we could experiment. We might change our minds a bit as we approach the concept of the human being and the equipment that surrounds him when he is in the library.

MR. SCOTT: Mr. McCarthy holds that retaining

every new standard is extremely difficult. He says it takes thirty years. By that time, obviously, the standards are obsolete; thus, we are never going to catch up. Further, I sympathize with his desire to get the library equipment manufacturer to furnish us with shop dimensions. We have never been able to get the information we really should have.

In my experience librarians, with respect to space, are the most parsimonious people I have ever worked with. Most of them want 6-foot 10-inch or 6-foot 11-inch ceilings so they won't waste any cubic space. I wonder if all of the present filing systems and arrangements of library materials are inviolate. Would it be possible to so arrange things that little-used materials could be filed parallel to the more heavily used books in less accessible space? Might it not be possible to have a compromise that would be both economical and more usable?

MR. McCARTHY: I propose this intensive use of space. I propose a storage library with closed stacks and special arrangements for little-used materials in such patterns that, if you have reasonable access, there is no need for constant traffic. Such areas need not be opened up. You must have the maximum use of the building and maximum use of that space.

An important planner on the West Coast a couple of weeks ago said that the library lacked glamor in the public eye. He called it an "institution." The library couldn't compete for the tax dollar because it did not truly reflect a public need. It wasn't human any more. It was an institution rather than something for public use.

Joseph Wheeler, in his book, points out that we should keep the library out of the civic center.[2] I recall a Denver planner who wrote a book about shopping centers in Las Vegas when Boulder Dam was in construction.[3] He pointed out that shopping centers—and the same applies to the library—cannot be located near public buildings because civic centers tend to produce obsolescence. Public buildings are not places of activity. They are an unpleasant thing to visit. The only time you go to the city hall is to pay taxes or to go to court, or, in general, to do something unpleasant. All you have to do is look around the country at your post offices. What are they surrounded by? Second-class hotels and rundown cleaning establishments. There is no life, no activity. I think this is the reason for having the public library at the center of ac-

2. Joseph Lewis Wheeler, *The Effective Location of Public Library Buildings* (Urbana: Univ. of Illinois Library School, 1958).
3. Saco Rienk DeBoer, *Shopping Districts* (Washington, D.C.: American Planning and Civic Assn., 1937).

tivity. The civic center tends to become simply an unpleasant institution. The reason I bring this in is to say that we should get away from the institutional concept and make the library a more pleasant setting to be in.

MR. HENDERSON: I can't quite agree with Mr. McCarthy's opinion about the civic center or his arguments against the civic center approach. It is possible to have a well-designed and well-landscaped facility there—a group of buildings with plenty of parking space for the city hall and the city offices as well as for the library. I think this is a debatable question and something we would never finally resolve. But doesn't everything depend on the library itself, its service and staff, as well as on the location? I wouldn't overemphasize location if there is sufficient space for parking and you are able to provide good service and a good book collection. It can be in the civic center or anywhere else.

MR. McCARTHY: I was simply using a simile when I used the word "institution."

MR. BLOSS: I would like to ask Mr. Scott or any of the other panel members if the question of the use of higher or lower shelves isn't rather a question of what we regard as maximum use. In other words, is maximum use of shelves for storage, or for making books accessible to people?

MR. McCARTHY: I think these slides I presented indicated that shelves were not for maximum storage; they were for maximum use of the space by the general public. Any piece of equipment that puts the strain on the user and not on the equipment I think should be reexamined. Moreover, I think that that is what is true of a lot of our library shelves today; they are not for storage.

MR. SCOTT: When I spoke of the "material," I was not necessarily speaking of the placement of little-used books or of attempting to select the little-used materials and separating them. However, would it be possible to use two lower shelves or perhaps a parallel shelf for research material, for example? Would that idea appeal to you or other ideas of that sort? Would you consider an arrangement such that you have two parallel shelving systems?

MISS HAMLEN: I think if we remained with the traditional type of service to the public in which there was a desk and a librarian and a page, we could have an arrangement of shelves by size. We would have the shelves arranged according to little use or much use; the users would be thrown entirely upon the card catalog. The minute you begin to open your shelves to the public, you lose track of what is little used and what is not. In the college situation, especially, when you must provide materials for term pa-

pers, the book that belongs in the shelves for ten years may be the very one that intrigues the student; he doesn't stay in the aisle looking at it. He takes it to a table. I don't see how we would store little-used books.

MR. HENDERSON: I am envisioning a public library and its branches, particularly the situation in which you have great variations in use. You decide to construct a branch and decide that it will house so many books. I am concerned with the cost of following this open arrangement or this "freeing up" idea of Mr. McCarthy's. I anticipate a greatly increased amount of floor area to get the same book capacity. Some of these books will be active and some will be less active, but you will have to have, say, a basic working collection of 35,000 volumes. We would like to consider the number of readers we would like to accommodate, but we give top priority to the space for the books.

It would seem to me that the space would have to be 30 per cent greater, or so, if we have only four levels of shelves as against six or seven. This would be extremely expensive. We might have the money for it, but then we wouldn't have the money to put the books into the building after we got it. This is what bothers me.

MR. McCARTHY: Maybe I can clarify something here. I was not advocating the installation of a four-shelf-arrangement shelving. In San Leandro the books are opened up; they are not in cages. A kind of transparency is introduced so that the library does not look empty. Say you plan to double the book stock over a period of years. You can put in four shelves but don't put up all seven. You can space your books out to 6-foot 8-inch aisles, then move them back in five or ten years from now if you have to.

MR. METCALF: We must remember that college and university libraries are different from public libraries; they have different problems. In a large university library, you have the problem of storing a lot of books. If you have a 2,000,000-volume collection, you cannot afford to waste any space. You cannot use simply a third of the space by avoiding the use of the top shelves and having wide aisles. The use of any one aisle at a particular time is comparatively small, and people can pass close together. You don't need to have 10-inch shelves when 90 per cent or more of the books are only 6 inches deep. A good many libraries can go to 50 inches on centers. Circumstances alter cases.

Now as to the question of the 4-foot shelf. At my age, anyhow, I can't look at the shelf even if it is 12 inches above the ground level. A 48-inch shelf would have other disadvantages. On the other hand, if it would save 30 per cent of the cost, that is an important matter, but I have to be shown that a 48-inch shelf will save 30 per cent of the cost when you get into production. These are simply some general comments.

MR. McCARTHY: With the 4-foot shelf the economy is this: If you have a 12-foot range, you have one less vertical column. If you use seven shelves, you have 28 fewer end brackets to support the shelving. You have a lower shelving cost because you have 14 fewer pieces to handle in the fabrication in the plant.

Our experience in San Leandro was that we saved about $3,000 as against shelving in 3-foot sections. With respect to aisle spacing, we find that in a public library at three o'clock, when school lets out and the students arrive, there is much more activity than wandering around in limited-access areas. Again, my observation is that the use of the card catalog in the public library is not the same as that in a university library.

Tables are very interesting. An architect always prefers a round table. I have participated in the design of a lot of hotels. A circle can be put into a rectangle and the pattern is not disturbed, but if you carelessly put a rectangle into this space, you end up in visual chaos. At banquets I dislike sitting at a long table. A round table always has more life. However, my library consultant always said "No" to round tables; there is no place for the girls' bags and no place for the books. At the library of the University of California at Riverside, we found round tables in abundance. The librarian liked them but said they were conducive to conversation. That is precisely why I like them in restaurants, but I must admit they have a disadvantage in a library.

MR. BROWN: I am surprised to hear that there is a lack of information available on the prices of equipment for libraries. I myself am in this business; I send out a lot of information and I think the problem is that the information is not used, or not used properly. Here is what happens: I send out information and answer a lot of questions. I suggest, for example, that you can get a lot more equipment in the same space without inconvenience. I send such information to the architect at his request. He shows it to the librarian. Quite often the librarian is one who never comes to a meeting such as this. However, the architect isn't impressed, so the information or suggestion is never used.

Discussion

Question: What does the university library do when the librarian is faced with long runs on fairly heavy periodicals? If the shipment is to be stored on a 4-foot shelf, you would have to use

heavier steel in the columns. I wonder if there would actually be this big saving you have indicated.

MR. McCARTHY: Actually, with the loading of 50 pounds per square foot on a shelf, in our tests we did not get excessive sag. I have seen library shelving specifications written many ways, for example, 3/16-inch maximum deflection for a 3-foot shelf. I have finally come to the conclusion that we should limit the sag or deflection to 1/250th of a span. My own experiments show that with 1/250th of a span there is no discernible sag. However, if the shelves are to be used for indefinite storage, then a reinforcing channel would have to be installed. I think the savings arise in the elimination of the extra steel parts; however, all I have is the one application of this idea at San Leandro.

Question: Peabody College Library, built in 1918, has shelves 22 inches long. We recently installed additional shelves. We have 42-inch shelves loaded with heavy periodicals. The shelves are sagging in the middle and, of course, your stacks aren't very attractive when they are sagging.

MR. BOES: We are faced with a practical problem here which is very serious. Perhaps it is a problem of the equipment manufacturers. It is too bad that there is not a representative from one of them on the panel. Being from an engineering school, I happen to know there are better materials available; for example, there are certain types of coating materials that could be used. These are just as economical, but they are not used by library equipment manufacturers, and I am curious as to why not. It is unfortunate that this matter can't be discussed and perhaps solved here today.

MR. WOJI: I am also from Polytechnic. I am not a librarian. Actually, I am a professor of mechanical engineering and I have been a consultant to some of these manufacturers of equipment. I would propose that we examine Miss Hamlen's suggestion a little bit further—this idea of moving shelves up and down. My suggestion would be that people like Miss Hamlen and a few other librarians push these manufacturers a little bit further. I think it is up to the manufacturers, not necessarily the architects. I don't think the architects themselves are in the market for this equipment. In short, I think it is up to you librarians if you want something —if you have new ideas about equipment—to contact the manufacturers and force them to do further research.

MR. METCALF: I have no doubt but that a 4-foot shelf can be made strong enough so that it will not bend. However, I am interested to know whether the people who come to my library can use 4-foot shelving of this height. When you are squatting down, it is hard to see the extra foot of shelf, and, of course, that is the important thing.

MR. SCOTT: Mr. McCarthy was speaking about new standards for libraries. I would think that librarians would be deeply interested in creating better libraries. It seems to me they are too often frightened by thoughts of money. We have never had real difficulty in this country paying for better houses when we had designs for them. Don't any of you believe it would be possible, as Mr. McCarthy suggested, to build better libraries, instead of worrying about the length of shelves?

MR. METCALF: I agree with you that we ought to try. Suppose you build a university library for six million dollars instead of four million. I would rather spend the other two million for books and service.

MR. GOODWELL: I agree with Mr. Scott and Mr. McCarthy. Libraries are more than just books and buildings. Libraries are people and service. If we want people to come in—and, of course, many of us now have more people than we can get into the space we have—and if libraries are going to become anything more than mere distribution points for books, we have to go along with Mr. McCarthy's idea of opening up the library, of providing greater access, more interesting areas, and things of that kind.

MR. ROTH: One of the reasons we have been forced to make a great many qualifying statements here —primarily because each library situation is unique—is that there is a tendency among individuals to keep their own formulas and solutions to problems to themselves. Here, perhaps, we are trying to open up the problems, trying to understand the language of other groups, and this makes the whole business extremely difficult.

MR. McCARTHY: Suddenly we are all talking about the intense use of space, this economy of building structure. The same thing happens in dwelling construction. Twenty years ago, before the war, we used to build a house for so much money. Mechanical elements made up 9 per cent of the total cost. Today, mechanical features are running 25-30 per cent of the cost of the residential structure. The homemaker wants a dishwasher, so we put in a dishwasher. Then she wants a clothes washer, then a drier, and an electric stove. So we keep installing all these gadgets. However, we keep reducing the size of the building. We have reached a point where we must and can make the best use of the limited space available. I think we have reached a point in residential construction where it is cheaper to build more house than to buy the gadgets neces-

sary for making the smaller house livable. I think we are working toward this point, too, in libraries. It would be cheaper to build more building than simply to buy gadgets and not be able to use them.

FATHER BOUWHUIS: I want to emphasize the objection to round tables in college and university libraries for the reason given. We find that, more and more, students want to work quietly and by themselves without interruption, and round tables *are* conducive to conversation. I prefer to work at rectangular tables where you have space at either side.

The second question I would like to raise is whether you have done any studies on the effect of carpeting in a library; that is, the effect of improving the general atmosphere for that advantageous arrangement of working by yourself?

MR. McCARTHY: The only carpeting we have introduced in our libraries—they have been public libraries—has been installed in areas for children. That was so we could eliminate the effect of having furniture directly on the floor. There are several libraries in southern California— including a new one in Arcadia, and some others —that have installed carpeting. I don't know how successful such installations have been. In my experience with carpeting in hotels, we figure the life of a carpet to be six years. That is very expensive public carpet at $25 a yard. However, it does take the beating given by heavy traffic. Frankly, I don't know how libraries can afford it. Perhaps the library doesn't have such heavy traffic. At the same time I recognize that the impression gained from carpeting is one of elegance and of luxury.

Involving Others in Planning: A Panel Discussion

Chairman:
 RALPH T. ESTERQUEST
 Librarian, Harvard Medical Library
 Boston, Massachusetts

Panel members:
 WILLIAM CHAIT
 Director, Dayton and Montgomery County
 *   Public Library*
 Dayton, Ohio

 JOHN B. NICHOLSON, JR.
 Librarian, Kent State University
 Kent, Ohio

 VIRGINIA McJENKIN
 Director, Fulton County School Libraries
 Atlanta, Georgia

 ALFRED N. BRANDON
 Librarian, Medical Center Library
 University of Kentucky
 Lexington, Kentucky

MR. RALPH T. ESTERQUEST

I have had the opportunity to visit the new central building of the Seattle Public Library. This, as those of you know who have seen it, is an excellent building. Functionally, it is superb and it is also a thing of beauty inside and outside. The people of Seattle are pleased with it and proud of it. In fact, this was brought home to me when I checked in at the Olympic Hotel in Seattle, which is two blocks from the library. The bellman who showed me to my room didn't know I was a librarian. As we walked down the corridor, he said, "You are very fortunate to be on this side; you will have a good view of our beautiful library."

This pleased me and I reported his remarks to the staff of the Seattle Public Library, which I proceeded to visit. I talked to seven department heads. (The head librarian was not present.) In each case, I met with great enthusiasm on the part of the department heads for this wonderful new building, and in the course of the interviews, I heard how each had participated in the planning from the beginning to the end. Through all stages of planning, each department head was consulted by both the chief librarian and the architect and by others.

To repeat—this is a beautiful building and a functionally perfect building, and I have never visited a library where staff morale is higher.

One more item to set the theme for our program tonight: I have had the pleasure of a number of conversations with Walter Gropius, one of the great architects of our time. On each of these occasions, Mr. Gropius has taken pains to describe architecture as that art which cannot be practiced by the individual in isolation. It is the art which must be practiced in collaboration and in cooperation with the owners, with builders, with consultants, and with many others. That Mr. Gropius really believes this is reflected in the name of his firm which is "Architects Collaborative," not as you might expect, "Walter Gropius and Associates."

The planning of physical quarters for a library is a serious undertaking, whether these quarters are to be a separate building or a few hundred square feet in a building used primarily for other purposes. The librarian is, or should be, the chief planner. It is his responsibility to develop the basic data by which are defined needs for space and its arrangement and requirements for equipment. Then he must work closely with the architect to develop a plan which meets these needs.

Around the librarian there are many who can help him and some who can hinder him. His own staff can help plan functional areas and work specifications for equipment. In the college setting the president, the library committee, a building committee, individual faculty members, and others are on hand to play a part. In other types of libraries other groups and individuals are potential collaborators.

The librarian in each case must make up his mind as to how each person or group can best make a successful contribution, and then he must try to shape and exploit the useful and pass over the unrewarding efforts. How he goes about this is the subject of our panel discussion tonight, and we have four librarians to discuss various aspects of it, each from the point of view of a different type of library.

MR. WILLIAM CHAIT

The Situation in the Public Library

A good way to describe the function of a librarian in planning a library building might be to borrow a chapter heading from Gerald Johnson's book, *The Man Who Feels Left Behind*.[1] The chapter is entitled "The Conquest of Inner Space." Librarians, working with architects and consultants, have the responsibility for determining how the space should be arranged and how best to use the space they can afford to build. The conquest of outer space—or,

1. Gerald W. Johnson, *The Man Who Feels Left Behind* (New York: Morrow, 1961).

rather, the planning of the exterior of the building—becomes much more the responsibility of the architect than of the librarian. Nevertheless, even the outside of the building may offer some problems of concern to the librarian.

My personal experience in public library building planning began many years ago as a staff member working in a new building. More recently I participated in three campaigns for funds for main library buildings; the preliminary planning of one main library building; the complete planning and construction phases of another; and the planning and construction of four branch libraries. This experience has led me to believe very strongly that, in planning, it is essential to engage the board, the community—especially community leaders—and perhaps, most important of all, the library staff.

The involvement of the community becomes most important when the proposal for a library building must be brought before the public for a vote for funds. In many places, people have become quite indifferent to professional administrators pleading for additional funds, staff, and buildings. They have adopted a "show me" attitude when it comes to voting additional tax money. It becomes essential, therefore, that the demand for a new library building be made by citizens and not by librarians. In our project, for example, we organized a citizens' committee which studied the needs and, when they were convinced, issued a public statement that a new building was necessary and that the old building could not, economically or efficiently, be remodeled or enlarged. A subcommittee of the citizens' committee also worked with the library director and his staff in drawing up the program for the new building, so that the end result was a building of which the citizens could say, "This much space and this much money are required."

Of course, we were prepared with facts and figures on what we needed and how similar needs were handled in other comparable communities. We were prepared, but we were also willing to listen and adapt to citizens' wants. A subcommittee on the library site made this hurdle easier to cross. As we worked with our citizens' committee, we also worked with the architect and presented our preliminary plans to the citizens, with the result that the citizens' committee approved the preliminary plans and the building budget which was presented to the people for final decision at the polls.

At this point, the exterior appearance of the building becomes important. Just as a community is not likely to vote for more funds than it believes it can afford, it will not vote for a building exterior it cannot comprehend. The level of sophistication of the community will determine what type of building you can create if you have to work with a voted levy or bond issue. What better group for the architect to try his ideas on than the citizens who are

convinced of the need and who themselves are working toward the creation of the new building!

There are many dangers in working with a citizens' committee and these must be met with persuasion and facts. Individuals in the community will have particular hobbyhorses which they will want to ride; others will be eager to keep costs far below the need for adequate facilities; and some will want a very large, impressively monumental structure to help bolster the community pride manifested by so many civic leaders. These forces must be reconciled, the librarian's ideas explained, and a plan developed which can become a citizens' plan and yet not be in conflict with good library practice.[2]

My experience with board members may have been quite unique. In one case, I worked with a school board which was so busy with school activities that very few of the members had any suggestions or comments on the library building program. One board member, however, regarded himself as an expert on interior decorating and furniture selection. To counteract the dangers involved in this, we managed to place the responsibility for these items on the architect so that the librarian would not be in the situation in which he had to combat the wilder theories of a particular board member. In my experience in Dayton, I found the board quite willing to accept the recommendations of the citizens' committee; the board did not argue with the plans as developed by the library staff. If a board and the librarian have confidence in each other, there is no need for conflict so long as the board is kept informed of progress on the building plans.

The most ardent critics of a new library building appear to be the staff members who work in it. I found this to be true twenty years ago when I worked in a new library building, and also true in the last few years while visiting new libraries. I discovered that some staff members tend to be very critical of the magnificent physical plants they had acquired. This leads me to believe that it is most important for the staff to be involved in planning, and that all suggestions from the staff be either incorporated in the building or answered in such a way that the majority will be satisfied with the results.

A staff that is consulted and participates in the planning of a building feels better about it than a staff that is simply presented with the final product and not asked or told about what goes into the building or why certain decisions were made. Every building is made up of scores of compromises, and the staff must understand this and help in arriving at the best compromises. In addition, we must remember that no library director or architect knows

2. Further details on how we used the citizens' committee in the levy campaign may be found in my article, "Library Building Campaigns," *ALA Bulletin,* 54:513-15 (June, 1960).

as much about the internal workings of a building and the equipment as the staff operating it.

At the same time that we organized our citizens' committee, we asked our department heads to submit their needs with respect to floor space, seating capacity, book space, workroom space, special equipment, and so forth. We also faced the problem of converting from a library which had been organized by function to one which was to be organized by subject divisions. We had to consider the need for planning the building so that a minimum number of staff personnel could operate it, because we knew the limitations on our ability to pay and recruit sufficient staff. The members of the staff participated in every step from the beginning. They helped to determine the service pattern through the proposed departmental organization. This was a good procedure, since those working with the collection and with the public in the old building were able to contribute much of value from their experience.

Once the over-all program was established and the preliminary plan prepared, staff members participated in a point-by-point discussion of the preliminary plan. Alternatives were fully considered in the light of experience, and all aspects were discussed in detail. The entire preliminary plan was presented to the complete staff in staff meetings; then each department head discussed his area with his departmental staff in greater detail. Suggestions were encouraged and questions welcomed. These all came back to the director who, in turn, took them up with the administrative council (consisting of major department heads) where they were considered and acted upon.

Some of you may not agree with our method of handling staff participation. The staff worked within the chain of command—through their department heads to the library director—although any staff member was permitted to go directly to the director with suggestions or questions. At no time did any staff member have any contact with the architects; we felt it would be confusing to the architects to have to deal with so many different personalities. On the other hand, when we worked with our furniture and equipment consultant, each department head met with the consultant and in the presence of the director outlined his needs and reviewed the suggested layouts.

One item about which the staff was not consulted in advance was the color scheme. We believed it was essential for our color scheme to be fully coordinated; thus individual preferences could not be given consideration. When the color scheme was determined, it was submitted to the administrative council for approval and suggestions, and when the scheme was in final form, it was made available to the whole staff for review and explanation. Staff participation in our main library building planning may be summarized as follows:

Assistance in the preparation of the building program
Review of preliminary plans
Suggestions for furniture and equipment
Review of furniture layout
Determination of signs and directories
Preparation for moving (Consultation with the staff resulted in a decision to close the library for one week during the moving process even though the director believed that the moving could be done without closing)
Operation in the new building (We hope to keep in close communication with the staff so that difficulties arising in the new building can be worked out with a minimum of stress for both staff and public)

We have also had some interesting results from consulting some of our staff with respect to branch planning. At the time a branch is started, we usually have not yet appointed a branch librarian; therefore, he cannot assist with the planning. This work has been done by the coordinator of branch and extension services, the coordinator of children's services, and the director. In the case of our last two branches, we called in the branch librarians of the more recent buildings and in consulting with them were able to obtain some valuable suggestions. By the time we are ready to choose a color scheme for a branch, we usually have appointed a branch librarian and we have let him work on the color scheme together with the two coordinators.

Staff involvement in planning is not easy on the director, and the staff does not always respond automatically. The library atmosphere must be such that the staff feels free to make suggestions, to criticize the director's suggestions, and to discuss with department heads the requirements for the performance of the work. This atmosphere must be built up over a period of years in all phases of operation if it is to be present when a building is to be planned. Of course, the staff will recognize that the final responsibility rests with the director and that his recommendations to the board must be of the kind he can support and substantiate. If the director cannot justify all parts of the building plan, even though they were recommended by a large number of staff members, he has no business recommending them to his board and incorporating them in the final plans.

We hope that working closely with a citizens' committee of more than one hundred members, asking our staff for suggestions, and submitting our plans for staff criticism will result in a building which is not a one-man show, but a composite of the efforts of the total staff and community. Such a building will undoubtedly better please those who work in it and the community who uses it.

MR. JOHN B. NICHOLSON, JR.

The Academic Library

I believe it is vitally important that the development of any kind of library, certainly of an academic library, be a total planning operation. It cannot be —it must not be—a one-man job or a job done simply by the head librarian and the architect, by the business manager and the architect, or by any very small group of people, because when the planning group is so limited, the worst things that can possibly happen usually do.

Frankly, I think much of the planning problem is a matter of politics. I believe that the librarian of a university or college must be a politician. He must know how to deal with a large and complex group, each member of which has a great number of vested interests. He must know how to mold those separate vested interests into a cohesive whole. I wish I knew how to do this all the way.

Planning a library building must also be an effort of a large group of people, for the most part made up of librarians. If you don't engage a large group of librarians in the enterprise, one person will have to take a lot of blame for a lot of mistakes. In our case, I didn't propose to take that blame and so, when we were planning our building, I enlisted as many people as I could find who could be induced to tell us anything about what they wanted. When we achieved almost all of what they told us they wanted and, later, some of those things were wrong, we were able to say, "But you asked for it," and this has helped us a great deal.

There are a good many groups on the academic level who must be included in planning for any kind of library building program. The most important group is the library staff, although involving this group is perhaps the most difficult. There are several reasons. Generally, librarians below the administrative level are poorly prepared, both in training and in experience, to be articulate about what exactly a library is.

Most librarians become so engrossed in the details of their jobs that they appear to be unable to describe what they do. I believe that I have some understanding of what the library under my supervision does and what the librarians' jobs are; however, this is because I happen to stand in the position of head of the library. The staff people too seldom have the opportunity to gain this kind of perspective; by and large, the staff are unable to talk about their positions and duties easily and forcibly. I think we have done them a disservice in not involving them more often and earlier in all types of library planning. As a result, librarians have tended to become too localized, focused too much on their own individual situations.

A moment ago I referred to "the library under my supervision." Of course, it is not *my* library; it is *our* library. In fact, it is *the* library. To the individual, the library becomes a very personal thing. And this personal involvement makes many librarians fearful of expressing ideas which they somehow feel are held by them alone. The result is a breakdown of communication between the librarian and the architect, and between the librarian and others, which creates a very real problem.

A certain skill is required to outline one's needs, to state clearly what one's problems are. This is a skill often lacking in librarians. Too often, the librarian asks the architect to solve a problem of which the architect is completely unaware; yet no nonlibrarian can understand library problems as well as the librarian, who obviously must be able to state them.

To illustrate the kinds of changes that should occur, I can tell you a brief story out of my own experience. Six or seven years ago this library, which had a staff about a third of what it is now, was, in effect, a one-man operation. Major planning was done by one person; he received all the blame or all the credit. It was as simple as that and, incidentally, as frightening.

However, the process of involving various groups in the planning has produced some astonishing changes in the staff at Kent State. From a group of people who worked separately—although they liked their jobs—has emerged a group that argues and fusses and fumes, but which *produces* as a team. This is the most valuable single outgrowth of enlisting the support and assistance of the staff in planning. I would hope that, sooner or later, every good-sized library staff would become involved in planning a building, because the same thing would probably happen to them. In my case, the increased participation in library activities by the staff has almost eliminated the need on my part for serious administrative decisions.

The total effect is a matter of group enrichment. I would always prefer to have a staff that has gone through the experience of collaborating in the planning of the building; such people become more mature and more professional.

The second group involved in planning a university or college library is made up of members of the faculty, the department heads, deans, the top administration, and, if there is one, the library committee. This is the most difficult group to deal with that can be imagined, as all college librarians know. With respect to the top administration of the institution, the problem is largely a matter of education—that is, education of the administrators. This is a difficult process. Most academic administrators are quite willing to pay lip service to the importance of the library in the academic setting. Getting action, however, which would make administrative statements something other than lip service is quite another matter. For the most part, it seems to me that the problem is largely a matter of convincing the administrators that all along it is they who have actually wanted what, in fact, you as the librarian have wanted.

College deans generally do not present much of a problem in library planning because—to put it most simply—they are so often heavily engaged in activities which keep them out of the librarians' offices.

Other than the library staff itself, perhaps the most useful group in library planning are the senior faculty members. They tend to have the larger perspective on problems of the entire university or college, and they very often present the librarian with ideas which represent a long-term appraisal of real facts and good ideas. Quite often, the younger faculty members provide valuable assistance in library planning because, in many cases, they have been irritated by things that happened to them on other campuses and this kind of irritation tends to produce valuable new ideas.

At the risk of voicing what may be heresy, I must say that, for me, library committees are anathema. Obviously, as individuals, the library committees are made up of wonderful people, but as committees? Let me illustrate with what has been said about the giraffe—"The giraffe is an animal that was planned by a committee." What I say is that library committees have planned a great many giraffes.

The last group I would like to mention as being important in library planning is the student body. For the most part, when you ask them for help, the students present almost no problems at all. This is because, ordinarily, they are quite enthusiastic and eager to have their suggestions taken seriously. And, very often, their suggestions are quite useful because students tend to raise entirely new ideas. At the same time, it is well to remember that, before you ask students to tell you what they want in the library, you should already have decided what you will, in fact, be able to give them. Another reason why it is good to let the students make suggestions on what they would like to have in the library is that you can appear to be generous in offering to give them what they ask for. Obviously, the public relations advantage in this procedure is enormous.

Specifically, the student groups to approach in library planning are the student council, the interfraternity councils, and, best of all, the student library assistants. The latter group can be especially useful. Student assistants in the library can help more than other student groups for several reasons: they usually have picked up some of the library vernacular and they recognize and at least half-understand many library problems. Thus, in their contacts with their fellow students, they tend to publicize many ideas of the librarian and many of the policies of the library and to interpret them.

Conversely, in their contacts with the library staff, they tend to reflect or express the ideas, suggestions, and complaints about library policies, practices, and procedures gleaned from their student associates. In short, I am convinced that there is not a single member of my staff who is not persuaded that many members of the student body have made it possible for him to do his job in the library more easily and more effectively.

To sum up this overview of the groups I would suppose to have been most useful in library planning —that is, the groups I would propose to involve in library planning—I would say that I have found it to be an extremely exciting and stimulating experience to engage the assistance of as many people as possible. Thus, the point I made first is also my last— the more groups and individuals you have involved in the planning of your library and in bringing the plan to fulfillment, the fewer headaches you, as librarians, will have, the better the building you will have, and the more satisfied the general public (whether this be in respect to an academic, a public, or a school library), and the more satisfaction you will find manifested by those with whom you work.

MISS VIRGINIA McJENKIN

The Situation in the School Library

School library quarters, which are usually a wing or a part of a total school building, must be planned in relation to the whole plant. The library suite is an integral part and, at the same time, an extension of the classrooms, laboratories, and other learning centers.

The concept of school planning and design has changed greatly in recent years. Formerly, the planning group was limited to the architect and the administrator. Frequently the building was copied from some other school design.

Experience has shown that successful school planning is done from the "inside of the building out," and that all persons and all interests must be involved if the resulting designs are to be functional and satisfactory. Thus, in many parts of the country, cooperative techniques have evolved and all interested groups (citizens, faculty members including the librarian, students, school building consultants, administrators, board members, and architects) participate in the development of school building plans.

The first step is to make a careful study of the philosophy, purpose, and program of the school so that the physical facilities will meet the needs of the present and developing educational program. This task is more difficult because of the accelerated pace of change in our modern world. Educational programs must anticipate the world of tomorrow. Moreover, this is the heyday for educational critics, who must be reckoned with. Designs for school buildings must be functional; they must meet the needs of the present educational program; and at the same time they must be imaginative enough to be adaptable to change.

The library plan develops as a part of this over-all effort. This cooperative planning is emphasized as a basic principle in *Standards for School Library Programs,* published by the American Library Association.[1] In describing the contribution of the present-day school library to all levels of education, Margaret Rufsvold has said, "The library is not merely a place in today's school; it is also an area of the curriculum, an instrument of self-education; in fact, a method of education. With its varied materials, its exhibits and displays, the library supports teaching and learning throughout the school plant, including the library quarters which become the center of its activity."[2]

Who, then, should be directly responsible for school library quarters which will encourage this flexible, imaginative, and challenging type of library service? The school administrator serves as the coordinator in all of the planning, but he should stimulate and rely on his school librarian or the local or state school library supervisor to be the "concerned person" in this part of the planning process. This person must assume leadership if he is to play a decisive role and if he is to make helpful contributions in designing library quarters in accordance with new developments in educational programs and new instructional methods, such as team teaching, changes in class groupings, and television instruction. Patterns of local school control will determine who the "concerned person or persons" are to be. If there is a school-system library supervisor, he should be permitted to work closely with the administrative group responsible for overall school planning. In turn, this supervisor should solicit suggestions and evaluations from local librarians, teachers, and principals in schools constructed previously.

In school systems where there is no supervisor, the local librarian and the administrator should seek the assistance of the state school library supervisor. If this is impossible, the school librarian must be ready to participate actively in the planning group.

In accepting leadership responsibility for planning adequate and flexible library quarters, the librarian and/or the local and state school library supervisor should:

1. Know the objectives and educational programs of the school or schools. These may vary from school to school within a system. As a member of the faculty planning group, he must be able to speak with authority about those library activities which will further these objectives and programs. He must be able to show that the activities carried on in and from the library will determine the space, areas, and equipment to be included in the library quarters.

2. Study and analyze with other members of the cooperative planning team the curriculum, the teaching methods, and the functions to be performed in each aspect of the school (and library) program. This requires a knowledge of current educational trends and instructional innovations —such as ungraded elementary schools, individualized reading programs, ability grouping, and advanced placement programs—to provide essential library facilities for existing and experimental programs.

3. Be familiar with helpful publications, films, and filmstrips on planning and building libraries, and encourage their study and use by all persons concerned with school planning. The national standards[3] for school libraries offer concrete guidelines and goals toward which to work; the film, *Planning the School Library,*[4] illustrates the principle that school libraries should be attractive, colorful, and well equipped; and the filmstrip, *Remodeling the Elementary School Library,*[5] assists those interested in providing for and in remodeling library quarters in existing school buildings.

4. Collect pictures, blueprints, and equipment catalogs and be acquainted with sources of other similar materials.

5. Visit other school libraries and learn from the librarian, teachers, and administrator the good and bad features of each library. If possible, arrange for other school personnel to be included in these visits.

6. Outline ideas of requirements, specifications for space, arrangement, and equipment. Frequently, these are incorporated in a manual or bulletin of specifications used in designing the total school plant.

7. Recognize the skill of the architect as he uses his imagination and creative ability to translate the needs of the library into a functional design. A nationally known architect presents the viewpoints of his profession in this message: "We feel that an architect has not done his job by

1. American Library Association, American Association of School Librarians, *Standards for School Library Programs* (Chicago: American Library Association, 1960).
2. Margaret Rufsvold, "School Library Design," *Bulletin of the National Association of Secondary-School Principals,* 43: 101 (November, 1959).

3. American Library Association, *op. cit.*
4. *Planning the School Library* (film; New York: Remington Rand, 1957). 23 minutes, color.
5. *Remodeling the Elementary School Library* (filmstrip; Chicago: American Library Association, 1961). 63 frames, color.

just creating a library that works, he must give it character. The character of a school library is unique for it must be quiet and restful, conducive to study, but at the same time it should stimulate the student's interest by allowing the student freedom to browse among the books and view exhibits.

"As for pitfalls to be avoided, we believe there is only one, the librarian or library specialist should not be so bound by the function of the library as not to permit the architect to use his imagination and his design ability. I have found that there are too many specialists, library, hospital, school, and others designing buildings that might *function* beautifully, but are not beautiful to the eye. Of course, the same rule applies to the architect; he must listen with respect and sympathy to the needs and wishes of the librarian. Only by mutual and pleasant collaboration can a beautiful and functional library be designed to the satisfaction of all."[6]

8. Establish channels of communication with administrators, the visiting school building consultant—if one is employed—and the architect so that they realize the librarian can and will assist in determining the essential library facilities. It is important for these people to understand that the librarian can bring to the planning process a knowledge and experience in library activities and that, at the same time, he can understand over-all construction needs and budget limitations.
9. Work with the art teacher, or the art consultant of a library system, and the architect in planning the decorations and colors for the library.
10. Suggest items of equipment and include specifications for durability, function, and beauty.

In summary, let me remind you that I have stressed cooperative planning for schools and school libraries; I have pointed up the importance of fitting physical facilities to current and anticipated educational programs; and I have indicated the necessity for librarians being included in each part of this planning. All of this study and educational planning is a basic part of our striving toward excellence in school and school library programs for young people who are preparing to live in a constantly changing world.

MR. ALFRED N. BRANDON

The Special Library

The word "special" has several different meanings. Some of them are: (1) having an individual

character or trait; (2) distinguished by some unusual quality; (3) designed or selected for a particular purpose; and (4) particularly favored or loved. I believe all these meanings can be applied to the medical library field, which I represent. Those who enter the fold of special librarianship soon come to believe that they are particularly favored. Early in their career, they realize that they have been selected for a particular purpose and that their library must be distinguished by some unusual qualities.

We as librarians recognize that a university library cannot serve the same purpose as a medical library, nor can a school library function administratively as would a public library. To provide an adequate basic arrangement and to select equipment for the particular needs of a special library, it is mandatory that the librarian as the chief planner quickly define the needs of the library under his direct administration. Neither the university librarian, nor the public librarian, nor the school librarian can define the needs of a library whose clientele, administration, and function are so different from those with which he is familiar.

The architect and the administrator of the institution cannot define the needs in terms of library experience. In establishing a building program, it is essential that the special librarian develop a plan to meet the requirements of his institution. In consultation with an architect, the space requirements should be discussed, and the best location within a building or group of buildings should be determined that will permit the development of a facility to meet the particular needs of the library.

The librarian alone cannot define all of the needs without consulting his administrator, faculty or research workers, other library patrons, and his library staff. As soon as the basic needs of the library are established, the librarian should enlist the support of his administrator for the recommended plans. To gain not only administrative but also financial support, it is important that the librarian keep his immediate superior fully informed about the progress of library building plans.

The librarian should welcome the appointment of a library building committee, which should function in an advisory capacity. Each member of this committee should be delegated to poll the faculty or research workers in his department concerning their individual needs for library service and facilities. By this method, the whole institution can be surveyed quite easily with the results being tabulated and evaluated by the library building committee in conjunction with the chief librarian. Very often, researchers will need special facilities for dictating, typing, and audio-visual equipment. Although the librarian should be aware of these needs, ideas from users of this equipment can often lead to the planning of more suitable quarters for these purposes.

Similarly, the role of other potential library

6. J. R. Wilkinson, "An Architect Speaks," *Library Journal (Junior Libraries)*, 80:5-6 (May 15, 1955).

users might be to answer a simple questionnaire which would elicit the needs of those noninstitutional patrons for whom service and facilities might be desired. Very often, additional financial support can be obtained from these patrons. The librarian need not use all of the ideas produced by the questionnaires, but serious consideration should be given to those suggestions that might help to provide a particular arrangement or special equipment that had not been contemplated before.

If there is a Friends of the Library organization, the librarian should discuss with its officers the proposed features of the new library which might be of interest to them. If this group, for example, is primarily supporting the rare book collection, it should be consulted in the planning of quarters which would accommodate special collections. When plans are fairly well formulated, they could be outlined at a meeting of the members of the group. Usually the librarian has one, two, or more "right-hand angels" who contribute funds, books, or whole collections. These people are worthy of special consideration. They should be consulted about the facilities and equipment under advisement to house and care for their gifts. Perhaps, in this connection, the key word should be "tact." If it is impossible to provide exactly what one prominent patron feels desirable or essential, the librarian should judiciously explain the reasons for his inability to accept those recommendations. All but the most narrow-minded patrons should understand the need for adaptation, conciliation, or capitulation.

It would be impossible to speak on the subject of involving others in planning without mentioning the vitally important role played by representatives of library equipment manufacturers. Not only will they advise the librarian of the latest trend in library furniture design, but they will work carefully with him on his equipment layout. It is extremely important to plan for the placing of equipment in each area before the final plans are approved and before construction is begun. This will ensure that the lighting is properly placed, that electrical outlets are provided where necessary, and that telephone connections are in desirable locations relative to desk placement. Preliminary planning with consultants will prevent many expensive change orders, eliminate spider-web extension cords, and assure the librarian of a more efficient arrangement of office and work space.

Most library equipment companies will furnish samples of each item under consideration. Their representatives will draw blueprints to scale showing suggested arrangements of reading areas, stacks, offices, audio-visual rooms, and so on, and will offer open or closed specifications for all equipment. These specialized services are generously given without obligation, and sometimes without compensation.

Visiting other special libraries and consulting librarians who have planned similar facilities can be most instructive. The librarian can learn much from the errors of others. As he sees other libraries in operation, he can more easily devise ways of adapting space to equipment.

The librarian should cultivate the friendship of those special librarians who are also planning new quarters to compare notes and blueprints. He should be advised of pitfalls to avoid by reviewing his plans with others who have recently moved into new libraries. This will be a reciprocal endeavor. Once a given librarian has completed his building, architects, other librarians, and administrators will descend upon him for advice, and they will benefit from his errors.

Each member of the librarian's staff should be consulted about his individual requirements for carrying out his responsibilities. The reference and circulation librarians, the catalogers, and the acquisitions librarians will all have preferences as to the best location for their operations and the arrangement of their equipment and working tools.

Although it is impossible to please everybody, each member of the library staff should be given the opportunity to express his desires and opinions. It may be that a particular librarian insists on a window in his office; if there are no windows available in that area of the library, it will be impossible to provide this convenience. The best that can be offered, perhaps, is to have a picture of a window painted on his office wall. Although such facetious remarks may be out of place in talking with such staff members, it must be remembered that some people are simply unreasonable in their demands and suggestions. It may be necessary for the chief librarian tactfully to ignore them in future planning, or advise them that because of budget or building limitations their suggestions are not feasible.

Library staff members can be extremely helpful in formulating specifications for equipment they will be using. In addition, the feminine members of the staff might assist in selection of *décor* and color. By soliciting the help of all of the groups and interested individuals mentioned previously, the chief librarian can much more easily fulfill his responsibility to submit the best possible plans to meet the needs of his institution.

Discussion

Question: I should like to ask Mr. Chait a question. How does one appoint the citizens' committee? Is it the librarian's responsibility or that of the trustees?

MR. CHAIT: We did it two ways in two different cities. Here, again, we had the staff involved. Since I was fairly new in the situation in Dayton, having been there only a year at the time we started our citizens' committee, the first thing I did was to ask the staff for suggestions of names of people who might be invited to serve on the citizens' committee. Then we had a list drawn up of about 150 names and had our board president send a letter of invitation to each person. These were individually typed letters, signed by the board president, inviting them to a meeting where the problem could be outlined.

In advance, we had prepared for an election of officers and appointment of a bylaws committee. I can't remember all details of the process we used in Kalamazoo because that was a much smaller community. I knew the people better. I had been there for about six years at that time, and we worked with about 40 people, while here at Dayton we had about 120.

Question: To whom was the citizens' committee responsible?

MR. CHAIT: To the board of trustees. The board of trustees appointed the committee and asked the members to study the situation and report back. The idea was that the board wanted broader representation of citizen opinion than its own seven members could provide on a problem like this.

Question: I would like to ask Mr. Chait the following: What if you have a Friends group to do this? Do you ignore them or decide they won't do? Second, have you had any experience in building a library within a total city improvement plan where you might have a citizens' advisory committee for the total program?

MR. CHAIT: We did not have a Friends group as such; in effect, the citizens' committee becomes a Friends group for this purpose. After I left Kalamazoo, I understand that the citizens' committee was later organized as a Friends group.

In Dayton, the citizens' committee wanted to organize as a Friends group. Our board of trustees did not want other parties "to become involved in the actual management of the library," as they put it. In effect, they asked, "Why should you have these people involved? The building has been voted; let the citizens' committee be a stand-by group in case it is needed again, but, meanwhile, the group should be deactivated." In one case, the citizens' committee became a Friends group; in the other, it did not. If you have an effective Friends group, it can serve the same capacity as a citizens' committee. You must get the group involved in the planning from the beginning; thus, it is better if they are the ones who say you need a building, than if you or some member of the library staff say you need a building.

Now, as to your second question, I am not quite sure I understand. Are you asking what

happens when the library is part of a total capital improvement program prior to the voting situation?

Comment: In our case, we have some friends available for many different projects as parts of general city capital improvements.

MR. CHAIT: Do you mean that city money has been voted and the library will be included?

Comment: That is the case in one of the projects under consideration by our committee.

MR. CHAIT: Then you have no problem with fund raising unless you want committee involvement. I'd say you can forget about that aspect of involving others in planning. On the other hand, such a course may be advisable if you want to have some expression of opinion from citizens—opinions about what they want in their building. You may decide to have them appoint a subcommittee to study the library situation and work with you.

Comment: Our primary problem is achieving a high priority for the library.

MR. CHAIT: I encountered this situation once. We had a library campaign in Kalamazoo in 1949 in which we were working with the citizens' committee on a total campaign for schools and libraries. We were defeated six to one. The citizens' committee was activated primarily to bring the school issue to a head. As I recall now, the committee set up priorities and it gave the library a very low priority. Thus I had to keep arguing with that committee in an attempt to get the library's priority raised. I was not successful. I therefore asked our board to appoint another citizens' committee to study the library situation because, as I said, the existing committee was too busy with the school issue. I got permission from the first committee for a second committee to be organized, and the situation worked out that way. Perhaps you will not be able to do this; you may simply have to work with that original committee. However, the action we took is always a possibility.

Comment: I would like to say that these capital improvement listings are all very nice, but you know they are not inviolate. In 1954, we were included in such listings, and then a freeway was constructed. In the meantime, the city decided that the board of education needed more classrooms, and they took priority over everything that had been planned over a ten-year period.

It seems to me that wherever you can get cooperative help—that is, wherever you can develop interest in your community in what you are trying to do—the community will be benefited, and this is all to the good. You may not have to use a citizens' group for pressure, but you may want to use it to spread the word, which is quite different; in fact, it is no pressure at all. In the long run, such influence comes voluntarily from a seed you, yourself, planted. This is a very worthwhile thing to consider at all times.

Question: As trustee of a public library, I would like to ask a question. I wonder whether the speaker for the public libraries had taken into consideration in his program the possibility that he might have been telling too much to the community. Is there a danger here? In other words, are you trying to convince the entire community to vote for this particular thing? How much of the community uses the libraries? For example, there will be many people with the opportunity to vote who do not use the library. When these people discover that you want to use some of their tax money for things that they do not especially want, don't you have to be somewhat careful about what you tell them you plan to put in that library?

MR. CHAIT: I believe that when you are working with a citizens' committee or a Friends group, you are working with people who are usually successful in their own right, in their own occupations. They are people who are leaders in the community. Many of them may not be library users, but they are interested in the library because they know that the library is something presumed to be good for the community. So you don't have to worry too much about that. In your preliminary planning, you have not gone into detail about what goes into the building. People don't know, for example, about the $1,000 carpet in the director's office, because that carpet hasn't been selected yet. They don't know, shall we say, about the gold-plated plumbing fixtures that might be going into the building. These things have not yet been determined.

All that has been determined at the genesis —the layout, the exterior, and how much is going to be spent—is what goes to the people for a vote, and the people aren't too much concerned about details. In my own experience, a building is not sold to the people through their knowing what is to be inside. You sell it to them by showing them attractive pictures of the outside of the building. I am quite convinced that you must have a model of a building for exhibition. You simply cannot sell the idea without a model. I hope there are communities where it could be done, but I have not seen one.

Bold, New Steps in Education

DR. FRANK J. WOERDEHOFF
Associate Professor
School of Education
Purdue University
Lafayette, Indiana

My topic has a very simple theme. The stage is set for American public schools to take some larger steps toward providing quality education. Victor Hugo once said, "Right in the course of marching feet is an idea whose hour has come," and today in education that idea is *quality* education.

Serious questions have arisen regarding the quality of education in the United States. There are some obvious defects in a system which prides itself on making education readily available to all youngsters and then fails to educate them to their fullest capacity. I am of the opinion that, if we were to understand and apply modern knowledge to educational problems, we would have to label our schools as obsolete.

I don't think I have to tell you about the conversation and current literature that abound with comments on what is right or wrong with the educational program of our schools. In the main, this dialogue stresses the notion that our educational programs must become preoccupied with an effort directed toward quality education; specifically, the suggestion is made that, in the curriculum, educators must blaze some new trails in the pursuit of excellence. Yet it is not quite clear what conditions are essential for the forward march. Our predicament in this matter is that, while the challenge for quality education is clear and our enthusiasm is manifest, we have no model to follow for meeting these educational requirements.

What is happening? Some educators envision an educational model which calls for getting tougher, bearing down more heavily on students, piling on more homework, requiring students to take more science and mathematics, and increasing the requirements for graduation.

Another group contends that quality education is essentially a matter of consumption; in this model, the teacher is expected to raise standards and teach the same specific material in the same sequence with the same activities for all pupils. Here the model deals with subject matter. The one way to deal with subject matter is to memorize it; what is produced is a walking encyclopedia.

Still another model is called to our attention. The people who subscribe to this model contend that, if we do a little tinkering, things are bound to get better. We will add a course or take a course away. For myself, I know that superintendents stream into my office, saying, "Let's add another course in mathematics," never asking, "What can we do better with what we now have?" This kind of model suggests: Let's just change the arrangements. Something is bound to happen that will get people off our backs. At least this might give the appearance that we are moving toward quality education.

These three models—and perhaps there are others—have been tried, but have not been successful in producing quality education. I think that teachers as a group are anxious to find how to do it. Perhaps it is not so much a matter of having a model to follow, however; perhaps it is more important that we have a clear view of the *promise* of education, a clearer picture of the ends of education.

It is in the promises of education and the objectives of education that we have taken some bold steps. We have begun to think our way through to a better concept of education.

Today we have a bolder vision of education as the life-giving principle of national power, of national necessity. Within this context the overriding objective of education is to develop in the individual the intellectual skills and knowledge which will make him capable of the kind of problem-solving and decision-making that will be required in his personal life and his life as a citizen in a democracy. If we are to work intelligently toward such goals, we must see more clearly the contributory objectives for the student, for the teacher, and for the curriculum.

In a program of quality education, with this kind of promise, the student must be helped to develop more appropriate methods for dealing with problems and conditions; he must be helped to think more critically, to marshal and organize information, to draw hypotheses, to find analogies and conclusions, to try out and evaluate courses of action, and to acquire the proper tools for thinking and learning—general and technical—and for leisure. He must be able to construct and apply defenses personally and sociably, and to maintain satisfactory relations with others. He needs to understand the values, purposes, and dedications of others in the world in which he lives. Of utmost importance, he must understand the educational process in such a way that he can pursue education, independently, both while in school and throughout his life.

To achieve quality education in terms of these promises, the teacher must guide this process for the student with a high degree of professional skill and knowledge. The teacher must continue to grow in service. His responsibilities must be such that he is not burdened by repetitive and nonprofessional chores. He must be deeply interested in the students. His working conditions should permit him time to give the greatest attention to the various learning needs of his students.

The curriculum in the quality education program must be the vehicle for enabling students to develop intellectual power and knowledge. It must be developed in the direction of how information can be understood and used, rather than in the giving and receiving of information as ends in themselves. The content of the curriculum must be *relevant* to the present and future needs of society, not burdened with obsolete and irrelevant units. It must be related to the objectives of the students. It must be flexible enough to meet the varying needs of interest and ability.

In the light of the promises of education just described, quality education is used boldly as a creative process. It cannot be effective if it is restricted to the rigid formulas that have grown up in some of our schools.

There can be no magical model that yields or guarantees a high quality of instruction. In order to advance, we must free ourselves from the entrenched rules that we have set up. We cannot afford to depend upon "more of the same" when better solutions are available. Recognizing this, we have begun to engage in widespread experimentation in meeting educational requirements. Never before in the history of our schools have so many new approaches been developed in such a relatively short period. New methods of organization, the use of new technological devices, and new concepts of the role of the teacher now bear promise of lifting the level of American education.

What, then, are some of the promising means to these bold ends? I have selected ten of them. There are others, but these seem to me to be most pertinent.

First, we have taken some bold steps in the organization and development of course content. Education, of course, as I pointed out a moment ago, has been criticized for its inadequate efforts to keep the curriculum relevant, to keep pace with the new needs, and to incorporate the new knowledge brought about by social and scientific change. Obviously, much of what is in our curriculum is now out of date. Courses and books become obsolete in a single year, and if this rate of change is to continue, it provokes a serious curriculum problem.

Here are some of the steps that we have taken and some of the directions that are being followed in developing and organizing course content. One of the points that I should like to suggest is that we have brought together in education teachers and scholars from the various disciplines. This is something that had not been done extensively in the past. They have been brought together for a program of curriculum revision, to eliminate some of the dry rot that is in our educational programs, to add content, to add subjects, and to eliminate some subjects. These teachers and scholars have come together to introduce a body of new teaching materials, such as films, filmstrips, and so forth. They have come together and discovered that the principal objective of education is not limited to mastery of information, because information changes.

This may not be new; it may be a great *rediscovery* of something we have known for some time. These people have very boldly suggested that change must take place in methodology—specifically, that teaching must be of the discovery method. There must be more integration of subject matter: for example, mathematics as it bears upon physics, biology as related to chemistry.

Then, too, the teachers and scholars today say that the arrangements must be *psychological* rather than simply logical and functional. There is a certain boldness in bringing these people together, bold in that the sights have been set and still bolder in that collaboration has brought greater understanding of the subject matter among educationists and the scholars. The two groups are able to appreciate each other, to respect each other, and to cooperate with each other.

A second bold step in education has been the downward, and upward, movement of subject matter. I think that psychology has yielded enough information about the mental growth and development of children to show that we have underestimated the toughness of the minds of young children. We have continued to serve them pablum too long—too much balloon busting and bead stringing. Word lists are now out of date. Children come to school with large vocabularies. Junior high school students can understand many of the principles, concepts, and problems formerly tackled at the senior high school level.

We have had a downward movement of subject matter, and at the same time we have had an upward extension of subject matter. We have extended skill-building activities from the elementary school up into the secondary school for some youngsters. So a second bold step has been this downward and upward extension of subject matter.

A third bold step in education has been the reorganization of school districts. This has been undertaken to produce larger school units, particularly at the high school level. In my own state, we are undergoing an exciting program of school district reorganization with a hope that our high schools will develop in size. The objective is for them to carry on more comprehensive educational programs, to expand curriculum offerings to meet the needs of the students, and to broaden the services offered, including library services. As we develop larger high schools, it may be that the school librarian will need on his staff specialists in subject matter. High schools with 3,000 to 4,000 pupils may need a science library. It is possible that, as staffs grow larger in libraries, there may be a librarian who

will work exclusively with teachers, namely, an educational librarian.

This leads me to a fourth bold step: we are beginning to develop a new plan for the school day and a new calendar for the school year. There is a challenge to the Carnegie unit which said that we must have classes of an hour each, five days a week. But this no longer makes sense for all subjects in the curriculum. Why not some classes for seventy minutes and others for fifteen minutes? Why five days a week, when possibly two days a week for some subjects and three days a week for other subjects might be better? There is nothing sacred about this. The rigidity is primarily a matter of tradition.

Why have we been frozen to certain concepts of class size? People say, oh, you have to have twenty-five pupils, or some will say, fifteen. Why should we restrict ourselves to this idea of the sacredness of classes? The fact is that, for some educational purposes, large groups will do the job and small groups for other purposes at other times; individual study periods are necessary for some and perhaps free times for children to pursue their curiosity.

So we have a new pattern for our school day. The school day will probably be extended to evenings and Saturdays. The school calendar is being extended through the twelve months. Summer schools are expanding, and this is a bold step. Not many years ago, summer school was designed primarily for those who failed in a subject or two. Summer schools today are for all youngsters: those who need to satisfy their curiosity, to expand their horizons, to pursue a subject in greater depth, and to accelerate their educational program.

A fifth bold step we have taken is that we have become concerned with the organization of teachable groups. The experiments deal not only with class size but also with the composition of classes. We have introduced a lot of ideas and a lot of experiments dealing with groupings of various types: according to ability, achievement, interests, readiness, skills, reclamation development, and common cause. We have begun to group children according to support needed from friends, from teachers, or from methodology. We have come to the conclusion that, while there is not unqualified empirical evidence to support grouping, there is enough for us to take some bold steps in experimentation; we no longer must leave grouping to chance.

A sixth bold step that has been taken, I think, is that reflected in the experiments that have upgraded schools—the schools, for example, without grades. We have given lip service to the doctrine of individual differences for many, many years. However, seeing educational people in practice, you would not recognize that they had ever heard of individual differences. They seem to try to form all students in one mold, force all to use the same textbooks, insist that all pursue the same kind of activities, and that all be graded by the same standards. What could be more contrary to the doctrine of individual differences?

We keep saying, "Not all children need the same things," but in practice we box them into grade level programs. This, of course, as a consequence, makes education dull for the bright children and frustrating for the less able. Actually, some children have lost their grades before they have begun. The ungraded school, however, strives to acknowledge the doctrine of individual differences. Progression through the school program is accomplished in terms of pupil growth and development. Pupils move at their own rate of speed. I believe the ungraded school at the elementary school level is almost past the stage of experimentation. The idea has been tried in the junior high schools, and there are some high schools presently engaged in the elimination of grading.

In the light of the promises of education, we have taken a seventh bold step when we have emphasized the need for independent study. The idea of independent study is boldness itself in education, I am sure, but the prime reason for encouraging and providing for independent study is that it benefits the student himself. As the student grows up and leaves school behind, too much of the factual information he has learned has become obsolete. He will need to study independently to be able to analyze new knowledge and to be able to think through problems and make constructive decisions.

Thus, in the quality of education, a bold stroke has been taken when we have provided for and encouraged independent study. This technique ought to be acquired early in the student's life so that he can become a self-propelled learner and not dependent solely on the teaching. As a matter of fact, I tell my own students this: You learn very little in the classroom. If that is the extent to which your learning proceeds, you will be uneducated people, because education *is* independent thinking, thinking which is pursued beyond the classroom, beyond the guidance of the teacher. So today, in keeping with the concept of independent study, we have provided additional resources for learning in the form of audio-visual aids, films, books, pamphlets, research monographs, and so forth.

An eighth bold step, as I see it, for quality education has been the emphasis on quality *teaching*. Teachers have been burdened with mimeographing lesson plans and teaching in subject areas in which they have little or no interest. This, of course, has had a great effect on the quality of education in our schools.

Today we are boldly experimenting with team teaching. Elementary school teachers who have been expected to study the whole gamut of subjects now can use a teaching team. High school teachers who have been expected to be expert in all phases of their subject matter now can specialize in certain aspects of those subjects.

A teaching team at the elementary school level might be directed to the problem of language arts for all second and third graders. One teacher would handle the writing, another speaking, and so forth. In the high school, with respect to the language arts, one member of a similar team could handle creative writing, one could cover poetry and the novel, a third speech and drama, and so forth. In brief, we are doing more about bringing teachers together both in the specialized and the generalized sense so that they can do a better job of presenting an entire subject area to the students.

There are no general formulas for the design of a teaching team; they are tailor-made to fit the needs of a particular school or a particular situation. The team concept has the advantage of helping the less-experienced teacher on the team. As a result, new teachers tend to be upgraded. More students can be handled without the sacrifice of quality. The teacher can make better use of his or her particular skills. There is the advantage of several people planning and executing, which obviously saves the teacher's time.

In addition to teaching teams, we have tried to reduce the nonprofessional tasks of teachers by developing a scheme in which the schools employ teaching aids. Such personnel prepare the mimeographed teaching materials and care for the equipment. This procedure is much cheaper and much more efficient than having the already overburdened teacher attempt to do these things.

Teachers are paid $5, $7, and $10 an hour to collect tickets at basketball games; but this can be done for 75¢ an hour. You absorb the teacher's time with many unnecessary tasks which are not professional, which do not exploit his professional training and experience; this is why we have recommended the use of nonprofessional teaching aids.

Progress has been made by the teacher training institutions. We are trying to find a break-through to the preparation of more qualified teachers. Schools of education are no longer willing to take the leftovers—people who are not equipped for anything else. Throughout the country, colleges of education are adopting selection programs for students; they are beginning to raise their standards and are beginning to attract better students.

Ninth, we have taken a bold step in the business of special devices for learning. One of the most promising learning devices entails programmed instruction and automated teaching machines. Moreover, we are developing program texts and, with these machines and program texts, students can pursue at least part of their education quite independently of the classroom setting, requiring a teacher only as a guide and counselor.

Some people have estimated that about half of the learning in the elementary and secondary school mathematics program could be done through program textbooks and/or teaching devices. Three fourths of the spelling, one half of the grammar and geography, one third of the language instruction, and one fourth of the science and history teaching could be accomplished in this way. There might be an over-all saving of as much as 10 per cent of the pupil's time—that time would be ordinarily used up in classes—and estimates suggest that as much as 15 per cent of the teacher's time might be saved by using program instruction in the school.

While the emphasis here seems to be on the economy of time, let me add that experiments have been conducted in which students can take a course in logic, for instance, and complete it within six weeks. All of what is important in any course could be learned in six weeks through self-guided, self-instructed program learning.

Another device is educational television. This is not new, and yet it is a bold stroke. Educational television has been used quite successfully for a number of years. I think we will find more and more schools engaging in instruction via television. Great emphasis in our own area has been given to an airborne television technique—the Midwest Airborne Television project—which happens to be centered in our university. This project has the potential ability to bring several million youngsters daily into the classroom. It has the further potential capacity to bring quality instruction to schools not fortunate enough to have fully qualified teachers or a broad enough curriculum.

This, of course, is an experiment, but it is a bold stroke. The potentialities of airborne television are great not only throughout the United States but also with respect to the underdeveloped countries of the world.

Another aspect of the development of new devices for learning is the increased use of recordings—taped and plastic—and films. A recording on a tape used in the classroom has saved teachers many, many hours. In surveying schools for the Central Association of Secondary Schools and Colleges, I have found the teacher standing before his or her class throughout the entire period, and then the next period, and the following period. Why not put the instruction material on a tape and have the children listen to it; then let the teacher devote his time to helping the individual?

Where will we use such devices? One thought is that they will be placed in skill-development centers within the schools. With much more experimentation these devices have great promise. I do not mean to oversell such devices, but I am suggesting they ought not to be underestimated; they do free the teacher from drudgery so that he or she can turn attention to discussion and individual assistance.

Such techniques help the student to move ahead and to progress at his own pace. They encourage the student to self-study and they offer great economies in time—advantages that will permit expansion in the scope of learning.

As a tenth and last bold step, I envision the development of new centers of learning in the school. I believe that books and libraries will gain a new importance in our new approaches to improving education. A single textbook will no longer suffice. We are going to have to use a multimedium approach to learning. Quality education demands the use of a wide variety of books, films, scripts, teaching aids and program texts, radio, television, and so forth to meet the expanding needs of youth.

The setting for learning will be not only classrooms but instructional source centers and laboratories—many kinds of laboratories. One question in my mind is: To what degree is the school library going to become a learning resource center? What will be its design? What media will it handle? I believe that it will not be unusual in the next decade or so for children to charge out programed lesson films for teaching machines, and take them home for evening study.

I don't think the new schools will necessarily be palaces; nor do they need to look like a series of egg crates. Buildings will need to be flexible. Walls will have to be changed with the turn of a screw driver. All the new kinds of materials will be used. I expect classrooms to be carpeted with rugs. I hope that libraries will be. Carpeting is much cheaper in the long run in maintenance and upkeep, and consider what is done for the learning environment!

I have given you ten main points which I regard as some of the bolder steps in education. I think they all have some bearing upon librarianship. I would like to close by raising six questions:

1. To what extent will the school library services be organized to become an active force in the newer educational programs and how will they be designed for quality education? I think this is a most important question.
2. Will the school library be designed to be a skills-building operation, or will it simply be a place to house educational materials?
3. What kind of librarianship and what kind of staff will be needed to implement, foster, and promote quality education? Will the librarian really be a significant part of such education?
4. To what extent will the design of the school library be planned to accommodate the new technology in education?
5. How can the school library be designed for continuous flexibility to accommodate a continuously changing educational program?
6. Finally, how can the school library be designed

and located for full utilization in the daytime, for evening school activity, and for the entire calendar year?

These six questions, among many questions, I think are especially pertinent, but briefly they sum up the highlights of what I believe to be some of the bold steps being taken in education which have a direct bearing upon school librarianship.

The Place of the School Library Facilities in the New Curriculum: A Panel Discussion

Chairman
    MARGARET MOSS
    Director of School Libraries
    Madison, Wisconsin, Public Schools

Panel members
    IAN IRONSIDE
    Warren Holmes Company, Architects
    Lansing, Michigan

    KENNETH I. TAYLOR
    Chairman
    Center for Instructional Materials
    West Leyden High School
    Northlake, Illinois

    JEAN CRABTREE
    Librarian
    Garden City High School
    Garden City, New York

    LEONELLA M. JAMESON
    Librarian
    Saginaw Township Schools
    Saginaw, Michigan

MRS. MARGARET MOSS

This morning it is our turn as school librarians to talk about the things that are most important to us. I think that, in everything we have heard in the last two days, we can agree that there is definitely a green light for education and for all the new media for helping to make that education better.

Obviously, there are many innovations to be encouraged on the ground that they will help the individual teacher to provide better instruction. He will have greater freedom in the use of these new media. We know that there is an unprecedented amount of printed material—books, pamphlets, periodicals, and newspapers—and along with those we have, of course, filmstrips and film, the opaque projector, the teaching machine with the program of instruction, and all of the other new media of education that are of such great importance to us. I believe that it is time librarians began to think seriously of what our place is in this new educational milieu.

MR. IAN IRONSIDE

The problem that architects often have in dealing with librarians, school officials, and school boards is to get from them expressions of such bold concepts of education as outlined by Dr. Woerdehoff, and also to be sure that they are fully aware of these bold concepts. One of the things that we have noted when we have worked with people is that, very often, these new concepts have not been expressed by the administrators or boards, nor have they filtered down to the staff and the librarians.

Another problem we encounter is not being able to discuss many of these things with the librarian before arriving at definite decisions, before the goals have been established and the amount of money to be spent has been determined, even before the bond issue has been passed. Sometimes, after the financial limitations are set, and you try to backtrack and elicit people's ideas, some of those brought into the discussion will say, "If I had only had a chance to have brought these thoughts out, we could have had this in the beginning."

In other words, it is most important to do your thinking beforehand, to make your corrections on paper, and then proceed at full speed with a very good over-all plan. Then you will have something very constructive, something that will, in fact, accomplish the purposes of education that were mentioned earlier.

I wonder sometimes about the definition of the library. There is a definition *I* think rather interesting, and perhaps it may be interesting to you—a library is a function whose responsibility is systematically to collect and acquire information, classify it, store it, and, upon demand, retrieve it and assist in adapting it to its use. That may be what we, as architects, should think of the library as being—the use of the library, its future, and how we should deal with it.

Now, to get to the bold concept of library design and location of the building. I would like to say that the design of a library can vary a great deal. With respect to such concepts as the instructional materials center and the audio-visual center, there are many questions to be asked of the school officials, the school board members, the librarians, and the staff members. The most general question is: How is this element going to work in your system?

I would like to present a number of secondary questions, simply to show how an architect could, if he wanted to, raise the kind of questions that would elicit your thinking, so that you could, in turn, help him in his planning. For instance, here is one: What will be the function of this area? Will it serve as a complete instruction materials center in everything that implies, or will it deal mainly with printed matter and its use by students and faculty?

A second question: If the practice is to divide the above function, what plans have been made for handling such materials as films, recordings, maps, charts, and so on? What is their relationship to library services, if any are to be required? Will this center serve the whole school system or only a single building?

In fact, I have a list here of about thirty questions which will be distributed to you later. From these questions I believe that you should be able to arrive at solutions to some of the questions in your minds as to how a particular type of center will fit into your over-all philosophy of a school educational program.

It is most important that the librarian be fully informed as to the philosophy of a particular school system. In every system we find extraordinary differences of opinion as to how one is to work. For instance, in some communities certain phases of community life have a part in the system, in others they do not. I remember North Chicago as an area in which the community was very interested in science, because a chemical plant was located there. That was where many of the students went when they left school; not all of them went on to college.

You have an entirely different situation in Detroit. Go into Indiana and Illinois, and you will find that the thinking varies between various sectors within the states—sectors in which the people have a different philosophy of education. Thus the particular area—say, an instructional materials center —as designed to be used in the future, would depend to a great extent upon what you in your own community believe to be most important and upon how this center will fit into those activities.

I believe that in Mr. Taylor's system, with all the facilities available, there is certainly a very highly developed plan. Of course, not all schools are able to have as much space as may be desired; but, again, you make use of the space you have. As to the location of the materials collection center, we find in many cases that it should be at the center of the academic area—the center of the quiet area of the building, not the noisy area. It probably should be close to the entrance to the building.

Also, there is the matter of future expansion. Flexibility was mentioned in connection with library planning. Many things in a building actually become too flexible. Flexibility, to me, means primarily the ability to use various areas in various ways; that is, areas should be multiuse areas. This is related to economy in construction. If you have areas that are large enough so that you can use them for various purposes—meetings and conferences—such areas in the library are most economical in our experience. At all events, economy is foremost in the thinking of many school boards.

I think the future of any library design will depend upon the librarians. The architect can design to meet your needs, and that is what he should do. I don't think any building should be designed so that you have to fit your operation into it. Rather, I think the building should fit into your thinking and serve your purpose. It shouldn't be the place to store a child, but it should be a place to serve the educational philosophy and thinking of the community.

MR. KENNETH I. TAYLOR

I would like to make a few comments about this. We call our area a "Materials Center," but I don't think there is any magic in a name. I think it could just as well be called a "library." I think this is a decision by the individual school, but its importance, I believe, is that a school library must define its role in the curriculum. This will be different in every school, but it has to be defined and interpreted to the people in that school. My feeling is that the program must be defined in terms of service.

You need not have a lot of facilities and a lot of equipment to have a successful program. If your library is too small, for instance, and you cannot store the number of books you want, it seems to me there are possibilities for putting books in the various departments—in the offices of the English department, for instance—or in a classroom. Central records can be kept to show where the books are. As you can see, I believe this must be the solution for many schools.

One problem we had was that, having been given an instructional materials center and a budget, we were still required to tell the board what we were doing with it. Very seldom did they have the opportunity to come into the building during the day. Moreover, when they had their meetings, they would talk mainly about money.

For this reason we created a kind of explanatory device to show people what we were attempting to do. This is a completely individual tool—made up of three teachers with some slides and a tape recorder —which interprets our program to the school board and other audiences.

MISS JEAN CRABTREE

When we were asked to be on this panel, we were told we were expected to react to what Dr. Woerdehoff had to say, and I reacted. Now I have reacted again, and I am so overcome with images of the future that I can scarcely focus on the change that will come to us.

Last week I spent three days at the Columbia Workshop on Audio-Visual Services in the Libraries, and there was a great deal of discussion about educational TV, teaching machines, 8-millimeter sound

projectors, program learning, and overhead and overlay, and now today we have even more of these new things; they come to us as a challenge.

My first reaction, I will say, is one of inadequacy. I can operate projectors, opaque slides, motion pictures, and filmstrips. I can run a tape recorder. I can even switch the needle on the record player from 78 to LP, but beyond that I am relatively untrained. I just do not happen to be a very mechanical type of person. However, I intend to learn about the educational use of all of these new devices and methods, and I intend to promote their educational use in our school.

I don't intend to do it, if I can help it, with my present quarters and staff. This year we have had 1,051 students in Grades 10-12. We have two specially trained librarians and a half-time audio-visual person, who administers and operates the projectors and does the routine work connected with rental film. We have an almost full-time clerk. She also runs the textbook room and issues working papers. Then we have the help of 34 students; and whoever said that using students as help in a school library relieved the librarian of work?

At Columbia Dr. Hyer, who, as you probably know, is Executive Secretary of the Division of Audio-Visual Instruction of NEA, gave us some figures to think about. There are no precise statistics —that is, quantitative standards for audio-visual services—as yet. Dr. Hyer said that each building should have a minimum of 2,700 square feet for audio-visual services alone, and an additional 800 square feet if there were going to be teaching machines.

At my school, which opened in the fall of 1955, we have now completed our sixth year in a new building. We are planning an addition. We have not proceeded very far as yet. We have not achieved the bond issue or anything like that, but we are having study sessions. We are planning to add some rooms to this already obsolete building, and we think we are going to get additional space for the library. We envision an expansion of the audio-visual area and the addition of a reading terrace. Our climate is not conducive to outside reading most of the year when we are in session. Perhaps in the future, if we are open all summer, we may be able to make more use of the terrace, but I think of that terrace as providing room for expansion, namely, the addition of another reading room. I visualize part of the collection as being moved in there. I see our extra reading room as probably devoted to social studies and history, but also as equipped with quite a number of carrels for individual study.

All of this means that we are going to have to have additional staff. I anticipate not simply one librarian for each 300 children; I think we need more than that. If we have a truly full-scale program based on our American Association of School Librarians standards, we are not going to be able to do the job of working with teachers, curriculum development, teaching the use of books in libraries, and helping individual students—even with one librarian a specialized librarian or consultant, whatever you wish to call him—with one librarian for every 300 children. We are going to need more than that, and we are going to have to use people who have had special training.

I often think that school librarians are so glad to have a centralized library in their school at all that they sometimes are willing to view it as a sort of one- or two-man operation. It is not that. Let's look at even a small college library. How much in the way of staff do they have? Let's set our sights high. Let's really dream a dream. Let's dream it so far that, when we go to our administrators, they cannot help but agree with us that we need more in the way of facilities, and that to operate those facilities to the best educational end, we need staff.

MRS. LEONELLA M. JAMESON

This morning I come to you with much enthusiasm for a new school district that has been established in the state of Michigan, in Saginaw Township, where we have an opportunity to implement the very things our speaker has talked about.

Because we are a residential area on the outskirts of the large city of Saginaw, and because people in the area preferred not to be politically annexed to the city and wanted to build their own educational system, we have a marvelous and almost unique opportunity to provide facilities in our school that will coincide with many of the things we have heard this morning.

These plans were very carefully thought through, and with the fine leadership of George Mills, our superintendent, who came to us with considerable experience of his own and with a tremendous understanding of the educational possibilities, we are going to try to prove that many of these ideas actually do work.

One of the problems mentioned this morning by our speaker was: Will the libraries of the future be designed so they are simply storehouses for material, or are they going to be research centers where youngsters can actually develop research skills? The latter is what I hope for, and this depends so much on the librarian and the abilities that she or he may have. It also depends a great deal, of course, on the facilities at hand.

I think the one word that has been stressed here so many times has been service. Each of us knows that if the librarian, given large facilities, is not able to make use of those facilities and provide the type of service that is needed, all the good facilities in the world come to nothing.

One of the things we have found in our school

system—and that we will find in the future, I am sure, because we are only two years old—is the fact that we are trying to build instructional materials centers intended to be central repositories. But, as has been mentioned also, we would like to see much of the material out in the classroom and in other areas besides the instructional materials center. This is not the old concept of the classroom collections. These are materials that are all purchased essentially in series, and then go to the instructional centers or to the high schools and the primary schools. The materials are indexed so that readers and teachers can find immediately where they are located.

If the collection is going to be kept permanently in a particular area of the school, this will be indicated for the reader. If, however, it is simply on loan for a specific period of time, this also can be quickly ascertained by checking with the clerical staff at the desk. It is possible, therefore, with sufficient flexibility for a librarian or instructional materials person, to give the type of service that is necessary within the framework that we have been working in for many years.

There is nothing sacred about a two-week, a three-week, a one-week, or an overnight loan. There is nothing sacred in providing that certain books must always belong to a particular period of time or to the particular areas to which they may have been assigned.

Again I mention the word "flexibility." I have begun to realize how inflexible one can become in a short period of time. I think it does us all good to move to new situations and to try to introduce more flexibility. I think that many of us in the past have been very anxious to please and give good service, but have not been able to reach out and do this to the fullest extent of our ability, and I think now is our time to reexamine how we do these things and actually see if our service is coming up to what the educational pattern of the schools demands.

Another belief that I have very strongly is that a librarian should not always feel that her own bailiwick is the instructional materials center and that she will never leave this sanctuary. A librarian should feel as much at home in the classroom as in her center, and I mean that in the sense that she should be able to work very carefully and easily with all types of materials. This is a good way to get your service across.

One of the other problem areas mentioned this morning was that of staff, and I would like to say something else on this. By inference I feel that Miss Crabtree, in her remarks concerning student assistants, has really hit on a problem some of us others have had. The student assistance program, with the general purpose of substituting student help for paid adult clerical help, was suggested as a way to involve youngsters in a school program, to make them conscious of citizenship responsibilities, and to teach them skills.

My own feeling is that, if you have a school of any given number of students, the very small percentage of student assistants you are using is too small a proportion to justify spending all the hours you do in preparation and revision. In short, that number of hours does not warrant continuation of the student assistance program. This, of course, means that we must provide adult clerical assistants who are paid to do the work.

I mention this—perhaps with some diffidence—because I come from a state where the Student Library Assistants Association is a very strong and very well-regarded association. I do think it has helped in many ways, but I also think there are tremendous limitations. I came from a school smaller than the school in which I am now and in which I, too, was using student help and working closely with the youngsters. It was a good experience for them and it was a good experience for me, but I spent hours in this type of work when I should have been spending them with other boys and girls in the entire school program.

This is something I think we all ought to consider. In our plans for the future, we should hope to relieve teachers of nonessential duties. I think that one of the things we should emphasize is the professional nature of our job, in order to get the most mileage out of the time we are spending in school.

Discussion

Question: To what extent do you think high school teachers in general are ready for new, bold steps in education? Mr. Ellsworth, in a previous conference, expressed the opinion that college libraries could not as yet go very far in planning for technological facilities because college and university teachers were not ready for them. Can the high school library lead in providing facilities before the college faculties begin using these methods?

DR. WOERDEHOFF: I would say that teachers are, very often, conservative individuals. I don't believe that all these people in education know, understand, and visualize the school of two decades from now. The central fact of the matter is that teachers are trying to resist change. They have grown so accustomed to their standpat manner of teaching and using a single textbook that it is hard for them to change. We need to build more fires under our teachers.

I recall preparing a talk to be given before the Indiana Teachers Association—a talk in which I was encouraging the experimental development of nongraded junior high schools. I took the opportunity with students in my graduate

course to test this idea out, to see what I might encounter with another audience. These students fought the idea for three quarters of an hour simply because they saw it in relationship to what they were accustomed. However, they have broadened their vision. Teachers don't do this. Librarians don't either, as a matter of fact. Maybe we grow old and comfortable too rapidly. Whether teachers and librarians accept these new ideas or not, we cannot afford to continue pursuing educational programs that are totally obsolete, totally inefficient.

Somebody said that when you build a school, the librarian ought to take a look at the philosophy of that school. I say the librarian ought to be *shaping* the philosophy of the school. He or she is not simply a consumer of philosophy. I have heard a librarian say, "Well, we use only one book in the class." I wouldn't stop there, if I were a librarian. I would do something about it.

Why do we have requirements for school librarians to become teachers, and then they are not teachers? This is a ridiculous requirement. However, the alternative is simply to train them as librarians, just custodians of books. If you are asked to become a teacher, along with becoming a librarian, why don't you act like a teacher and influence educational philosophy and the concepts of education? Of course, some of you do, but I think, as an educationist, that we have to do a lot of rethinking in the field of teacher preparation.

These people we have trained were trained only yesterday. We trained them yesterday and now they are fifty years behind. So we can't look for the millennium tomorrow, but we can be pushing our sights higher, our vision on to further horizons. I admit that teachers are a restraining force at times, and even in institutions for quality education.

Comment: We have ten college professors working on the Ford Foundation, and they met in the month of April and the month of May, trying to become familiar with the high school curriculum. Now they are working as consultants and advising on units of study.

DR. WOERDEHOFF: That is one of the bold steps I mentioned. I think we are going to push teacher education and curriculum improvements by raising the quality of academic specialists (if I may call these scholars that) who are working with the education of teachers. We will have greater respect for each other's task. We will work more cooperatively. There is no need for building fences around the various disciplines, around education, and around the classroom teacher. We have to have a lot of communication back and forth. This will improve the program. We will all achieve greater respect for each other.

Educationists—and I don't apologize for being one—are generally imposed upon by the university staff. It is only when we make efforts to let them know and understand that we, too, begin to know a little, only when we show appreciation for their efforts, that we get the kind of cooperation and teamwork necessary to build a strong teacher education program and move toward improvement of the public schools.

Question: May we have a discussion of the procedures which take place when materials move from permanent loan in one department to student use of materials in another department?

MR. TAYLOR: The materials kept in a department office tend to be reference books, rather specialized books, because the teachers ask for this kind of material. If a student needs some of this material, and we don't have it in the materials center, or if it is out on loan and the departmental copies are the only ones left, the student can go to that departmental chairman and ask to borrow it. But the length of time for loan depends on that departmental chairman. He has complete control over such material. We don't tell him what policies to set up. If he is using that material at the time and he needs it the next day, he may tell the student he may take it home overnight. On the other hand, if he is not using that material, he may let the student have it for two weeks.

In these cases, the departmental chairman is frequently the most highly trained specialist in that particular subject, and is the best-qualified person in the school to help the student wanting that kind of material. However, in any instance where the departmental chairman feels burdened —that is, too many students are coming for a particular book—he is in the best position to recommend that we buy duplicates. Thus, as soon as the loan becomes a burden we buy more copies.

Question: If materials in classrooms, conference rooms, and study centers are not a part of the library—not serviced by the library in any way, such as through inventories, circulation control, and so forth—are they considered expendable in regard to losses and damage? If the responsibility is placed upon the teacher, how is it carried out, and is it successful?

MRS. JAMESON: I speak from an infant school system, because we have been operating our middle school for only two years. We have loaned materials directly to the teachers, using the card system in different colors. We keep one copy. The teachers have the other for checkout. The teacher is responsible for this material; we call it in. If they want it for only a month, we call it in then. If they want it for the entire semester, we call it in at the end of that time. We inventory once a year. We then tally up how we stand and we come out pretty well.

I think if there were any loss involved, some teachers would volunteer to pay for it on an individual basis. However, high school will not open until fall. I cannot tell how successful the system will be. After five years I will have statistics on how this works.

I was pleased with what happened this spring after we had used the system. The teachers felt they wanted the additional service. We asked them: Are you willing to do it? Do you think it is an extra job? They felt it wasn't. We have movable trucks in each classroom. There is plenty of room for materials and the materials are there to pick up, if students want to take them home. There is one student monitor to a classroom, keeping tally on the other youngsters. This is better than having a librarian keep track, because the students will get the things back.

Presentation
of Plans

College and University Libraries

Panel of critics
  MARY AMNER
  Associate Librarian
  Kent State University Library
  Kent, Ohio

  RAY DELA MOTTE
  Architect
  Cleveland, Ohio

  HORACE HILB
  Librarian
  Fredonia State College
  Fredonia, New York

  HELEN KALTENBORN
  Order Librarian
  Kent State University
  Kent, Ohio

  EDWIN LARSON
  Architect
  Cleveland, Ohio

  RICHARD E. LAWRENCE
  Architect
  Canton, Ohio

  ARTHUR SIDELLS
  Architect
  Warren, Ohio

University of Pittsburgh Library

Pittsburgh, Pennsylvania

Presentation of plans
    DR. ALAN C. RANKIN
    Assistant Chancellor
    University of Pittsburgh

    LORENA A. GARLOCH
    Librarian

Building data
    Architect: Celli-Flynn
                McKeesport, Pennsylvania
    Type of library: Central building
    Population to be served: Graduate students,
            undergraduate students, and faculty
    Area: 225,000 square feet
    Book capacity: 1,500,000 volumes
    Seating capacity: 2,200
    Dimensions
        Ground level: 70,000 square feet
        First floor: 35,000 square feet
        Third-fifth floors: 40,000 square feet
    Size of module: 25 feet 6 inches

DR. ALAN C. RANKIN

Since the library of an institution reflects that
institution's educational philosophy, an understanding of ours at the University of Pittsburgh should
help explain some of the unusual things that we have
done in planning our library. We consider the arts
and sciences so central to our educational effort
that we are moving away from professional education at the undergraduate level. We are eliminating
training in business, teaching, and pharmacy at the
undergraduate level.

We believe that every qualified student should
have a liberal education and a professional training.
In the years ahead, these will not necessarily be undertaken in the traditional fashion: four years of
liberal arts, and then three or four years of professional education. We believe that these two can be
interlocked. Our educational philosophy recognizes
the value of a close relationship between the arts
and sciences and the professional schools.

The proposed library is a large square structure among a complex of buildings. Three adjacent
towers are to give 1,900 more dormitories for students. One of the towers is twenty-one stories, the
second eighteen, and the third fifteen. These are
being built for approximately $13,000,000.

The complex consists of the professional schools
in the social sciences, the graduate school of public

and international affairs, the school of law, the
graduate school of business, the school of education,
the graduate school of social work, and the common
resources building. These buildings must be related to one another and to the central library to
carry forward our educational philosophy.

To the right of the complex is a public plaza,
skirted on one side by the great Carnegie Institute.
Housed there are the Public Library of Pittsburgh—
the Central Public Library and the Carnegie Public
Library—a music hall, an art gallery, and a mu-
seum. This building is almost as large as our entire social professions and library complex—a consideration when we began to build in this area. The
buildings of the social professions were planned for
the site of Forbes Field. The University owns
Forbes Field, and as soon as the stadium was re-
located in another part of the city, we made plans to
tear down the baseball park to make space for these
six buildings.

The library will not be peripheral to our campus.
When the five schools of the health professions are
built, it will be centrally located. This is an important consideration because we would regret a
building as important as the library being off to one
side of the campus. This will not be the case in the
long run.

The broad terrace may be entered from three
points—from the courts in front of each building. A
steep slope creates an architectural problem, and
to ensure privacy and light, we designed an open
court at ground level. This is a large inner court,
approximately 240 feet by 200 feet. Glass walls
will allow natural light to enter the ground area,
which is not a basement. None of these buildings
has a basement or excavation below, except perhaps
for mechanical purposes.

To carry forward our conception of a close relationship between the professional schools and the
arts and science area, we have devised an unusual
library system. It is important for students in professional schools to have ready access to our graduate collections in the social sciences, and, in turn,
there are many occasions when the people in the social sciences programs need to have specialized
materials that are housed perhaps in only one of the
professional schools. It will be possible to leave
the professional schools through a corridor to the
common resources building, or if one wishes to step
into the law library, to move through the library
system. This should help to control the growth of
our professional schools.

In designing our library, we have tried to do
three things, two of them rather difficult under one
roof. First, we wanted to have a separate undergraduate library, housed in a separate area in this
building, instead of in a separate building. Second,
we wished to have a graduate library housed there.
Third, we tried hard to relate the special libraries

Architect's visualization
University of Pittsburgh Library
Pittsburgh, Pennsylvania

Jay-Bee Photographic Studio

to the specialized libraries of the professional schools. Our difficulty has been in getting all three under one roof in a workable, serviceable library for our faculty, students, and library staff.

The library is a five-story structure, approximately 225,000 square feet in size. This is about five and a half acres. Although this is about five and a half times the space we now have, in five or ten years we shall probably be overcrowded and wonder why we didn't build a larger building.

The library should house approximately 1,500,000 volumes and seat 2,200 readers. The module is 25 feet 6 inches. The building is air-conditioned throughout and subject to humidity controls.

The ground floor is level and comprises some 70,000 square feet. It is almost entirely above ground except on one side, where it is sufficiently above ground to allow three-quarter windows. The first floor, an overhang, is considerably smaller, approximately 35,000 square feet. The next three floors are about the same size, some 40,000 square feet, and space permits the extension of more floors.

The undergraduate area will be the first and second floors, and the graduate collection will be housed on the ground, third, and fourth floors. Why

did we split up the graduate collections, with the undergraduate area between them? We did this for a specific purpose. We wanted the graduate materials in social sciences to be on the same level as the materials in the social professional schools, and the only way we could accomplish that was to put our social sciences collection on the ground floor. The two entrances on the ground floor open onto an exhibition lobby 75 feet wide and 25 feet in depth. An elevator will service all floors.

These facilities are available to everyone in the building and to the people in the social professional schools. Here is the union catalog. The university now has several libraries and no complete union catalog.

Smoking has been a disturbing problem. Since we cannot permit smoking throughout the building because of the cost of the air-conditioning equipment entailed, glass-enclosed smoking rooms have been placed on each floor. Smoking is permitted in work areas of the staff and in faculty study rooms, but students who wish to smoke must go to the smoking rooms. Or, they may study in these rooms.

The technical services area originally included the offices of the librarian and assistant librarians, the reception desk, and the staff lounge. Everything

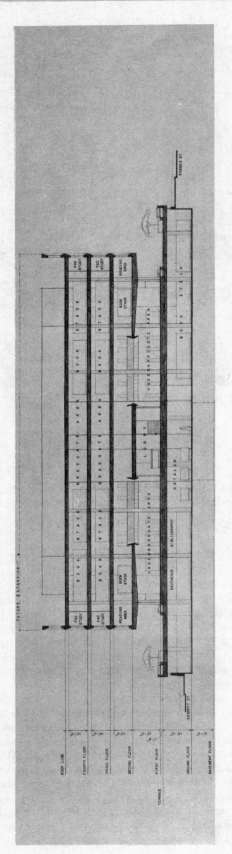

Cross section

*University of Pittsburgh Library
Pittsburgh, Pennsylvania*

Longitudinal section

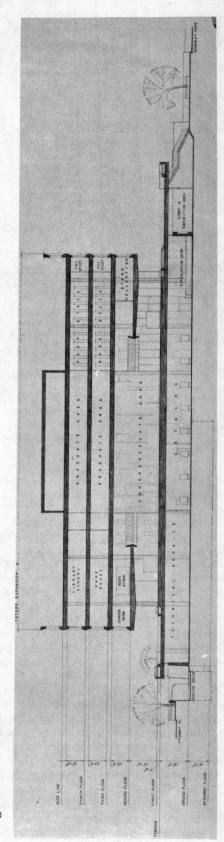

seemed to be needed on the ground floor. Since we had to move some things, we moved the librarian and the staff lounge upstairs, after we realized that other institutions operate successfully without the librarian's looking into the technical services room all the time.

An entrance here permits students and faculty to go back and forth to the social professional school libraries. These are all social professional schools, and people will have immediate access to the graduate, generalized, and specialized materials in the social sciences.

We have eighty faculty study rooms, but not enough on the ground floor. These are areas of about 8 feet by 9 feet for a faculty member who needs to use library materials. He can take these materials into his study and leave them. They are not intended to be faculty offices; there are no telephones, and no study conferences are permitted.

On the first floor will be the first level of the undergraduate social sciences materials, so they can be related to the graduate collection. On the ground floor will be a simple catalog. The undergraduate library is not intended to house more than 100,000 volumes, with room for 600 readers and 50,000 volumes on each the first and the second floors. There will be some duplication as well as some current periodicals, but not as many will be housed elsewhere in the building. The fourth floor is designed to house natural science materials at the graduate level and bound volumes of older publications. Space has been allocated here for a library school.

Seminar and conference rooms are absent because we have tried very hard to keep this a library and have resisted every effort to turn it into something else. There is not a seminar room in the building. The common resources building next door will serve meetings.

Critique

MR. DELA MOTTE: Obviously those concerned have been studying this building for a long period of time. The few minutes that I have heard it discussed this morning do not allow much criticism, I am sure. I think that the building is very well done.

As to the 25-foot 6-inch bay space, I think that the planners were here and found some of this information at this campus. I think that the openness and the feeling are very good. The stairs seem to be close together. In Ohio, under our code of laws, we wouldn't be able to do this, but this is something that may make the building function better. I think it is a very well-presented plan, and the enormousness of the thing floors me.

MRS. AMNER: I am impressed, too, but I want to ask about the booklift. Is there a booklift or some way of getting books up and down?

MISS GARLOCH: There is an elevator for a truck, which will go off on each floor; we think this is better than a conveyer.

Discussion

MR. NICHOLSON: I think you are making a mistake on the booklifts. You will find a book truck on an elevator a real block. No matter how good your shelves are, if you can't get the books up to the floors quickly, you will be tied up.

MISS GARLOCH: We won't have the conveyer unless we find more enthusiasm for it. I think Brooklyn College has been having a great deal of trouble with it, due to the architect. The floor was not level and so forth. We are studying this problem, and if we can find a successful conveyer, we will have it; if not, we won't. The book trucks will be small and will automatically exit onto the floor for which they have books. We will push a button and designate it. There will be no operator riding with the truck.

MR. KUHLMAN: I think the elevator is a must. You may have to have two in the big building. If you can get the books up rapidly and automatically, and get them up without any additional handling, you are going to save yourselves a lot of money. The libraries in this country waste tremendous sums of money putting books on conveyers and booklifts today, through extra handling done by boys who are careless with the books. The damage to binding is considerable. You put your books on the trucks at the charging desk when the book comes back. The truck is then sent to the floor. You save two handlings. You don't lose any time and are much better off than you are the other way.

The conveyer may be all right, but the booklift is a pernicious thing in my opinion. If you can get a good conveyer and carry the books on the conveyer in a basket so that they are not damaged, it may work. You will have to look for a good conveyer. It is hard to find. The best one is in the New York Public Library. It has been operating for nearly forty years very satisfactorily. There are very few in the country and very few have been made.

Our conveyer has worked now for twenty years through an eight-tier stack, without any complications at all. I think you said you will have a lot of self-service. You will find that many people can't find the books they want so that if you can communicate with the page on the top floor and have the page put the books on the conveyer, it will speed up the service.

Question: This is a building on a grand scale. I can't get down to the details, but I am interested in your concept of the undergraduates and the graduates under the same roof. Does that mean that undergraduates will not use the graduate level, or that they will be encouraged to use the level where they will be most at home?

DR. RANKIN: They will be encouraged to use the level designed for them.

Question: Is the undergraduate level mostly a duplicate of what is on the social sciences floor? How are you going to keep the undergraduate students in the same place?

MISS GARLOCH: Some of the undergraduates will have to go down to the ground floor, it is true. Our current journals will be there. There will be some duplication in the undergraduate libraries, but "A" students certainly will go to the graduate level, and we want them to. But I believe the mass will stay in their own quarters.

Question: Is there any provision made for the concentration of traffic engendered by a library school on an upper floor?

MISS GARLOCH: We have elevators that the people in the library school are bound to take, that is, they can enter at the ground level and immediately get into an elevator and go to their floor. We are fortunate in having a new building, with classrooms, constructed adjacent to the library so that all of the classrooms of the library school will be in another building. The offices and the laboratory—if our dean wants a laboratory—will be in the library, but I think the traffic problem under that circumstance will not be as great as if we had classrooms in the library.

Question: I was wondering if your faculty study rooms will be available to students. Can a student readily go into a faculty study, or will the faculty person be protected from intruders?

DR. RANKIN: We hope the students won't. The rooms are not designed for that purpose, but for a faculty member to engage in research and writing in the library center. The rooms are not to be assigned, as far as we can control the situation, to faculty members as offices.

MR. NICHOLSON: Mrs. Amner asks about the advisability of providing conference space or conference rooms for undergraduates.

MISS GARLOCH: We have conversation rooms, which will seat from four to six persons, in the undergraduate area.

MRS. AMNER: Does a professor never bring a class in?

MISS GARLOCH: No, indeed. We don't want classes ever brought in, because we have the special building adjacent. Originally we had requested a lecture room, to which to bring groups for lectures on the library, but we have even done away with that, which is a great advantage to the library building. The lecture room will be in the adjacent building.

Alma College Library

Alma, Michigan

Presentation of plans
HELEN MacCURDY
Librarian

Building data
Architect: Lewis J. Sarvis
          Battle Creek, Michigan
Type of library: College library
Population to be served: Undergraduate students, faculty
Area: 39,970 square feet
    Existing stacks: 5,280 square feet
    First floor: 14,450 square feet
    Second floor: 9,040 square feet
    Basement: 11,200 square feet
Book capacity: 120,000 volumes
Seating capacity: 400 students

MISS HELEN MacCURDY

Alma College is a residential, four-year liberal arts college with a faculty of 69 serving a student body of 750. Student enrollment will be limited to 1,200, and the library was planned to accommodate that number. In addition to the main library building, facilities include a science library containing a collection selected for upper-class science students in the Dow Science Building. The science library will be the only separate collection.

The academic program for underclassmen centers around a two-year Western Civilization course which makes heavy demands on library holdings in philosophy, religion, history, art, and literature. There is an independent study program for upperclassmen.

The present library is ideally located in relation to dormitories and classrooms. It consists of an 1890 fortress-type building to which a three-tier, 60,000-volume, self-supporting stack unit was connected in 1928 by an 8-foot corridor. We plan to remove the fortress and retain the stack unit. In the proposed campus development plan, the library retains its central location as a link between academic and residential areas. The building is to house 120,000 volumes, with seating space for 400 students, work space for a staff of 12, a study area for faculty, an audio-visual auditorium, and a curriculum laboratory. It is to be an open stack library.

A major influence on the planning of the library was the decision to retain the existing stack structure. This decision imposes some limitations on lanning, but elimination of the stack could not be ustified economically. The development of the plan ʼraps the new building around the stack structure, ith provision for reading space at the first and uird tier levels. The second tier is available to oth the first- and the second-floor reading rooms, y means of stairs at either end; in the proposed rganization this tier will be used primarily with ue first-floor reading area.

The entrance lobby area divides the reading rea served by the existing stack from the reading rea served by the new freestanding stacks. Part f the lobby extends upward through the second floor ɔ give this space greater importance and interest. ʼsychologically, this will help to promote movement ɔ the second-floor reading area.

The elevator must necessarily serve both the xisting stack levels and the new building floors, nd is located accordingly. This, in turn, controls ue location of the charging desk. The location of ue processing area is determined on the basis of s availability to the service drive.

At the present time there is fairly heavy student ʼaffic south of the library, between the administra- on building and the library. As the campus de- elops, however, this traffic will move to the north; ɘnce the main entrance to the library is on that ide.

Although planning is at a schematic level, the ɔllowing is contemplated. The foundation and ʼaming of the first floor will be reinforced in con- ʼete, with the floors above having fireproofed steel ʼaming and concrete floors. The floors of the ɘading and stack areas will be designed for a 150- ɔund live load. The roof deck will be of poured ʸpsum with a built-up gravel-finish roof. The ex- ɘrior walls will be brick and limestone, and the in- ɘrior finish in the principal public areas will be ʼick and plaster walls, vinyl tile floors, and acous- ɔally treated ceilings.

The main two-story block will have very limited lass areas on the east, south, and west exposures, hile the north will be mainly glass. The character f the building will conform with other recent build- ɪgs on campus. Year-around temperature and hu- ɪidity control is planned.

The stack unit is in the southwest corner, and ue main entrance, as I have said, on the north. here will be a connecting corridor to the east wing f the Reed-Knox Building.

The second floor of the new building is expected ɔ be level with the third tier of stacks. Just east f the stacks are the listening booths, which have ɘen placed there to separate them from areas here they would disturb people. On this level we ʼill house a music, art, literature, and science and ɘchnology collection, down through the eastern half f the building. There is a lounge area around the ɔening in the floor.

The basement has an audio-visual auditorium in the northeast corner, a faculty study area accessible outside of library hours along the eastern side, a curriculum laboratory just above that, an archive storage space, lavatories, staff room, the mechani- cal area to the south, and future library storage to the northwest.

The main floor is really the most important floor, since we have a small staff which will gradu- ally grow. It happens that east is toward the floor, west is toward the ceiling. The entrance is from the north into the main library that holds the circu- lation desk area, which is backed up to the old ex- isting stack unit, because the elevator has to be at the southeast corner. South of the existing stack unit is a flank of conference and seminar rooms, typing space, and the librarian's office. In the southeast appendage is the work space, which we expect may eventually have to hold as many as 8 people. We hope that will take care of receiving and all processing. The reference clerks will be just beyond that wall with the reference attendant beside the stairway to the second floor.

Critique

MRS. AMNER: The questions I ask are necessarily those of a librarian, not those of an architect. Have you made any provision for microfilm fa- cilities—perhaps the library is not large enough —or microcard facilities?

MISS MacCURDY: We had hoped that the conference and typing rooms could serve a double function as a place for using the microfilm or microcard reader, and we would keep those files near the main circulation desk.

MR. DELA MOTTE: Structurally the building looks as though it has rather large spans, being rather open. Probably you want to provide for a great deal of flexibility. It is difficult to carry stacks and floor loading on very wide spans. They look like about 32 feet, and we found that 25 feet was probably nearer the ideal for arrangement of stack spacing and loading.

Discussion

Question: Why don't you place the circulation desk right at the entrance? Why not put your public catalog near the entrance? The time is coming when we will have to have checkers even in a small denominational college, and if you are go- ing to plan along economical lines, you can save a lot of money by putting your circulation desk at the entrance.

MISS MacCURDY: We plan to have a checker at the door. We kept the circulation desk back partly to take advantage of using the first couple of aisles of the existing stack for reserve use.

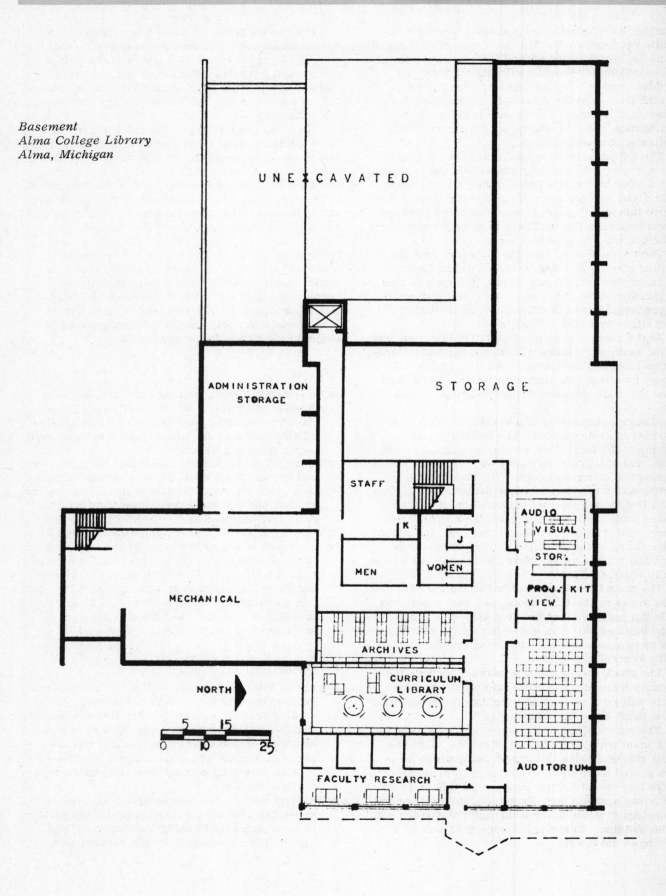

Basement
Alma College Library
Alma, Michigan

UNEXCAVATED

ADMINISTRATION
STORAGE

STORAGE

STAFF

K

J

MEN

WOMEN

AUDIO
VISUAL
STOR.

MECHANICAL

PROJ. KIT
VIEW

NORTH

5   15
0   10   25

ARCHIVES

CURRICULUM
LIBRARY

AUDITORIUM

FACULTY RESEARCH

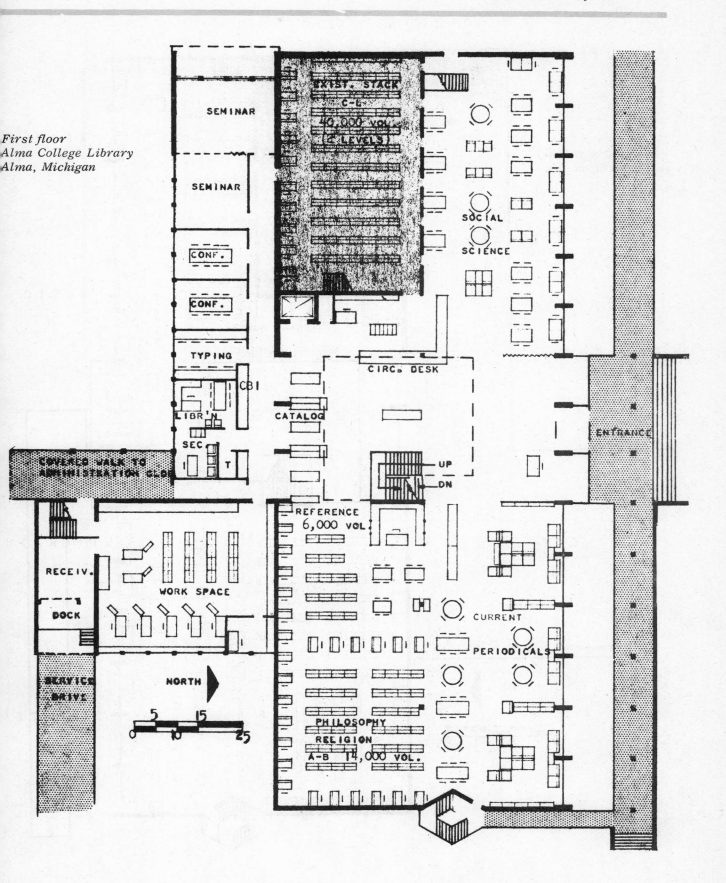

First floor
Alma College Library
Alma, Michigan

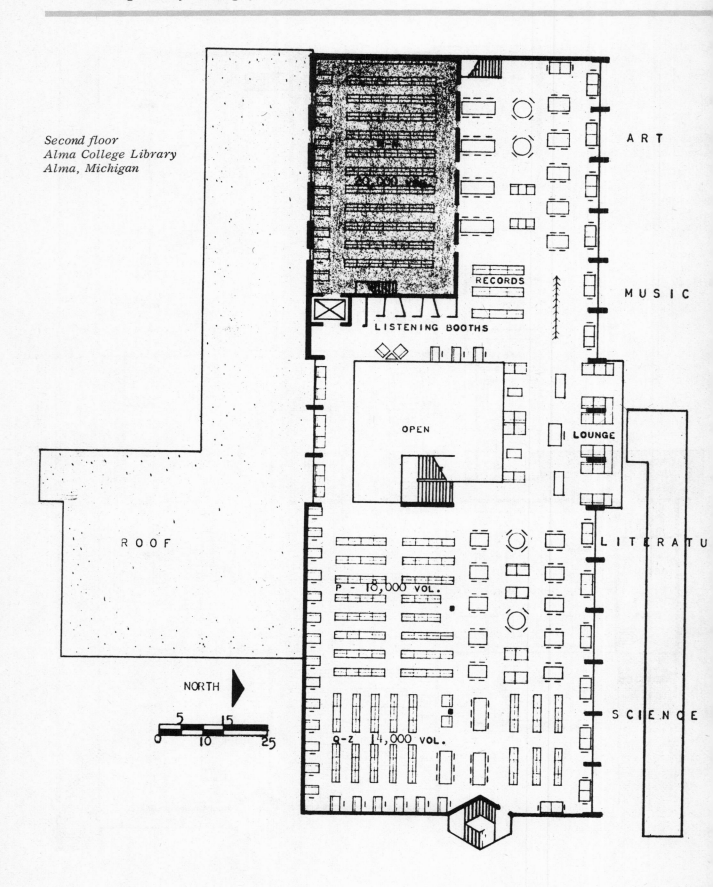

*Second floor
Alma College Library
Alma, Michigan*

RECORDS

LISTENING BOOTHS

OPEN

ROOF

P - 18,000 VOL.

Q-Z 14,000 VOL.

ART

MUSIC

LOUNGE

LITERATU

SCIENCE

NORTH

5   15
0   10   25

Question: What do you plan to do with reserve books? Where do you plan to put them?

MISS MacCURDY: In the first stack or two of the existing stack areas.

Question: Is there any difference between the building you would have liked to have and the building you finally got?

MISS MacCURDY: Yes. Keeping the existing stack has greatly affected the building. If we were completely free, I would like to see it a little wider and proportionately a little less long.

Question: With the ceiling height already 16 or 18 feet, I wonder about the advisability and necessity of having the open well from the first to the second floor. It seems to me this will create problems in heating and noise, and also waste space.

MR. VANDERPLOEG: The floor-to-floor height from the first to the second floor will be 15 feet, determined by the existing stacks. We had considered the possibility of dropping the second floor a couple of feet, but we were getting so close to the third tier of the existing stack that we thought we might as well hold to it. Also, with the very wide spans we are using, we will be involved in probably at least 3 feet of construction between the first-floor ceiling and the second floor.

The ceiling height in the open well will be approximately 25 feet. The purpose of the open well is twofold: (1) psychologically, to make a more impressive space as people enter the building and (2) to help move people up to the second floor. An important part of the library is on the second floor, and we want people to feel they can move up very easily, that it is not a separate part of the library.

Question: With the arrangement of the furniture in the technical processes area—in its relationship to the cataloging—you have given the priority to books rather than to librarians. You could have saved considerable walking to and from stacks.

MISS MacCURDY: My cataloging department likes windows, so we are going to let them walk farther and sit by the windows to work.

Question: As an architect, I am interested in whether the building is air-conditioned and humidified.

MR. VANDERPLOEG: We have planned to maintain year-around temperature and humidity control, but I question it for this installation. It is fairly far north in Michigan. There is no summer program at present, so that the cooling concern, as far as human use is concerned, is confined to no more than a month in the spring and a month in the fall. To install expensive equipment and to operate it through the summer simply for the benefit of the books, and possibly a half-dozen people, would appear to be of dubious economic

value. We might spend a thousand dollars a summer on operation alone. Possibly that money could be better spent for books.

Comment: If you don't have summer school, you don't need air conditioning, but you could have a small outlet for the workroom and, very inexpensively, make those people working throughout the summer very comfortable.

Question: Has any consideration been given to humidity control for the archives?

MR. VANDERPLOEG: That ties in with the total program, but we would provide special equipment for the archive room. That would be the one room where you would be concerned about preserving books.

Question: Is there any possibility of altering the stairs, which are hazardous in winter and difficult for a handicapped student?

MR. VANDERPLOEG: There is a covered walk along here. It will be possible to avoid the use of these steps by coming along the covered walk. The building is on a slight podium.

Question: Is the basement a real one, on the ground, or are there enough windows and air space for ventilation for the archives? If not, why not put them on the third floor in the present stacks?

MR. VANDERPLOEG: The grade falls off to the east, so the basement rooms at the east end will receive some natural light along the north. I think that in the case of the archives, it would be the intent completely to control the air in any event, so that it would not be particularly necessary or desirable to have them open to an outside wall.

The main problem is organization, and an alternative we have considered is an extension of the sections of the collection. With present organization there is a division on the first and second floors which may become inconvenient as departments grow. The chief disadvantage would be that it would force us to continue the kind of stack that is in the building now, rather than the freestanding stacks, so that students would have less direct accessibility to their books.

MRS. AMNER: Do you mean to use the existing stack area for self-service?

MISS MacCURDY: Yes.

MRS. AMNER: And if you enlarge it, do you expect that to be self-service, also?

MISS MacCURDY: Yes.

MRS. AMNER: It seems to me you would be pushing the books in one corner and the students in the other, and have little connection between the students and the books. If you wish to encourage students to use books, it would be better to have it the way it is.

University of Alberta Library

Edmonton, Alberta

Presentation of plans
    B. B. PEEL
    Chief Librarian

Building data
    Architect: D. L. G. Macdonald and William Wood
            Edmonton, Alberta
    Dimensions
        First unit: 140 feet by 165 feet
        North and south wings: 70 feet by 124 feet
        Completed buildings: 280 feet by 165 feet
    Type of library: College library
    Population to be served: 6,500 students
    Book capacity
        First unit: 456,000 volumes
        North and south wings: 748,750 volumes
        Completed building: 1,204,750 volumes
    Seating capacity
        First unit: 900
        North and south wings: 1,460
        Completed building: 2,360
    Size of module: 20 feet by 22-1/2 feet on
            column centers

Main entrance
University of Alberta Library
Edmonton, Alberta

University of Alberta Photographic Service

MR. B. B. PEEL

The Rutherford Library of the University of Alberta is a beautiful but inflexible four-story building constructed in the traditional plan with large reading rooms and concentrated stacks. Opened in 1951, its area is 83,000 square feet—7,500 square feet of it attic space above the monumental reference reading room. Originally, increasing needs for library space were to be met by doubling the size, but a new library building would be less expensive with better utilization of space.

At larger universities, when a second library is erected to meet the needs for reader accommodation as student enrollment rises, the usual practice is to use the original building as a research library with most of the collection and to erect a new building as an undergraduate library. On the Edmonton campus of the University of Alberta, the reverse is taking place. Since the design of the Rutherford Library does not provide—in close proximity to the books—the working space and privacy desired by advanced students and faculty, it was decided to make the new building the research library. The Rutherford Library is to be converted into an undergraduate library. In the initial stage, after the erection of the new research library, there may be criticism that we have too few books and readers rattling around in too many libraries. However, if the student enrollment and the book stock increase as rapidly as expected, time will justify the decision.

The enrollment on the Edmonton campus for 1960-61 was about 6,500 students. By the time the new library building is available, there probably will be an additional 2,000 students. By 1980 it is expected that the Province of Alberta will have some 28,000 students, with perhaps 20,000 of these on the Edmonton campus. Diversion of more students than expected to the new Calgary campus and a network of junior colleges would not necessarily affect the library space needs, since the Edmonton campus will remain the principal provincial center of graduate study and research. Since 1957 the Edmonton Campus has rapidly developed a graduate program in teaching and research. This trend, with its important implications for the library, can be expected to gain momentum in the years ahead. There will be more specialization and correspondingly greater demands on the library to build up research collections.

For several years in the 1950's the library added about 9,000 volumes a year; during the last three years of the decade the program accelerated until, in 1960-61, the library added 26,000 accessioned volumes and 10,000 documents. The rate of growth is likely to increase to 40,000 or 50,000 volumes a year. The assumption is that the library collection will reach a million books and documents by the end of the 1970's.

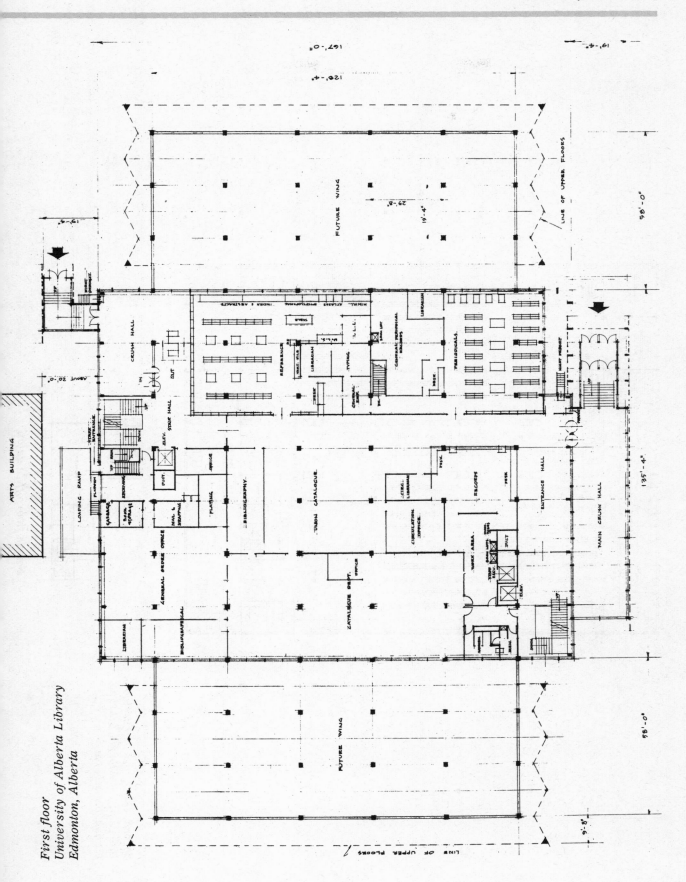

First floor
University of Alberta Library
Edmonton, Alberta

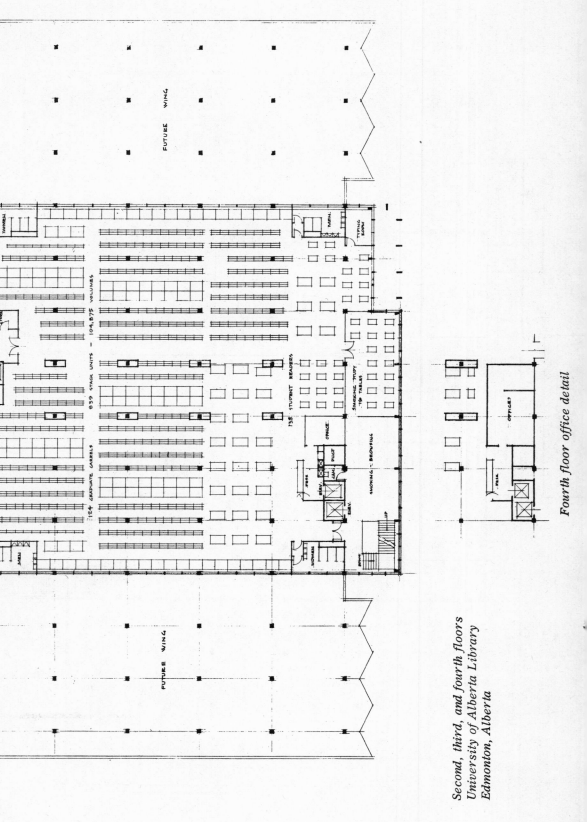

Second, third, and fourth floors
University of Alberta Library
Edmonton, Alberta

Fourth floor office detail

When the new research library is completed, it will receive all the materials used by senior undergraduates, honor students, graduate students, and other research workers in special areas. Thus, the research library will contain most of the collection. Undergraduate materials will be retained in the Rutherford Library at the prespecialization and general educational level.

The new research library will be located a city block from the Rutherford Library. This is at the center of the campus, with the university's major science buildings on three sides and the arts building on the fourth side. The first unit of the research library will occupy an open quadrangle between two long two-story buildings known as the North and South Labs. These buildings are expendable since they are low buildings which have outlived their usefulness while occupying choice space. The laboratories are to be removed when the library needs to add wings north and south of the first unit.

The principles of design and service include the following:

1. The new library is to be functional in design and have considerable flexibility.
2. The building, of modular construction, is to consist of a first unit, rectangular in shape, to which will be added two substantial wings as needed. The wings will practically double the size and capacity of the first unit. In designing the first unit, the ultimate building is to be kept in mind.
3. The building is to be air-conditioned.
4. The central location of the research library makes it appear necessary to provide a secondary entrance on the east side of the building. The subsidiary entrance must lead into the central circulation-catalog hall and control be simple and inexpensive.
5. Control of the library is to be at the exit. Although the library is primarily for the use of senior research students, it is not proposed to institute a pass system. Galoshes will be kept outside the control point, and brief cases allowed within. There will be provision both near the entrances and within the library for coats.
6. The circulation desk is to be near the main entrance, with circulation records centralized here.
7. The building is to have provision for adequate vertical communication in the form of elevators, booklifts, and pneumatic tubes. Consideration should be given to the use of modern devices to speed up and facilitate all library operations: for example, intercommunications systems and closed-circuit TV.
8. In its final stage the new library is to have storage facilities for a research collection of at least 1,000,000 books and documents.

9. In the first unit the building is to provide seating for 900 readers; in the completed building there will be seating for approximately 2,000 readers. Much of the seating should be provided at individual tables or at tables divided by screens.
10. The library will be on the open stack system with materials and services arranged to promote maximum self-help. The book collection and reader-seating facilities should be close together.
11. The basic organizational plan is to have essential library services and information on the first floor. Library users must pass these services before proceeding to the book collection on the floors above. The library collection is to be arranged in the Library of Congress classification sequence from the fourth floor down to the second floor, with one major grouping of subjects on each floor.

Organizationally, it is desirable to concentrate many of the essential library departments on the first floor. With this arrangement the library user can check the record of holdings and also quickly reach basic information without penetrating too far into the building. The master catalog should be close to the entrance. The processing departments should be adjacent to the catalog, and general bibliographies and general reference material should be housed in the catalog area. The periodical reading room will house current periodicals, arranged by subject.

The general reference materials and service will be on the main floor, with subject reference materials on the separate floors. The philosophy of reference service will be to emphasize instruction and guidance. Since the building is primarily a research library, the student user will be expected to find much of the information he needs on his own initiative.

The second floor will be typical of other floors above. Much of the floor space will be given over to freestanding stacks, with reading tables (perhaps most of them individual tables) arranged around the perimeter. This reading space will include some special facilities for the teaching staff. There will be a conference room on each floor. Near the public elevator and stairway will be a service point with an office.

Floor plans and stack furnishings on the fifth floor will be modified according to the needs of the special collections and services which will be grouped together in this area. The largest unit will be the documents collection, which is expected to expand rapidly. In addition, the library administration will have offices on this floor. The ground floor will contain coatrooms, public and staff lavatories, and perhaps the medical library.

Discussion

MR. NICHOLSON: The rooms which have to do with coats and parcels are called "crush" rooms. What does that mean?

MR. PEEL: That apparently is an architectural term which just means an entrance lobby.

MRS. AMNER: I don't know how many people you envision in technical processes, but if you are a growing library and adding new things, I suggest you think your wildest dreams and then add some. This is what is happening to us. We thought to our wildest dreams, and we added a little bit. Could you do that?

MR. PEEL: We have a staff of about 30 in the two processing departments. We expect to increase our accessions rapidly. We can seat 60 comfortably, and perhaps push this number to 70 or 75. Notice the wings. We expect in about ten years to be adding a wing, and then technical processing can acquire more room. I think we have sufficient room for processing staff there.

Question: Would the module be more satisfactory if it were divisible by 3 feet one way and 4-1/2 feet the other? Then, functionally, I think it would be very satisfactory.

MR. PEEL: I recommended that it be changed to 18 feet instead of 20 feet. However, the Library Committee felt that more room was needed. I think it is a mistake.

Question: Is this building air-conditioned?

MR. PEEL: Yes; our present building is not air-conditioned. The first floor, a ground floor, has no windows in it. We have spent ten years trying to get the proper quantity of air down there. We are all in favor of air conditioning.

John Carroll University Library

University Heights, Ohio

Presentation of plans
  REV. JAMES MACKIN
  Librarian

  ERNST PAYER
  Architect

  EMMERSON HUFFMAN
  (Construction)

  JOSEPH LEITHOLD
  (Financing)

Building data
  Architect: Rowley, Payer,
      Huffman & Leithold, Inc.
      Cleveland, Ohio
  Type of library: University library
  Population to be served: Graduate and undergraduate students, faculty
  Area: 66,230 square feet
  Book capacity: 340,000 volumes
  Seating capacity: 500
      Study carrel rooms: 96
      Lecture room: 150
  Size of module: 25 feet 6 inches
  Cost: Building—$811,924
  Cost per square foot: $17.80
  Cost per cubic foot: $1.32

FATHER MACKIN

John Carroll decided on the site for the university in 1886, and in 1906 it was built for 600-800 students. Immediately after World War II, enrollment jumped and at present it is 4,000, with 2,800 full-time students. The university is primarily a men's college, but it has an evening school and for two sessions of summer school there are women students. The original buildings were all College Gothic, and this building is the first across the road —in the new section of the campus.

The problem was that the old library was on the top of the Administration Building. The old library would seat about 110 and was designed to house about 80,000 volumes. It had 110,000 volumes by the time we seriously began planning a new library, and it was overcrowded. There was a small study hall for a large number of students. The faculty had been pushed out entirely. They could come there to get books, but there was no room for them to work. Therefore, we wanted to plan a library which would have a basic collection for undergraduates, would

Front view
John Carroll University Library
University Heights, Ohio

allow for some research, and would supplement books with plenty of microfilm. We hoped to divide the reading areas into large ones for students and smaller ones for faculty and have plenty of carrels and good control.

The Library Committee began to work about 1954. By 1957, when we started to engage architects, it had planned for a modular library of 90 modules, originally calling for 22-1/2-foot modules. Later, at the suggestion of the architects, in order to house 340,000 volumes and 500-600 students, the module size was increased to 25-1/2 feet, which increased the total size from about 48,000 square feet to 66,000 square feet.

MR. ERNST PAYER

No problem today is solved by one architect who does all the planning, designing, detailing, and supervision. Mr. Huffman and Mr. Leithold did the architectural work with me. We worked with construction engineers, lighting engineers, mechanical engineers, heating engineers, and others.

We feel that when you enter a building, you should immediately and easily be able to orient yourself; therefore, our entrance lobby immediately gives you a view through a glass wall in the back

into the bookstacks. You know you are in a library. It shows you the card catalogs. You see where the elevator is. You see the main stair. Through a glazed opening in one wall, you see a browsing room on the other side and a corridor leading to other parts of the library. I thought the honor system would work, but I found that almost every library today controls student entrances through a turnstile. When students leave, they pass a checkout desk.

The first point is that we feel a person should be easily oriented. The second is that in any building, whether a factory or a library, you, of course, have problems of circulation. You bring in services, books, service personnel, people who run the library, and then students.

We hear a lot about functional design, but you rarely hear that a building has to function emotionally—an omission I have found very disturbing. In three or four libraries we visited, all the rooms, regardless of whether they were small study rooms or large reading rooms with perhaps more than fifty people in them, had the same ceiling height. I found it a bit monotonous. We kept this very much in mind and achieved, without any additional expense, different room heights with our large reading rooms, for example—18 inches higher than the others. Another

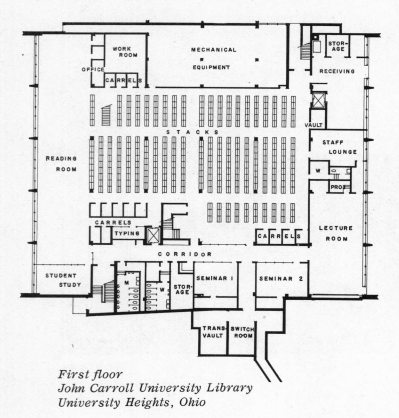

First floor
John Carroll University Library
University Heights, Ohio

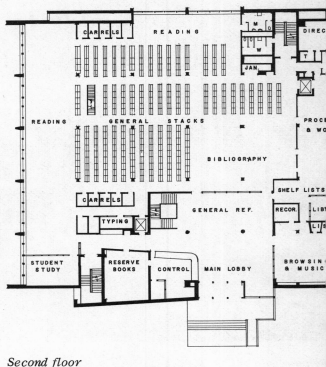

Second floor
John Carroll University Library
University Heights, Ohio

important aspect is, of course, color. A building can be killed by drab colors, and you can make a room wider, shorter, lower, or higher by using bright colors on one or the other wall. The same is true of lighting.

We work somewhat differently, I believe, from most other offices. We use electrical engineers for electrical work—for wiring our controls and electric outlets. We make our preliminary computation of foot-candles and have the electrical engineer check those figures. But since we work rather intensely and closely on all problems, and therefore are intimately familiar with what we want to achieve in each room, we confer again with the lighting engineer and tell him what we want to achieve; by that time we have made our own selections.

We do the same thing with color. There are certain standard rules; for instance, you should have cool colors on the south side and warm colors on the north side. But I think this is kindergarten talk, and you must treat each room individually. You try to carry a theme through a building and not listen to interior decorators (almost an offensive word in our office) who say, "Of course, your dining room will be in Renaissance, and the ladies' boudoir has to be in Louis Quinze. What could be more wonderful!" And every time you open a door, you fall from one century into another. You should have a feeling that a building hangs together. We also be-

lieve this is comfortable; many people may not be aware of it, but you must design for the few sensitive souls.

I have heard a great deal today about modules. You get the impression that modular design is something specifically invented for libraries and used only in libraries. In any structure where an element is repeated over and over again—in this case 3-foot bookstacks—naturally you will choose a column spacing. In libraries, of course, the module will be a multiple of 3 feet plus a small installation space, to get the stacks between the posts or columns, plus the thickness of the heaviest column in the building. In this case, our module is 25 feet 6 inches.

We feel very strongly that too many modern buildings today are completely devoid of art. We try to tie in art, especially in a college building. Students who come from the hills and the backwoods have had no contact with art, and if they do not get it in college, they may never get it. Therefore, one of our first moves was to incorporate a statue or sculpture with the outside of the building. I confess that we—shall I say "slyly"—included the cost of the sculpture in the budget.

We were given a very strict budget, and we are proud to say we built a building within four tenths of 1 per cent of the budget. When the final bids were in, I said, "Now would be the time to commission

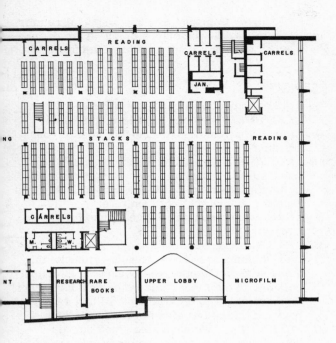

Third floor
John Carroll University Library
University Heights, Ohio

Mr. McVeigh"—who is one of the country's outstanding sculptors.

"But, how much?"

"Well, it is in the budget."

So, we got our statue.

There was a lot of talk about light and light intensity. We have a relatively small library for 340,000 volumes, and after some discussion we settled for 70 foot-candles in the reading room.

Lighting has to be very carefully modulated. If you are illuminating everything with the same light intensity, the whole effect falls flat. Therefore, in the corridors, we have 25 to 30 foot-candles, but in the display cases on the side, 60 and 80 foot-candles. In the browsing room, we have an average of 75 foot-candles, yet the pictures on the walls have 200 foot-candles. In the recordings booth, where you are supposed to listen, we have only 20. In the stackrooms, we have 50 at the top, 25 at the bottom.

Incidentally, after some experimenting, we ran our lights trusswise. That is subject to argument. We experimented and found that the average bookstack is a canyon. If you have one light in the middle, the light comes down. If you run the light crossways, the light comes at such a flat angle that even at the lowest point it will hit the book at the flatter angle, coming over the edge of the opposite rim of the canyon, than if it came from the middle. We find this to be some advantage.

We were very happy to find that we would build our library not in the Gothic row but across the street in a large undeveloped meadow. Everybody agreeing, we decided we would not build a Gothic library; yet we wanted a library which would not clash. I assure you we were perfectly capable of designing a beautiful glass box with a zigzag roof, but that would not go well with the Gothic. We decided to use the same brick as was used in all the other buildings. We decided to use limestone and keep the building of the same bulk as the other buildings, but there the similarity ends.

MR. EMMERSON HUFFMAN

The structure of the building is fundamentally of a concrete material and set up on a 25-foot 6-inch module. We built it basically for economy, being able to reuse a lot of the form lumber, and raised it a floor at a time. This resulted in our being able to complete the building in some eleven months.

We also used standard lumber sizes for the concrete. We have essentially a post-and-beam system with concrete joists in between the beams. This has allowed us to coordinate and install our lighting fixtures, which are recessed into the space formed by the ribs or the joists. The lights in the reading rooms are basically diffusing.

The air conditioning is hooked to the lights and diffuses through those areas. We are using the ceilings themselves as air-diffusing plants, pumping the conditioned air into the spaces, and the air filters through the ceiling.

The concrete structure is wrapped with insulation in its entirety, and in no place that I can find, do we have an outside material in contact with an inside material. The cavities in the walls are all insulated. This results in substantial savings in operating costs for room control and heating.

We used materials that matched the Gothic buildings on the existing campus. The main entrance is all stainless steel, for low maintenance. The ceiling is all glass with inset lighting fixtures which illuminate the entire area below. The brick aluminum sides are monumental.

MR. JOSEPH LEITHOLD

You probably noticed throughout this presentation that we have stressed low maintenance material. We were given a tight budget. That was two and a half years ago. The architects were called in then to establish a budget, and we came up with $1,200,000 for the building, $100,000 for bookstacks, and $350,000 for furnishings. We were probably quite conservative on the bookstacks, as the total cost of the stacks was some $63,000. Our base bid received for stacks was $1,450,000, which was about four tenths of 1 per cent below our budget figure.

This contract breaks down as follows: The architectural trades were some $811,000 or 65 per cent—I do not think the dollar figures mean much. We are talking about a million and a quarter for this building. Sixty-five per cent was for architectural trades; 19 per cent for mechanical trades. This building is completely air-conditioned all around, humidity control ranging from 35 to 55 per cent, depending on the outside climatic conditions. The electrical work was 10 per cent, and we should point out that in the large reading spaces we diffused the supply air through the ceiling fixtures. Many buildings have done this, and we think this method is gaining wider acceptance.

By diffusing the air through the fixtures, you eliminate Anemostats, and with an Anemostat the round or square ceiling fixture becomes slightly black around the outer edges. With low velocity diffusion the entire fixture will soil equally.

For the bookstacks we used some wood, but most stacks were of metal. We used some woods around the perimeter of the reading areas to give an added warmth, as compared to the cold steelwork on the stack areas. Finished hardware for stacks was 1 per cent, or $12,000.

In the beginning we had a tight budget and did not know quite where we were going. We made changes from time to time. We went from plaster to brick walls, and from vinyl asbestos flooring to rubber tile flooring, so that we set ourselves a lot of alternates, a lot of unit prices. You cannot save real money on cutting finishes in any building. The only way to save real money is by eliminating part of that building.

For instance, we have a stainless steel front entrance, with Herculite all-glass doors. All our plaster walls within finger-tip reach are covered with heavy-gauge vinyl plaque. We have rubber tile on all floors of the building. We have carpeting in the lounging room and the G. K. Chesterton room. We have superior finishes throughout the building by reason of taking all of our deductive alternatives and eliminating all other alternatives. We did not spend the $1,450,000. We have a net of $47,000 on the total building, and this is the goal for a minimum, quality building. That is less than architectural fees.

We had control of the manufacture and the selection of the bookstacks. We went to six manufacturing plants to examine the stacks. Generally, if you tell the manufacturers what you want, you can get it, although one manufacturer designed a stack that we did not accept. This manufacturer built a stack section that was really the Cadillac of the industry. I have never seen anything like it. It had a Cadillac price, too. Had we accepted their stacks, we would have paid some $85,000, but the stacks were so superior! If you have the dollars to spend, the manufacturers will come to you.

Our rubber tile was of sufficient quantity for the

B. F. Goodrich Company to make a special run for us. We did not like the colors or the graining in their stock tile and we said, "What can you do?"

Discussion

Question: What was your cost of furniture?
MR. LEITHOLD: I would say close to $75,000.
Question: What was the square-foot cost of your building?
MR. LEITHOLD: Including structure, plumbing, mechanical, electrical—everything but the architect's fee—it was $18.79 a square foot. This includes stacks, but not furniture.
Question: What provision did you make for future expansion?
MR. PAYER: On one side of the building the exterior columns are strong enough—although the same size as the others—to serve as interior columns in the future, and we can enlarge them. We have space to enlarge the building several bays out on the left side for reading rooms.
MR. LEITHOLD: We have also sized our air-conditioning equipment, the ductwork, and so forth for future expansion. Our technical processing area on the second floor takes in the right-hand bay and most of the plan. This is also to be expanded in the next bay to the left, and we have provided an underfloor deck system there to take care of electrical needs.
MR. PAYER: And we used prefabricated partitions, which can be reused.
Question: What is the air-conditioning system?
MR. LEITHOLD: Centrifugal air unit, 235 tons. We have a cooling tower on the roof.
Question: How is the building oriented?
MR. LEITHOLD: It is almost north. We are in a situation where there is some sun on the building at various times throughout the day and throughout the seasons; therefore, we have heat-reducing insulating glass on all sides.
Question: I wonder whether the reference area is proportionately large enough. It is quite small relative to the space for other parts of the collection.
FATHER MACKIN: As it is an open stack library, we felt it could be smaller than it otherwise might be.

Newark Colleges of Rutgers University Library

Newark, New Jersey

Presentation of plans
  DONALD RYAN
  Librarian

Building data
  Architect: Kelly & Gruzen
        New York City
  Type of library: College library
  Population to be served: 3,500 undergraduates
        and 500 graduate students; 250 faculty
        members
  Area: 52,100 square feet

Book capacity: 200,000 volumes
Seating capacity: 650
Ceiling height: 9 feet 6 inches and 10 feet
Cost
    Building: $1,350,000 (not including furnish-
        ings or site)
    Furnishings: $165,000
Cost per square foot: $27.50
Cost per cubic foot: $1.90

MR. DONALD RYAN

The Newark Colleges of Rutgers State University of New Jersey consist of several professional
schools, including a school of law, college of pharmacy, college of nursing, graduate school of business, and the Newark College of Arts and Sciences.

Our library serves all the schools except law
and pharmacy. We have two evening programs—a
university college and extension—and several grad-

Basement
Newark Colleges of Rutgers University Library
Newark, New Jersey

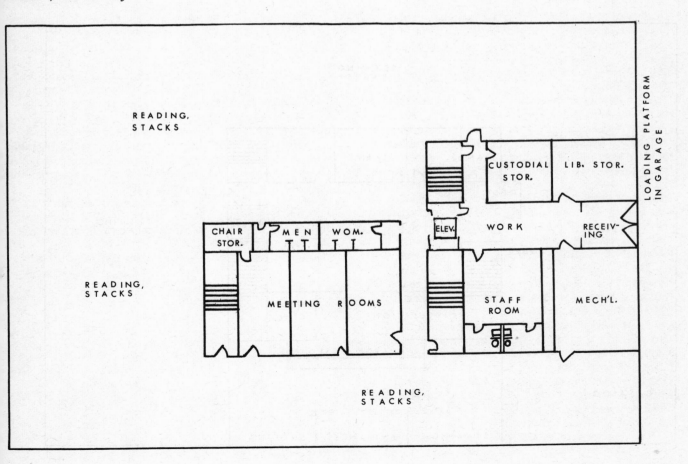

uate schools from the main campus also offer courses in Newark. These are the graduate schools of arts and sciences, social work, education, and library science.

We are serving some 2,000 full-time students, and by 1970 expect to be serving 4,000 full-time students. We expect most of these students will be commuters for the indefinite future; some of them travel twenty to fifty miles each day. We plan some dormitories. The library has about 70,000 volumes, and we are adding about 6,500 volumes a year. We check about 1,000 different periodical titles, and circulate 21,000 volumes a year on a semester loan basis.

The staff consists of 4 professionals and 4 clerks. We are on the third and fourth floors of a former brewery, without any elevators. Other buildings that Rutgers uses in Newark are former houses, office buildings, stores, a razor-blade factory, and a quaint little stable. In 1959 a state-wide referendum gave the university $9,000,000 to add to $2,000,000 from other sources to start a new cam-

pus. Steps were taken to acquire a downtown site of twenty-five acres with federal urban renewal funds.

The architectural firm of Kelly & Gruzen was asked to submit an ultimate plan for the entire campus. I will try to describe this plan. The buildings are grouped in a large quadrangle around a central plaza, with graduate and professional appendages and classrooms on the east end and science buildings on the south. Student facilities are grouped on the north end. The central plaza surrounds the library.

The library itself has one entrance, facing northeast, directly next to the classrooms. The site is very large. Fifty-five per cent of the open land is on the plaza. The only way the library could extend would be in the central area. There are other problems created by this situation: for instance, the architects wanted to make a monumental building out of it.

In our program we accented flexibility. The library, we feel, will be filled within ten years or less, and we know it is going to be a long time be-

First floor
Newark Colleges of Rutgers University Library
Newark, New Jersey

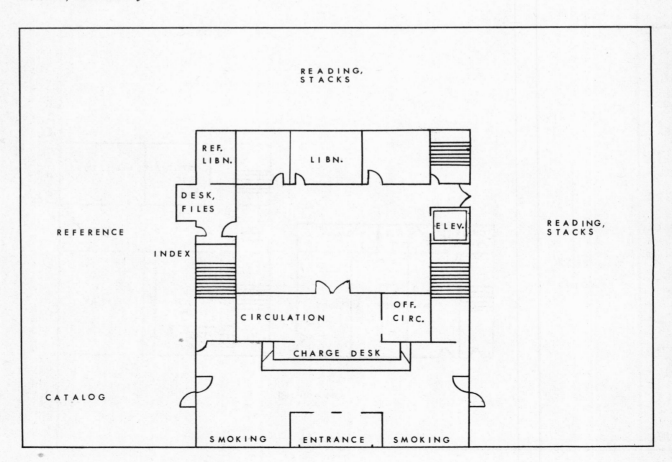

fore we get additional money, so we want to be able to utilize best the space we have available. We have eliminated all artificial spaces except those for microfilm and so forth, and tried to keep out everything not strictly pertaining to the library.

For instance, the basement is to have a 9-foot ceiling and the first floor a 10-foot ceiling. This is from the top of the floor to the bottom of the ceiling and excludes the fixture. The second floor is 9 feet 6 inches. Some persons have criticized the first floor, saying the lobby itself will not have a large enough ceiling height at 10 feet, while others have criticized other floors, saying 9 feet 6 inches is probably too much on the top floor, or somewhat of a waste, and 9 feet too much in the basement.

There is a vestibule lobby of 1,600 square feet, including the vestibule. The architect is considering removing the vestibule and installing revolving doors. The circulation department's location here will enable us to check people on their way out. To the left are a catalog area and a reference area. Behind the circulation area is the processing room, where most of the ordering will be done. Since our cataloging is done at the main library in New Brunswick, at this point we do not have to plan for catalogers. If we ever do our own cataloging, the librarian's office complex can be moved elsewhere, and the whole area expanded.

The architect hopes to get something like a 44-foot span without any columns or supporting walls. I hope he can do this. It would be a librarian's dream, and we have budget limitations. In order to get this, he will have to have a central core of stairs repeated on all three floors, which ties up our space between the stairs; but this is a relatively small percentage of the area. The walls at the stairway would be weight-bearing.

Critique

MR. LAWRENCE: Since the war we have used one revolving door. It was for the president of a large company and cost from $8,000 to $10,000.

Second floor
Newark Colleges of Rutgers University Library
Newark, New Jersey

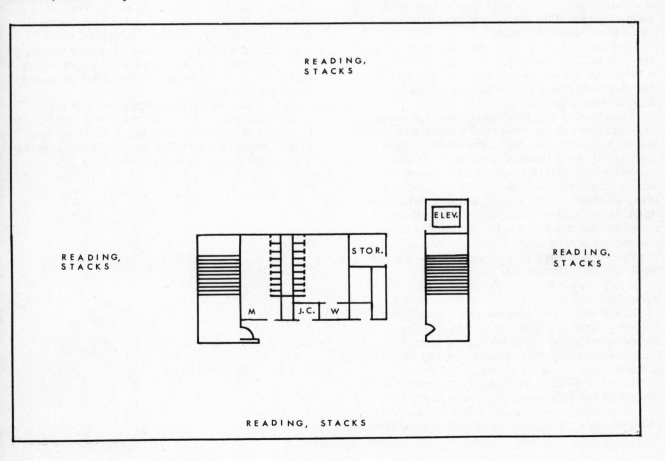

It is not an economy move. It is about the most expensive type of entrance. Most hotels do not use theirs—"This way is too windy today. Please come in the side door," and so forth. The big, excessive floor span would be wonderful, and I suppose you could do it at $27.50. I don't know how it can be done for that amount of money. I would not say it is a low budget job.

MR. RYAN: All I can say is that our architect gave us the estimate of $27.50 a square foot, and he claims Newark is one of the highest building-cost areas in the country. Most people who have to build think their own area is the highest. Our architect tells us that his estimate is probably too low, but we do not know. We are probably spending too little money on decoration and so forth. If we come out better, all of this will go back into the library.

MR. NICHOLSON: I think a central core of work area will have you running in circles all the time. There is no way through; you will always have to go around it. The work space could be rearranged for a more economical operation for the general public as well as for yourselves.

MR. SIDELLS: On another building, I thought that the librarians had overinfluenced the architect and that the architect had not really done a job of architecture. I am afraid this is just the opposite. This strikes me as a kind of architect's free-for-all up to this point.

The budget figure of $27.50 a square foot will buy a lot of long-span floor framing and that sort of thing, but you as librarians have been living with this holy module. The only question is: What is its dimension?

You claim it will take all of your equipment. Although these plans show open spaces with no stacks, they obviously will have stacks in them one day. If the columns and the spacing are correct, there will be no conflict. I see no reason why any architect should attempt to carry heavy loading on such a floor system. When you finish your books and stacks and carry them on a tremendous span with a 10-foot ceiling height, running the stacks up so close, you cannot tell whether or not there is a column there. This, I think, gets a little absurd.

It is possible that, if most of the mechanical equipment will be on the second floor—and I would assume it will because of the large penthouse—a vertical expansion of this building should be ended by using folding plate or something else. Since this is in downtown Newark, it probably would look all right.

This can be done as illustrated recently in the library at the University of Nevada at Reno—a 90-foot clear span—by using 4-inch folded plate, concrete roof. You need carry only a snow load.

This does not mean more stacks on that floor. It is simple and easy, and you can leave the columns out. Trying it on the first floor would not work. As an architect, I would never recommend that you turn the whole problem over to one person; a library can be over-"architected."

MR. HILB: I wonder whether the architect could plan better if the use of the facilities was indicated. For instance, on the second floor there is a space which indicates great flexibility, but there is no indication of how you might want to house periodicals, either bound or current. I would say that the one feature that seems excellent is the exit on the first floor.

MR. RYAN: Periodicals housing is not shown because we are not sure yet ourselves exactly how it will be done. I suspect there will be a separate room for current periodicals, and bound periodicals will be housed somewhere off the first floor in our straight alphabetical file. Beyond that, we hope the building will be sufficiently flexible so that we can place these rooms where we desire. We are fully aware that if we wait too long we may be in serious trouble and we should think about placing very soon.

Comment: When you enter the main Cleveland Library, you will see a sign at the revolving door: "Use at Your Own Risk." There are definite hazards. I cannot see a place for a revolving door in any modern library. In regard to the long span of 44 feet with a 9-foot ceiling height, it can be done. If you want to keep a decent floor dimension, you are going to have a 5-foot clearance on the beam.

Comment: If that is the only entrance, it is not completely practical to remove the vestibule. If you air-condition a building, a vestibule is a must. Anybody who wants air conditioning wants a vestibule for every outside entrance.

Oregon State University Library

Corvallis, Oregon

Presentation of plans
WILLIAM H. CARLSON
Director

Building data
Architect: Hamlin and Martin
            Eugene, Oregon
Type of library: Main university library
Population to be served: 8,400 students
Area: 127,000 square feet
Module: 22-1/2 feet
Cost: Building—$2,385,000, including air condi-
      tioning and funds for equipment

MR. WILLIAM H. CARLSON

Oregon State University is a science-oriented
institution, coeducational, with an enrollment now of
8,000, and it will be 8,400 by the time we move into
this building. We have $2,385,000, including funds
for equipment, from our legislature, and we are in
the early phases of preparing working drawings.

The building we hope to have for our $2,385,000
will be 127,000 square feet in area—that will be the
first unit. I emphasize this because the whole is
planned on a unit basis from the beginning. This
unit will be the first of three phases of construction;
by the time that the third phase is in operation, we
can have a building as large as that showed you this
morning by Dr. Rankin for the University of Pittsburgh. We can even have a separate undergraduate
library, if events turn that way. On the other hand,
if a miracle is achieved and everything is micro-
carded and so forth, we have a good-looking building, and it will not sit there unfinished or be waiting
for any additions.

The building will be built by the lift-slab method,
which means that slabs for all four floors will be
poured one on top of the other. As the workmen
pour the first floor, the concrete for that floor is
treated chemically; they then pour the next one, and
so on, until they get to the fourth floor. These are
then conveyed on electrically controlled jacks, which
balance and adjust themselves. The floors are
pushed up along the uprights that constitute the
modules for the building; thus all the concrete pour-
ing is done right on the first floor.

We are going to have the open access, dispersed
type of building. We have tried through preparation
to avoid falling between the two stools of the old
traditional style and of the newer methods, as some
buildings I have visited have clearly done.

Now I want to talk a little on the elements of
planning. One point is the selection of the architect,
and I was both pleased and flattered when I was
given the opportunity to recommend the architect to
be appointed. Thus I had my choice of architects.
We could have had big-name people and a large
firm, but we settled for a small firm in Eugene,
Oregon, a firm that had never built a university library building. The firm had built one small public
library in Eugene—the Eugene Public Library.

We selected these people because they had ex-
hibited some imagination in the work they had done.
They have a good record of coming out extremely
close to their budgets, and in our thinking this was
important. Then, also, a very important thing was
the opportunity to visit with them; we learned that
they were the kind of people we could work with and
that they would learn along with us. We concluded
that we could have a pleasant and mutually profit-
able relationship between the architect and the librarians.

The modules are 22-1/2 feet by 22-1/2 feet.
When the architects started engineering this, about
two or three weeks ago, they found they were going
to have to give us about 2 inches more on the modules, one way or the other. Actually, we are building a foot wider. In the preliminary planning, the
modules had not been refined to the point where the
bookstacks would fit in between them and provide
clearance room for the uprights of the end panels.

There will be a garden area and an arcade walk-
way which will come down to the main entrance. It
is actually at the on-grade level. We won't even
need a ramp for an incapacitated person, but such a
person can roll in with a very slight little rise. The
subbasement will contain all of the mechanical
equipment for the building.

The air cooling is going to be plenum chamber,
with the areas all open; the fans will raise air
throughout the whole area, and there will be no individual outlets. The air will simply come out
through holes spaced throughout the entire ceiling
area.

This is similar to the plan used in the New Orleans Public Library. We got some of our best
ideas from New Orleans and Seattle and, personally,
I don't think there is too much difference in the re-
spective problems encountered.

We are going to have a continuous screening;
this is somewhat similar to what they have in New
Orleans. It will be engineered so that it will give
us complete absence of direct sunlight from the
south. There is a southern exposure, and the
screening goes all the way around. The screening
will probably be Anodyte aluminum and will extend
3 feet out from the windows; the estimated saving
on both cooling and heating is approximately 17 per
cent.

Our first floor follows largely standard prac- tice, and I must say that this is an all-purpose building. It is intended as both an undergraduate li- brary and a research library, but it can as well be- come more of a research library or more of an un- dergraduate library. The technical processing people are going to have to go down the stairs (and down in the elevator) to service the catalogs below, but this creates little difficulty; they have been do- ing that for the last thirty years.

We have a generous allotment of space in square footage—I think about as much as Pittsburgh has—in the present plan. The top floor is really the core of our library, and this is the research part of our op- eration.

Now, here is a point where we have much debate among ourselves. We are divided in opinion. You will note there are three separate services offices: the science office, the forestry office, and an engi- neering office. These are in conjunction with the stacks which they service; we are doing this be- cause it constitutes one of the elements of strength in our present situation.

In the old building there are separate rooms— not remote from one another, but they are separate rooms. We want to retain our people as specialists in depth (to the extent that we can have them). We have decided that we do not want a really good ref- erence librarian. This is because, if you have a really good reference librarian, everybody asks for that person's services. The person is worked to death, and ill feeling is created on the part of other people.

I want to add this: Somebody asked me the other day if we had a consultant and the answer is yes. We had Metcalf, and Ellsworth, and the cost was very low. Primarily what we did was to read what they had written. In addition, we had Ed Lowe, from Oklahoma; Sidney Smith, from Georgia Tech; and Clem Purdy from Wayne. One of the penalties (or pleasures) of creating a good library—whichever way you look at it—is that a lot of visiting firemen come by and ask all kinds of questions. We have learned a lot from our colleagues and friends and from the proceedings of this Institute; the mistakes we make will be those of omission, not those of commission.

Critique

MR. LAWRENCE: As an architect, I would like to say that we must remember that architecture is like frozen music. On the other hand, it is something you can't have very strict rules about. Building programs and budgets vary a great deal, of course. Our buildings will proba- bly outlive all of us, and we should plan for ex- pansion. In buildings built fifty years ago people did not do what they could have done. I would suggest that we not be timid. We should shoot for the highest standards. I would fight the leg- islators, and I would fight committees, to meet the highest standards; even these in a very short time will seem backward.

The orientation of the site is good. You have a two-level solution, which I think you must have. There is, however, a danger in the plan- ning. The circulation seems tight, and it wor- ries me. For example, you say on the south en- trance you would have dormitories; and to get to music listening, for instance, students would come in on the lower level, go up a flight and over, and back down a flight. This doesn't seem like very good planning. I would have tried to avoid it. There may be good reasons why it is done, but I think circulation could be improved.

With a 22-foot 6-inch module you have many wide spaces. Why be niggardly on your module? At Pittsburgh and Penn State it seems that 25 and 6 works out better. Why not try it? It would free much of the circulation. You are working yourself into a tight corner which you can't get out of.

I would be a little suspicious of a sun screen in your part of the country. We probably would not use it in Ohio. In northeastern Ohio and Pittsburgh, in winter, the sun shines very little. I think that is the case in Washington. Perhaps in your part of Oregon it does shine a lot, though a screen is not something you would use in Indi- ana, in Texas, or even in Chicago, where you get a lot of winter sun. This screen is a cliché used by all architects when designing something that looks nice. I would worry about mainte- nance. If you don't use the sun screen, there are other ways of controlling the sunlight.

I would check on the lift-slab. People were going to save a lot of money on the lift-slab idea; however, it has not been talked about in architectural circles. I don't know whether it was a fad, or whether it was fact or fiction that it saves money, but it has usually been aban- doned on large projects. I could be wrong in your area. You would have to check that.

MR. CARLSON: Thank you very much. Our archi- tects will hear all of your comments when we get back. I think that the experience with the lift-slab on the Oregon State campus has been quite successful. Three or four buildings have been built this way. It will be optional with the contractor, if he thinks he can save money; if he wants to pour it up above, he can.

We certainly are going to fight for the maxi- mum building. I was interested in the comment of the speaker from John Carroll University— that the difference between a good building and one that might be inferior is really a small per- centage of the total cost.

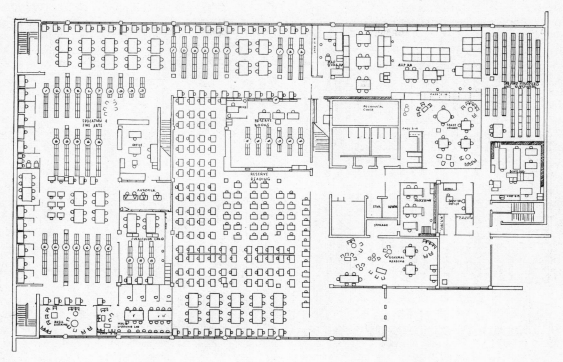

First floor
Oregon State University Library
Corvallis, Oregon

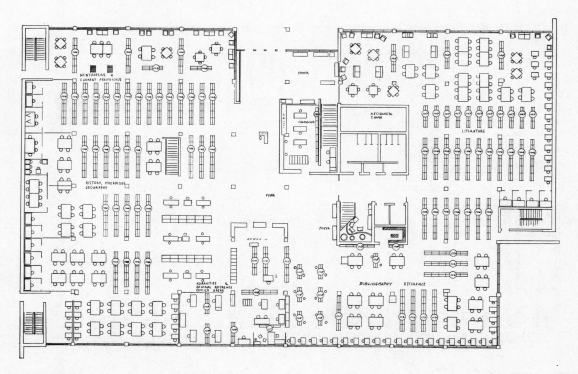

Second floor
Oregon State University Library
Corvallis, Oregon

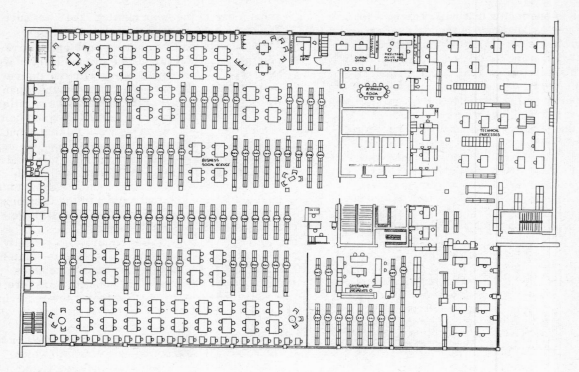

Third floor
Oregon State University Library
Corvallis, Oregon

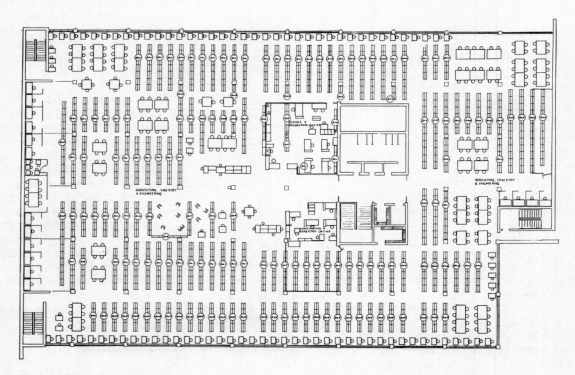

Fourth floor
Oregon State University Library
Corvallis, Oregon

There is one factor that will require a lot of fighting from us, and that is the air cooling. When I wrote the program for this building, I said that air cooling would be highly desirable but not an absolute essential in our climate. This was before I observed the amount of heat that is yielded by the high-intensity, low ceiling in our new Portland State Library; even on a cool day the library is unbearable. The weather hasn't been very hot, but our hard-nosed legislators will be impressed by the fact that even Alberta, Canada, needs air cooling. We will add that to the arguments. We particularly want to get some firm figures on the amount of heat the lamps actually emit and how much of it can be bled off, or how this situation can be controlled in the event we do not get the air cooling.

Comment: If you have fluorescent lighting, it should not be much of a problem.

MR. CARLSON: The architect estimates that we would have 4 watts per square foot. According to estimates for the Oregon mean temperature, we will have an exterior heat loss per hour of 2,300,000 B.T.U.'s, and the lighting will yield about 2,000,000 B.T.U.'s per hour.

MR. SIDELLS: You evidently need to incorporate some mechanical thinking before you decide on the structure of the architecture. Actually a library, as with a hospital and other functioning structures, cannot be considered as a building separate from its mechanical equipment. Statements have been made that solar screens such as in New Orleans and Texas will reduce the tonnage an estimated 17 per cent on air conditioning, and these statements indicate that there has been insufficient study of this point.

This is a very large building, with 127,000 square feet, and while your budget seems fairly ample, by roughly breaking out parts for equipment and similar factors you will be shooting for about $15 a square foot. This won't take you far if you are led astray by factors which are not definitely functional necessities.

This building doesn't particularly impress me as an architect. It has no real architectural character internally, such as a grand staircase or an open area of real impact. It seems to be a consolidation of many separate compartments, which does not make a good building. There needs to be emphasis on the architectural features. Vertical separation is a repeat which is set off by a counterfoil. But I did not like the little individual study tables all down the entire window wall. This is the kind of thing that gets monotonous rather than interesting.

Comment: As an order librarian, I would complain about having the technical processes division on the fourth or third floor, well removed from the main catalog on the first. We make a dozen trips a day to the main catalog, and I am sure the catalogers in your department do, too.

Also, wouldn't you have a problem with receiving being that far off the ground level? We have a problem in our library with our deliverymen; if they have to take anything farther than the door of a library, they complain very bitterly.

I noticed that you had a multilith room on the third floor, also. When we were talking about the plans with the architects, they thought—and I agreed with them—that equipment of this kind does cause noise through the building, which could be a problem. I do not know whether this equipment could be taken down to the basement, or your lower level, or whether this arrangement would be an improvement.

MR. CARLSON: We installed a multilith recently. We were mimeographing and were immediately conscious of the noise which those machines make. This department is planned, therefore, for the basement area. Regarding the receiving problem, there will be people in the bindery all day to take care of the deliverymen.

Comment: You said the lift-slab construction or the more usual construction—girders into which beams are trained—would be optional to the builder. These methods are not interchangeable. In a lift-slab you may have the entire slab. Lift-slabs are built one on top of the other. They are parallel thin slabs. A lift-slab may be 10 inches thick, which is very small, and you will need a great deal of reinforcing to keep the slab from sagging. If you use the usual girder and construction beam on a thin slab over the beam, your main girder may be 18 inches deep.

This construction may interfere with lighting and running of air ducts, and you may have to refigure all the mechanical equipment. Also, it may affect distances from floor to floor. Thus, the two methods of construction are not interchangeable.

MR. CARLSON: I obviously cannot comment from a technical standpoint. All I can say is that, within the past three years, three large buildings have gone up on campus using lift-slabs.

MR. LAWRENCE: If you want air conditioning and good control of lighting, lift-slabs are adequate for a dormitory, where you do not have mechanical problems, but I would be very much surprised if further study showed that you would want a lift-slab. Because a contractor could save a couple of dollars on the floor, the entire library might suffer.

Public Libraries

Downsview Regional Branch

Township of North York Public Library
Metropolitan Toronto, Canada

Presentation of plans
  WILLIAM GRAFF
  Librarian

Critique
  COIT COOLIDGE
  Librarian
  Richmond Public Library
  Richmond, California

Building data
  Architect: Paul Meschino
              Toronto, Ontario
  Type of library: Branch library
  Population to be served: 60,000
  Area: Approximately 10,000 square feet on each
         of the two floors, lower floor being base-
         ment level
  Book capacity: 100,000 volumes

Seating capacity: Minimum of 2 seats at reference tables and 20 seats for lounge
  reading
Cost: Building—$275,000 for full regional
  branch with air conditioning
Parking area capacity: Neighboring shopping-
  center space for 800 cars

MR. WILLIAM GRAFF

I want to stress that this is the regional library
in an urban situation. In the Shaw report on the
Metropolitan Library in Toronto,[1] one of the main
recommendations was the establishment of regional
libraries in metropolitan conditions of thirteen municipalities: the city of Toronto and twelve others
which range in size from 10,000 population to my
township, which has a population of 260,000.

What is the difference between a regional library and a neighborhood branch? The basic difference is the departmentalizing of your book collection and your services. Most metropolitan areas

1. Ralph Robert Shaw, *Libraries of Metropolitan Toronto: A
Study of Library Service Prepared by the Library Trustees'
Council of Toronto and District* (Toronto: Library Trustees'
Council, 1960). 98p.

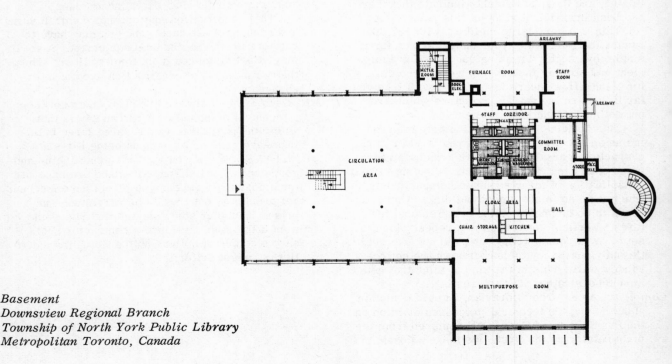

Basement
Downsview Regional Branch
Township of North York Public Library
Metropolitan Toronto, Canada

include an old, established city in the core of which is a main library. Perhaps this library has been rendering good service over the entire area without any financial remuneration from the other municipalities or their residents who are using it. However, in most main cities in Canada and the United States, the neighborhood branches offer weak service: primarily, book collection, circulating books for light reading, and reference services limited to a few encyclopedias and handbooks.

There is a wide difference in the service of neighborhood branches and that of libraries in smaller independent communities. I was a chief librarian in Peterborough, Ontario—a city of 40,000. There I had a building of approximately 15,000 square feet. This was similar to the building I now have, which is approximately 40,000 square feet with administrative space for a larger system, larger technical operation, and bookmobile service. Basically, this library renders a much higher standard of service than many of the neighborhood branches in the cities.

I would like to quote from the Shaw report, Recommendation 5: "Services to adults and young adults are far substandard in metropolitan libraries and the quality of service is low. This is particularly true of adult education services. Not even at the larger outlets do residents of metropolitan areas receive all the range and quality of adult services that they would have readily available if they lived in smaller Ontario communities, such as London (a city of 100,000 before annexing some areas recently, which increased it to 150,000). It is therefore recommended that regional branches containing collections of at least 100,000 volumes, with specialized staff, and providing the full range of bibliographical, reference and cultural services be given first priority in the plans for building libraries in metropolitan areas."[2]

I would like to emphasize recommendations in the Shaw report pertaining to children's services:
"Children's services and adult lending services

2. *Ibid.*, p. 97.

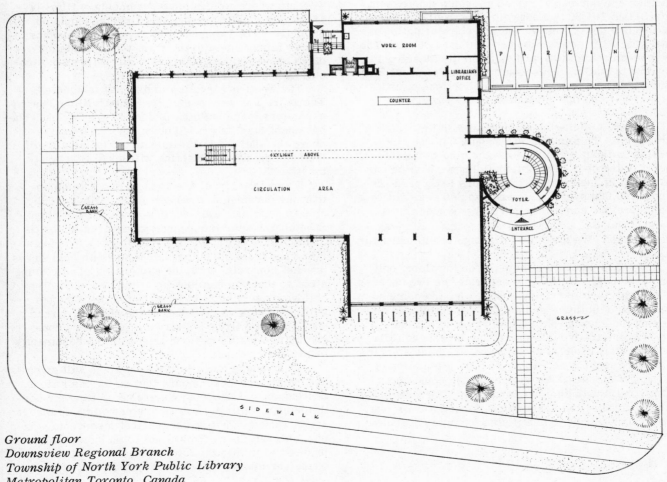

Ground floor
Downsview Regional Branch
Township of North York Public Library
Metropolitan Toronto, Canada

at the present level can be supplied in considerable measure by such low-grade devices as bookmobiles pending the development of first-rate children's library service."[3]

What we create inside our new building is space, and everything is movable and flexible. We are using three types of shelving: wall-mounted shelving with Visusels fixed to the wall, double stacks for nonfractionals, and frames adopted from the design in the Cincinnati Public Library.

In the section for the junior high school we have a trial system. We have allowed seventh, eighth, and ninth grades in the adult department, and find this very satisfactory because the older public school children hate to use the children's section. Also, the nature of the assignments given by the schools now needs an adult reference collection. We are helping the junior high school age groups rather than the senior high school groups. The senior high school students have one or two A-frames displaying specially suggested books; otherwise, they read as adults.

The control desk is in the center. We have two Recordak photochargers. The adult department circulates 455,000 books. Our children's department circulates 191,000. Last year we circulated a total of 655,000 books, the second largest circulation in any single library system in the United States. The reference room is separated from the other room by double stacks. This is a collection of about 5,000 volumes and is comparable to collections of cities of 40,000 to 60,000 population in the Province of Ontario.

We are building up our business in the technical collection. This means that people can use our facilities without traveling eight or nine miles into the heart of the city. The only building we have in our township is used mainly by readers in an area of about 740,000 people. We receive 300 periodicals and therefore can give much better service than a neighborhood branch which may receive 20 to 40 periodicals. We have the full range of bibliographic tools.

We have no clerical help out on the floor, only professionals. We have to separate the two because of the shortage of professionals, who are doing a basic job of building up the book collection and conveying the knowledge of the working collection.

Administrative offices are on the second floor, and the staff room is at the rear. We have a small viewing room for screening and for orientation of groups of classes. We have a garden court and a lovely patio with summer furniture. The staff enjoy it very much. The court below is used for a story hour, and we hope to use it also for outdoor sculpture exhibits.

The children's department looks toward the garden court. Here we have used the Visusel on the wall. Most of it is built-in shelving of oak; it is the only place we have built-in shelving. We have one professional librarian in charge, and she is a very busy person.

Our schools in North York all have excellent libraries consisting of about 1,000 books in each collection. Junior high schools have 2,500 and senior high schools 3,500 as a minimum. We find that the better the school library the more demand there is for public libraries, and I have yet to find the place in North America where there is too much library service, either school or public.

The foyer has art exhibits and a committee room to accommodate 16 persons with a small kitchenette. Our multipurpose room is a combination auditorium-art gallery with paperboard walls, where we have staff parties at Christmas. This room seats 150 people, and many of the regional branches we are building will be equipped with a similar room.

On Saturday afternoons we have music recitals and film showings. This is about the only place in Toronto where we can have documentary films of 16 mm. We have between 300 and 400 people on Saturday. The Downsview Branch has a shopping center immediately to the right which accommodates about 800 to 1,000 cars. It is on a main thoroughfare with bus stops on it.

The western elevation is difficult to handle. There are louvers—sun strips which will be done in gay colors. The building is done in gray brick. The basement level is graded down, and the windows above the shelves will eliminate a basement feeling. We hope the natural lighting will make it very attractive.

There is a circular entrance, and a ramp so that any paraplegic or wheel-chair patient will be able to come in. This applies to all our buildings. (The chairman of our board suffers from arthritis and is aware of people with handicaps.) The interior view from the entrance on the south side shows precast concrete; down the center is a plastic dome strip so that you can look up at the blue sky. The children's section is in front, with a little higher ceiling. There is glass below the shelving on the wall. There will be a staircase going down connecting the main top-floor area with the basement public service area.

What we are doing in the first stage will give us approximately 6,000 square feet on the main floor, costing about $120,000. We are not putting air conditioning in initially, but we are providing so that it can be added. That is the greatest disadvantage of our main building. We are not to include even the provision for it in the future. This annoys us because our municipality has invested $200,000 in-

3. *Ibid.*

stalling air conditioning in its building. It is a mistake to build a library without at least providing for air conditioning if you cannot install it at the start.

For lighting we are using a minimum of 70 footcandles, ranging between 70 and 100. We are hoping that all corners in the building will have adequate light. There are dangers in trying to do an over-all lighting approach, but that is all we can do under the circumstances.

Critique

MR. COIT COOLIDGE

Mr. Graff has worked out a plan of four regional libraries to serve North York. The basic concept on all four is in the 100,000-book range each. The main library unit has been functioning for more than a year and has circulated 655,000 books in the last year. This tremendous success demonstrates the validity of this concept of larger book units.

The general planning is excellent. I had to work hard to find fault but I felt that if I did not find fault with something, people would think the plans had not been studied. I will point out the good things in this building, which are many.

Having all the main service elements as far as possible on one level is sound planning, and this has been done here. Having the maximum (within the limits of the wall) free, unencumbered floor space as well as having everything movable are also sound planning. If five years from now conditions have changed, services have changed, and ideas have developed, all these things can be altered. The concepts on which this building has been planned are open.

Vertical louvers control the western sun. They stand at a little distance from the wall and function like the marker on a sundial. They cast shadows on the glass. This is an interesting solution to what I thought was an insoluble technical problem.

The main entrance appears to be in grade, and that is good. There is adequate parking. I was going to speak about the absence of parking, but I found the library is sharing the nearby market lot. Having the market there will draw people into the unit.

Now I would like to point out the line of design. I do not know just where it is proposed to cut the unit. This is the plan for the whole, and I understand from Mr. Graff that they are building a part. But I point out that it is laid out in modules or bays which are about 12 feet wide. This is a good layout. When the time comes to spend the other $100,000, you simply add as many of these bays as you can, 12 feet at a time. You do not have to redesign this part. This is a practical method of expansion and sound design.

The relationship of the workroom to the outside entrance should be helpful to the delivery people. With 100,000 books coming in, anything the architect can do to eliminate stairs and simplify access to the workroom from the outside would be helpful. The delivery people appreciate having an outside door to drive up to and unload. The girl here at the counter can step right in and receive, if necessary, and that is good.

The librarian is in a good location inside the door, in a glass section. This forces him to be a good public relations man and keeps him in the public eye. I believe the staff will increase to 15 or 20 people when the library is finished. A circulation of 300,000, then 500,000 to 600,000, will require more staff, and I hope no trouble strikes this room. When everybody is tense and whoever is in charge is trying to make things run smoothly, it is very helpful to have a place to work where people cannot see you.

Immediately below the workroom is a staff room, and if the plans would allow it, it would be nice to consider installing the smallest possible stairway for direct vertical access to the workroom from the room below. I have a prejudice against booklifts. In this building I am sure they are a good thing, but a little elevator that will hold a man with a truck greatly simplifies vertical transportation of materials. You wheel the truck into the elevator and go up with it to its destination, all in one continuous process. When you separate this movement on two floors, you need another person scheduled simultaneously to take the truck out at the top and find another truck to replace it. If another person is not there, you must go around the long way and find the truck and take care of it. This may be better than carrying it up the stairs yourself, but not much better!

The tremendous thing about these plans is the creative imagination used in developing all sources of recorded thought. It is marvelous that Toronto and North York are using all lines of recorded thought, and making a dynamic effort to stimulate people's minds by taking advantage of all the things you can do now that you could not do thirty years ago.

Downstairs are a multipurpose room, committee rooms, and so on. A glass wall there permits the supermarket crowd from next door to see the meetings.

I question the idea of separating the reference function by putting it downstairs; if possible it should be kept upstairs. Reference should be close to all the adult books, and the reference librarian should be able to work anywhere in the adult collection. As soon as you put reference material downstairs and adult books upstairs, you are in trouble.

I had some concern about the possible use of

basement space simply for books in such a large basement. I think the main part of this operation will wind up on one floor when this building is completed, and some thought might be given to such matters as having one basement to store books for the entire system with teletype connection and rapid delivery of wanted books.

In the main this is an effective plan. Planning is in units to expand as population comes in. The over-all concept for the complicated building, with area for expansion, is 20,000 square feet, with about 10,000 square feet on the main level and 10,000 below. The plan calls for a forceful approach to the community by bringing in people for all sorts of group activities.

Discussion

Question: What do you think of having windows underneath the bookshelves?

MR. GRAFF: There is only a small strip of glass of about 8 or 9 inches along the wall. This was done in the Westdale Branch of Hamilton Public Library and has worked successfully. I do not know whether it is important enough to justify extra cost. As long as you don't have direct sunrays coming in, using natural light with the sky dome can be an added feature.

Question: Is the purpose to increase natural light?

MR. GRAFF: Simply to give airiness to the wall—an outside effect. I see no harm in it.

Question: If the work space is to be expanded in the future, as it sounds from the report it might be, how will that be accomplished?

Comment: That is accomplished by laying out the work space a little generously in the beginning. I think that is adequate for a situation where the processing is being done elsewhere. It would not be adequate if you had to maintain your own order and acquisition department. This space is going to be for receiving as well as for processing books ready for use. What you do is design your workroom and your circulation space a little larger for your first unit, and when you add onto it, the space is big enough to handle the expanded building.

MR. GRAFF: We felt it was best to have additional work space because the staff members are going to need it. They are going to be under pressure. There will not be enough book space, and in trying to wangle any space for public service, we felt we should be a little more generous. In two of the buildings we have the work space for the full unit, but at the Bathurst Heights building, unfortunately—because of the entrance—we could give only half of the work space.

Question: What kind of telephone and teletype arrangements do you have in this building?

MR. GRAFF: In the main building I showed you, we are using the telephone for intercommunication.

We have twenty-two or twenty-three extensions, and I think there are six lines in the building now. When we get the three branches, the traffic between the main building and the branches will be heavier, so we will have to enlarge the system. Initially, we are starting with two telephone lines, and I am using an intercommunication system, recently brought out by General Electric, that consists of small transistor transmitters and so requires no wiring. It is reasonably inexpensive and I think it will work in the first stage. When we get into the second stage, we will have a combination of wired communication system and wired telephone.

Worcester Public Library

Worcester, Massachusetts

Presentation of plans
    THURSTON TAYLOR
    Head Librarian

    WALTER ROONEY, JR.
    Architect

Critique
    WILLIAM CHAIT
    Dayton and Montgomery County Public Library
    Dayton, Ohio

Building data
    Architect: Curtis and Davis
                  New Orleans and New York City
    Type of library: Central building, municipal
        library
    Population to be served: 186,587
    Area: 95,700 square feet
    Book capacity (proposed): 500,000 volumes
    Seating capacity
        Adults and young people: 275
        Children: 40
        Meeting rooms: 220
    Ceiling heights
        Basement: 7 feet 6 inches
        First level: 8 feet 16 inches
        Second level: 8 feet 16 inches
        Third level: 8 feet
    Cost
        Building: $2,140,000
        Equipment: $300,000
        Site: $325,915
        Contingencies: $34,085
    Cost per square foot: $25

MR. THURSTON TAYLOR

Worcester is an 100-year-old New England city with a 70-year-old library building. We have been waiting for fifty years for a new building and now are getting it. The city has a population of 186,000 and is in the center of a metropolitan area of 325,000. We are about to become, we expect, a regional reference library that will serve 622,000 people, except for more advanced reference and research services.

The Worcester Library adult department is divided into three subdivisions, a popular library, and a circulation division. Curiously enough, the organization is apparently almost identical with that of our critic and his library in Dayton.

Worcester is a city with unusual reading characteristics. There are five four-year colleges in the city, and there are two or three excellent college libraries. It is a city of diversified machine tool industry. The result of these characteristics is that we have heavy demand for reference service, although no one could characterize Worcester as a city of readers.

In our program we have decided to include with the adult department its three subdivisions and its operational library. The children's room is an integral part of the main library. This presents some difficult problems of planning, supervision, and communication about which we have no experience and are frankly worried. Our program calls for 275 seats for adult readers and 35 or 40 seats for children. It calls for provisions for 85,000 to 100,000 books on open shelves and for another 400,000 volumes on closed shelves, making a total book capacity of about 500,000.

We asked the architect to provide for our public services about 35,000 square feet on the main floor of a building which could be only a little over 25,000 square feet; he will tell you how he has solved it. The program calls for 20,000 square feet of work and office space in the basement and on the third floor, and for 26,000 square feet of closed stack area in the basement and some on the third level.

Although our budget requires a building that will be as economic as possible, the city of Worcester insists on a building that will have some of the characteristics of a monument. Worcester has waited fifty or sixty years for this building, and people expect things of the building that frighten those of us who are connected with it. This is the first public building that will have been erected for many years in Worcester.

It is in a redevelopment project that has been delayed eight or ten years and is a political hot potato in Worcester. The building will have to look about twice as large and elegant as the $2,000,000 which we have to spend for it would ordinarily make possible. This presents the architect with some difficult problems. Walter Rooney, of the firm of Curtis and Davis, will relate how he proposes to solve them.

MR. WALTER ROONEY

The library site is at the corner of the new urban redevelopment site. It faces across Salem Street, looking at a rather disreputable and dilapidated red brick building. Immediately behind the library is a large parking area which the library patrons will be able to use.

The original layout was a rectilinear site, the thought being that the library would front right on the Common, or as much as possible. Because of the shape of the site and access from two directions, we are proposing a different approach.

We have two principal means of pedestrian access. Many persons will come from the shopping district and the Common, entering from the front of the site. Almost an equal number of people will enter from the south end. Right away, this indicated that an entrance at one end of the site was wrong. We wanted to make access as convenient as possible to people coming from both directions. We have made a control point about halfway back from the side with access in the minimum reading levels on the floor, providing views both to the north and to the south and shielded on the south with some screen planting. Our bookmobiles and service vehicles will enter from the major thoroughfare from the back, on a ramp down to the service and shipping department in the basement.

This is how we arrived at the total necessary area of 95,700 square feet. As was pointed out, the original goal was to put all the public spaces on the ground floor, indicating a total of 41,000 square feet. The next best thought was to put at least all the adult areas on the ground floor, which would have made a total of 35,000 square feet. However, because of the shape of the property, the necessity for control within the building, and the way the other spaces shaped up, we had to deal with an optimum floor area of between 25,000 and 30,000 square feet.

Our first breakdown was a two-story building, grouping most adult areas on the ground floor and

Architect's visualization of interior
Worcester Public Library
Worcester, Massachusetts

some adult areas and the children's room on the second floor with administration and staff areas, and, of course, the stack development on the ground floor. We were not too pleased with this because it isolated some of the adult areas, and we had no fair way of deciding which of the departments should be put on the upper floor and thus be less accessible to the public.

Although the floor is some 8 or 10 feet high, it acts as a kind of mezzanine or second floor. We hope to give the feeling and illusion that this area—which contains all of those parts of the library that the public will use—is more or less an entity and that none of the departments is relegated to less desirable space.

We hope to encourage the use of stairs rather than elevators. For play of light we have introduced some features to get north light in the interior reading areas, rather than trying to put a lot of glass on the east and west sides.

The main facade, with 16-foot columns, faces Franklin Street. There is a conscious effort to give the building some dignity, some feeling of a public building, some monumentality, without the applied ornamentality of the past. We hope to make it as inviting and appealing as possible and with lasting dignity—a building that will wear well over a long time.

The ground floor will be raised some 18 inches above grade because we have a very dense rock ledge beneath most of the property that limits the depth to which we can economically sink the basement. There will be pedestrian ramps at each end so that people in wheel chairs and elderly people will not have trouble going up. Access will be along an arcade from the street parking into the main circulation areas and past the circulation desk which acts as a control. Beside the circulation desk is the circulation workroom and behind that the information center and the union catalog.

The floor will be kept as open and flexible as possible. We plan on no partition other than at the four vertical corners which house service elevators and staff in the rear, a mechanical pipe, a storage lockup, and the janitor's closet. In the center of the building, immediately visible as you walk into the library, is a passenger elevator and open stair which leads not only down to the stack level for the staff but also up to the upper reading room levels for the public. This floor contains the major adult areas: the popular; the humanities and fine arts and literature; and the social studies and literature. As the plans on the interior space are developed, we hope to have these departments flow one into the other to encourage browsing from department to department and make the library as interesting as possible. The combined meeting rooms have a capacity of between 200 and 250 people, and when that many people come out of a meeting room they must

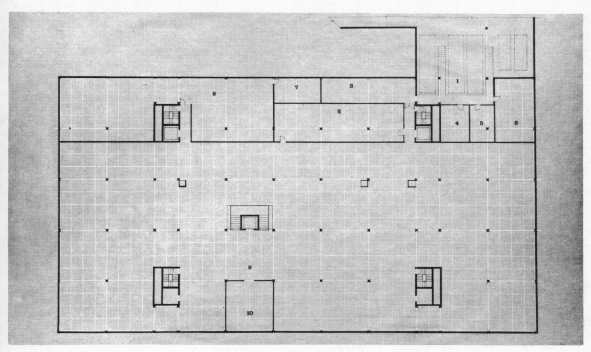

Basement
Worcester Public Library
Worcester, Massachusetts

1 bookmobile loading	6 shops and storage
2 bookmobile workroom	7 electrical equipment
3 shipping	8 mechanical equipment
4 men's locker	9 stacks
5 women's locker	10 circulation workroom

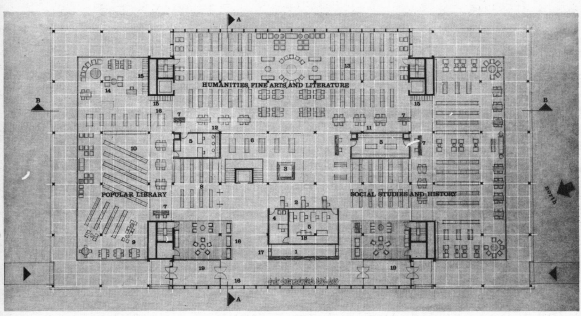

First floor
Worcester Public Library
Worcester, Massachusetts

1 circulation desk	8 browsing	15 files
2 registration	9 young people	16 display
3 information	10 fiction	17 bookchute
4 office	11 directories	18 switchboard
5 workroom	12 magazines	19 vestibule
6 union catalog	13 reference	
7 service desk	14 music, films, etc.	

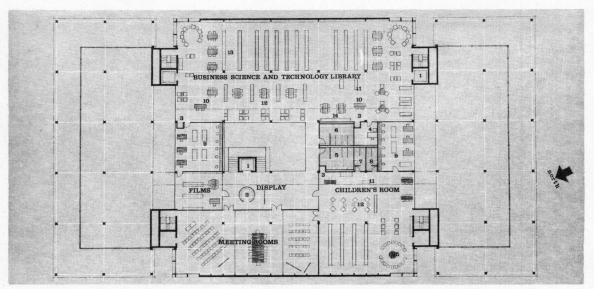

Second floor
Worcester Public Library
Worcester, Massachusetts

1 elevator	9 workroom
2 coats	10 service desk
3 booklift	11 catalog
4 office	12 magazines
5 men	13 reference
6 women	14 directories
7 girls	15 story hour
8 boys	

Third floor
Worcester Public Library
Worcester, Massachusetts

1 business	11 general office	21 book selection
2 extension	12 boardroom	22 catalog
3 personnel	13 first aid	23 order
4 asst. librarian	14 women	24 serial
5 librarian's sec'y	15 men	25 darkroom
6 librarian	16 staff lounge	26 storage
7 conference	17 reception	27 office
8 exhibits workroom	18 binding	28 printing
9 exhibits storage	19 office	
10 gen. office storage	20 gen. storage	

have some place to go. We provided for that purpose space that will double as a major display area.

Immediately off this display space are the business, science, and technology department with its
work space; the children's library with its work
space and separate lavatory facilities; and the only
public lavatory facilities, which serve the library
itself, as well as the meeting rooms for previewing
and showing films. We propose to use, by partitions, a portion of the meeting room areas as the
storytelling room for the children, although we also
propose to have a small storytelling circle which
might be enclosed in soundproof drapes or left open
for quiet reading.

At the third level, we have the stacks which
serve business and technology, as well as some
children's enclosed stacks. The administrative
area is on the left, with receptionists, board room,
librarian, various business offices, staff lavatory
facilities, the main staff lounge and kitchen, and
first-aid rooms. On the other side, near the service elevator, are binding, cataloging, book selection, catalogs, and printing.

The stack level, which is immediately below the
ground floor level, has four points of access from
above. Also on this level are the bookmobile garage
and shipping department, extension division, shipping and receiving, staff lavatory facilities, general
storage area, mechanical equipment space, and as
open and uninterrupted space as possible for closed
stacks.

Critique

MR. WILLIAM CHAIT

The program for this building is so much like
the program for the building which we have under
construction in Dayton that I was amazed when I saw
it. The space allocation for most of the public departments is almost alike. The subject division is
the same, and yet the solution is entirely different.
Because it is different does not mean it is worse,
but after living with one solution for two years, to
be presented with an entirely different solution
comes as a kind of a shock.

This building has 275 adult seats and 40 children's seats, and 90,000 to 100,000 volumes on open
shelves and about 400,000 volumes on closed shelves.
This plan has dimensions that are about the same as
the dimensions of the Dayton building—about 240
feet by 120 feet compared with 220 feet by 140 feet
in Dayton.

Some other comparisons: The Dayton plan is
about a fourth bigger. Instead of 90,000 square feet,
we have 126,000 square feet. We did it very simply.
We went down one more layer, into a basement, and
added to the book storage. Instead of having 90,000
to 120,000 books on open shelves, we estimate we

will get 150,000, and we are building for a total cost
of slightly over $2,000,000, including wrecking the
old building, landscaping, and everything else.

I am a little disturbed about the estimated price;
what bothers me is a lot of waste space. I think
some of the problems can be solved by eliminating
the waste space and making use of it for other
things.

This is one thing I do not like, and most of the
things I will discuss are things I do not like. I may
not be able to suggest a solution in each case. I do
not like, in New England winter climate, a ramp
down to a bookmobile garage; in addition, there is
the problem of backing out a bookmobile and turning
it around in a heavily traveled street. Get your
bookmobiles out of downtown. We have found this a
very satisfactory solution for our bookmobiles. We
do not want to tie up downtown traffic at eight o'clock
in the morning, and I think Mr. Taylor ought not to
tie it up either. If he is going to, he had better plan
to get the bookmobiles out forward instead of backward. Whether the bookmobile will be able to back
out and then enter the street forward, I do not know.
I do not think any decent-size bookmobile can get
out that way into the traffic.

The advantage of the bookmobile garage being in
the basement is that the workroom space for bookmobile staff is here. By relocating the freight elevator and by vertical plans, the bookmobile entrance
can be put on the first floor, thus eliminating the
headache of the ramp.

I had better go on to the first-floor plan because
I will have to discuss anything else in connection
with the first floor. I like the openness of the first
floor. I think it is excellent. One thing I was very
much impressed with was the imagination that was
used by the architect on that plan. I think the plan
is unusual, it is exciting, it is not just another library building. It is a different library building,
and I think the planners ought to be commended for
this.

On the other hand, I sometimes wonder if, in
order to achieve architectural effect, we do not lose
the value of a simple, attractive pattern inside the
building. Yet, plans are sometimes very preliminary, and a better traffic pattern can be worked out.
I do not think there is any major danger. Here,
again, let me explain what I mean by waste space.

An arcade projects in 12 feet to bring people in.
I like that. I think this is good, even though it
wastes some space. But when you have 12 feet all
along the sides of the building for an arcade, you
can move this wall out and simply by adding some
lighting and air conditioning at very little extra cost,
have an additional 2,000-3,000 square feet. I think
this might be worthwhile. You will lose the sun-
shading value, but we were able to drape our entire
building for $5,000, and by using gray glass and
draperies we think we will take care of our sun

problem. By gaining that floor space, perhaps a bookmobile garage could be developed there without the objection of the elevator shaft. I think this is too bad in a very unobstructed plan. You can get your children up on the second floor much more easily. You can get them inside the library and make use of the same charging desk, which is a wonderful economy, and get them to the second floor and somehow or other to the children's room. If that can be worked out, I think that will be a great advantage.

One of my major criticisms of this building is one I have of almost every library I have seen—that is, not enough workshop area. In visiting other libraries, the comment I got from more office staffs has been, "It is a beautiful building but there is no room for us to do things, not enough workroom space, or the space is not where we can use it most conveniently." I think this is too small a workroom for the circulation. Another workroom could be put in.

The Cincinnati Library has the workroom in the basement. I know of nothing more wasteful than to take every book down to the basement for slipping and then send it upstairs again for distribution. Probably 75-90 per cent of your distribution will come from open shelves, so why send all the books down and then up again when you can enlarge the workroom? Perhaps the thing to do is to block off a few windows and switch the workroom to the side, which would open up the building even more. I do not think the two workrooms will be large enough for the three divisions located on this floor. I think this is a problem.

I definitely do not like this barrier type of information desk. The staff should be behind an ordinary office desk and able to get out to help people and show them the subdivisions, rather than behind the railroad type of information desk. I hope this type is really not being planned.

If the elevator was moved to the corner, the children's room could probably be adjoined to these meeting rooms. I think that could be done easily. On the second floor my greatest criticism would be the very narrow access to the business, science, and technology area for people coming up the stairway or the elevator. It is a long way around and up into the business, science, and technology area; perhaps there should be direct access. You would have a better arrangement.

You get a marvelous open effect looking up these wells, but I wonder if it is worth using this space for the light. The light will shine on the tables, but people will seldom look up a deep well to the top of the building.

I suggest that the workroom be enclosed, or members will be unable to relax because they will be in full view of the public. The staff should be kept under supervision, but walls should at least separate the staff from the public so there can be some conversation without being overheard or observed to any extent. I suggest building a wall, perhaps of glass, and moving the children's room down.

On the third floor, remember, you have your open wells to take care of the children's room and meeting rooms. These rooms are 16 feet high. That is another thing I almost do not like; a 16-foot height seems to be excessive. It may be dramatic but I keep thinking of the money that might be wasted.

The staff toilets are in a beautiful location, on the best corner. I am pleased that the staff was given such fine accommodations, but frankly there are also some staff toilets down in the basement. If I were a staff member working on the first floor, I am not sure I would want to find my way over to this corner every time I wanted to use that facility. This arrangement could create a very difficult situation in loss of time, and through the years would add up to many man-hours.

Our library system has about twice the budget of the Worcester Library, as we serve the whole county. We are at least as large as Worcester will be when it becomes a regional library. If I had this many people in my administration, I would have to spend my time thinking up things for them to do. There is entirely too much space given to administration. I counted something like 15 or 16 work spaces in that area, which is too many for a library that has a budget of about $600,000 a year; even if the budget rises to $1,000,000, the number is high. I have the same impression of the processing of 80,000 books a year with 25 people; 26 work stations is what we have in our building. Why there must be provision for 40 or 50 stations in this much space I fail to see.

There is a big printing office. If the library wants to do printing there, that is fine, but I like to leave the printing to the printers. There is no reason why the library shouldn't have a printing office, however. I wonder if the office could not be in the basement, unless the department needs outside windows.

The book preparation department has a wonderful window arrangement with glass all around. I was wondering why our solution could not be used. We think our book preparators are the least skilled people and the easiest to replace. Our catalogers and clerical assistants work along the windows—that is the best space—and we put our book preparators inside. Why should a cataloger or skilled typist work 24 or 40 feet away while all the book preparators are within reach of a window?

There is a switchboard in the circulation workroom. I see no sense to that at all. The switchboard should be in the administration area or some other place, rather than in one of the busiest spots where the staff is working on overdues or registra-

tion or other things. A switchboard operator should
be as undisturbed as possible in her work. That
function would be well combined with that of a re-
ceptionist if the switchboard is not too busy, but I
would not put the board in the circulation room.

Discussion

Question: I would like to rush to the defense of my
colleague. I feel that the architects have done a
magnificent job, and I would like to plead for in-
clusion of some of the architectural amenities
in the budgets. I feel that, as you have set aside
a budget for work and reading areas, so should
you consider setting aside some of your budget
for space advantages an architect can give you.
The more ingenious your architect, the more he
can do at reasonable cost because he certainly
has your budget in mind, too.

I do not mean to make a sales pitch here, but
I feel that the originality of the idea of the north
light would set your library apart. Certainly
you can build a cinder-block structure with 20-
foot column spacing and get a much more reasonable building, but it will not be an inspiring
building in which to read, in which to study.

I wondered why the children's area was set
upstairs. Why could that not be downstairs? It
seems that it would be easier for the children to
reach, and it would be pleasant to see as you are
passing. Also, you might be able to incorporate
a pleasant little terrace for the children and a
wall terrace next to the children's area.

MR. ROONEY: We shuffled the various departments
trying to allocate the second-floor space. In the
final analysis, we thought the children could
climb the steps better than elderly people could.
The areas fell neatly into place that way. We
have a strong feeling—and I don't know that I
have completely convinced Thurston Taylor that
it is the right feeling—that the children should
be an integral part of the over-all library plan.
They should not be shuttled back to a dark corner and caged there, and the library proper be
kept as a kind of forbidden fruit. The children
should have limited access to the adult areas so
that they acquire some sense of responsibility,
some feeling that there are areas they can enter
and other areas they cannot enter. We do not
trust them completely, and they will be under
observation all the time; but we feel strongly
that by letting the children be a part of the total
library they will grow up to love it, rather than
to feel it is a place where they are held down
and put back in a corner. It would be delightful
if we could get a garden, but it was lost by putting the children's area on the second floor.

As to the extension—bookmobile and service
areas—we felt that the ground-floor space was

much too valuable for them. The flexibility of
the ground-floor space and the bookmobile area
is reduced. We are not sure what the regional
program will do in the way of extension, so we
want to keep it as flexible as possible. We will
have coils under the drive so that trucks will
have no snow problem. There will be space at
the bottom for trucks to turn around. A stop
light at the corner will halt traffic periodically
so that trucks will have no difficulty entering
and exiting.

Although the arcade which extends along the
north and south of the building does cost money,
there is nothing worse than large glass areas
which must be continuously draped and Venetian-
blinded in order that the people inside are not
blinded by the sky glare or broiled by the sun.
Large glass areas demand protection. We feel
they are necessary to make it pleasant for people sitting inside to look out, and to make people
outside want to come in. When we accept the
fact we want glass, we have to protect it. On
the north and south sides, overhangings of 12 feet
do a satisfactory job of protecting. The overhang up at the roof level will do us no good. We
needed the overhang at the ceiling of the reading
room. We pay no premium for extending the
third floor and the roof. We estimate that the
arcade space will cost $8 a square foot.

We do not consider the elevator shaft an ob-
struction. It has been pointed out that it is un-
desirable to walk into a building and feel as if
you needed a map to find your way. The elevator shaft will be in the middle of the building
and either painted or finished in a bright color.
We want it to be the first thing a person sees
when he enters. I concur that we do not have
enough workroom space on the ground floor. A
smaller information desk, informal in nature,
would be much better.

MR. FRANKLIN: What about the signs?

MR. ROONEY: We have done nothing on signs yet,
but we certainly will. The interior plan of the
building was hastily done to have a plan for this
meeting. It needs much more study, and we are
aware of it. We hope that the workroom spaces
will not be formed by solid partitions, but with
bookshelves. If we can talk the staff out of a
sound barrier, we will not install glass from the
top of the shelves to the ceiling. I do not know
if we will be successful or if we really should be
successful. It will take more consultation with
staff members to get their reaction to this complete openness of space. At any rate, the partitions will be of such nature that they can be
moved around next year or next month at very
little trouble and expense.

The whole thought has been to keep the
ground floor as flexible as possible so that, as

library needs and the public taste in reading change over the years, we can open a new department, and the library will be as up to date as we hope it is now.

In regard to comments of excess cubage in the building and the attendant extra cost of heating, air conditioning, and so forth: There is no excess cubage. There is simply a different allocation of cubage. If we had two floors in the building, in an area of 62,000 square feet, we would certainly need a minimum 12-foot-high ceiling. In such a vast area even a 12-foot ceiling over 26,000 square feet would be a little oppressive and not too high. All we have done with the two floors at the 12-foot level is have one 8 feet and one 16 feet so that the total volume in the building, the total cubage that has to be heated or cooled, has not altered, and we feel the excitement of the various levels—the visual relief of going from a low-ceilinged to a high-ceilinged area. The ever changing roof pattern and the openness of space will make the library inviting. You can be in the high-ceilinged areas or a little cozy corner, depending on your personal wants and disposition and the type of work you are doing, whether studying or lounging with a good book.

Mr. Taylor will have to justify the area in the administrative portion and processing area. If we can cut it, we certainly will. We are always worried about budgets. We would always like to do a building at a little less money and put aside a few dollars for some artwork.

Lincoln Public Library

Lincoln, Nebraska

Presentation of plans
    CHARLES DALRYMPLE
    Director

Critique
    DAN WILLIAMS
    Librarian
    Des Moines Public Library
    Des Moines, Iowa

Building data
    Architect: Hazen & Robinson
                Lincoln, Nebraska
    Type of library: Main branch library
    Population to be served: 128,000
    Area: 54,000 square feet
    Book capacity: 181,900 volumes
    Seating capacity
        Adults and young people: 123
        Children: 48
        Meeting room: 100
    Cost
        Building: $321,000
        Equipment: $71,900
        Site: $11,000
    Site: Rebuilding on owned site
    Location: Core area, downtown

MR. CHARLES DALRYMPLE

The population of Lincoln, Nebraska, is 128,000. The city is a governmental and educational center. We have a strong university with an agricultural college division, both located in Lincoln. The university provides service to the community on citizen cards. Cardholders can freely borrow all their special material there. The agricultural college has a separate library building. We have a strong historical society, the Nebraska Public Library Commission, two other colleges, and seven branches. Three of these are new; four are about sixty years old.

The service of the public library is largely in the area of true public library programs, with no special extensive technical service because it is readily available. This means, however, that we must have a strong program because the university faculty and government officials are good library patrons and expect us to have good auxiliary or special services that suit their needs: for instance, a strong children's program, a strong film program, picture loan service, recordings, and a good basic collection of popular and contemporary materials. We have some extensive business and technical service, although we have a School of Business Administration that does a good job of providing much direct service.

The state extension program has a library of some 10,000 films, which is unbelievable as far as the usual public library service program is concerned; we have a collection of 250 to serve community needs. In many ways we can afford to be a little more extensive in our collection aims; that is, we can buy art materials and some of the things that are unusual because we have this resource in the community.

We do not give school service, and with seven branches in a community of 128,000, we obviously do not need bookmobile service within the city limits. In the near future we expect to expand into the metropolitan area, which covers Lancaster County. The county population is 152,000.

The library plan was developed over a long period. The need for new facilities was noted in 1924. In 1945 a bond issue was proposed. The community kept growing. In 1950 it was 99,000. In 1951 a plan was submitted to the City Planning Commission for a complete review of the library service program. The critical need, the Commission stated at that time, was for a new main library and the possible addition of two neighborhood branches for more service centers in population groups of 10,000 to 17,000.

In the next five years we were able to proceed with the program; two new branches were built and one older branch rebuilt. In 1957, a proposal was submitted to the voters for a bond issue of $1,250,000 to build a library on a half-block site downtown. This was turned down. As a result, the board suggested that the plan be redescribed.

We have one of the most fortunate sites. It is in the center of town, midway between the state capitol building and the state university. It is one block from the heaviest traffic thoroughfare, but buses from every part of town circle the site. We thought it might be well to occupy this site, which was only a quarter of a block. To achieve further economy we thought we might add to the old building. It was substantial, although completely obsolete from the standpoint of elevators, communications, stairs, and so forth. In studying the plans to build an addition, a proposal was submitted to the City Planning Commission and endorsed as an intermediate possibility. About this time a loyal friend of the library, who had helped us through a couple of campaigns for funds as well as the bond issue proposal, came forth.

His first suggestion was that he would give us a building, but this was not acceptable. Then he considered giving the addition, but in going over the plans it was decided that a better solution would be for us to take the full-scale plan and cut it in half to make one new building twice as large as the present facilities, with ample provision for expansion to a building large enough to satisfy the usual planning requirements and formula. With an initial gift of $300,000, plans were made for construction.

The city council agreed to support us and provide some of the demolition and site clearance. Special funds were made available for consultant and architect fees. The Lincoln City Library Foundation, which had been established in 1951, agreed to raise additional funds for furnishings. We again submitted to the City Planning Commission a proposal to complete the entire building in six years, and made the capital outlay proposal of $300,000 for the next year for construction and furnishings; this is the stage of the plan now.

The total plan calls for more than 54,000 square feet, and initial construction will be about half of that. I say about half because we have not yet proposed a full basement. If you put in a large basement, the tendency is for public services to be pushed into this area, rather than for provision to be made for an additional public service area. The full basement is an additional extensive phase. If funds become available and it looks as though the full basement will not jeopardize expansion on the first

Edholm & Blomgren, Photographers

Staircase corner
Lincoln Public Library
Lincoln, Nebraska

and second floors, we will probably put it in. It would increase our square footage in the first phase of the plan from about 29,000 to 35,000.

The building is located on 14th and N streets, in central downtown. The plan is to open up the entire first floor and put the secondary and some public service areas on the second floor. The corner entrance is not in the immediate corner; it is just north of the wall. The children's room has a separate entrance, on the far side. All the general services will be offered in this area, which is not sub-

ject to departmentalizing. There is one general meeting room, with reference and technical assignment in the northwest corner, the children's service, and a break straight through the center of this area of the building.

On the first floor there is plate glass around the base of the building. It has a planting screen, and the solar screen overhangs the first floor by about 36 inches. It should give sufficient light control.

There is a public parking lot across the street. It will take about 350 cars on five levels about three

Main floor
Lincoln Public Library
Lincoln, Nebraska

Basement
Lincoln Public Library
Lincoln, Nebraska

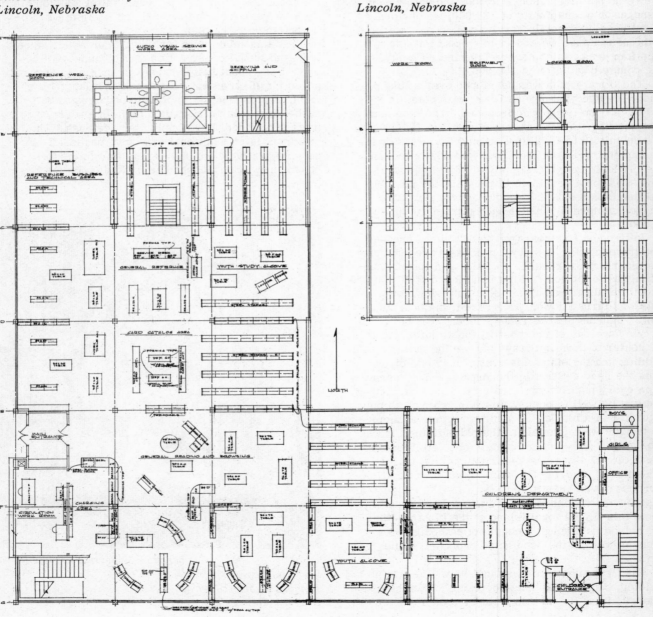

stories high, and it offers shade and protection on the west. There are two tall buildings immediately south of that to give afternoon sun control. We have no direct sunlight. On the south is a telephone building which will give some protection, although we will have some light control here. Until the second stage of planning is completed, we intend to use this area for a garden. These windows open onto the area as if it were a court.

The second floor would have the technical division, a multipurpose room, and the staff room, with elevator service. This, again, is a multipurpose area for small group meetings. While we are a block from the municipal auditorium, we do have a group of meeting rooms ranging in capacity from 80 to 320 persons as a public service. It was thought we should not consider an auditorium larger than an area for small discussion groups, music groups, and exhibits.

This is a relatively simple plan—all elements are movable, interchangeable. It varies from the construction plan. We are actually at the beginning state of construction, but because the funds were given to the Foundation and there was a special arrangement with the contractor for completion of the building, we have no problem changing our plans as we go along. We can adapt. The plans were not put out for bid.

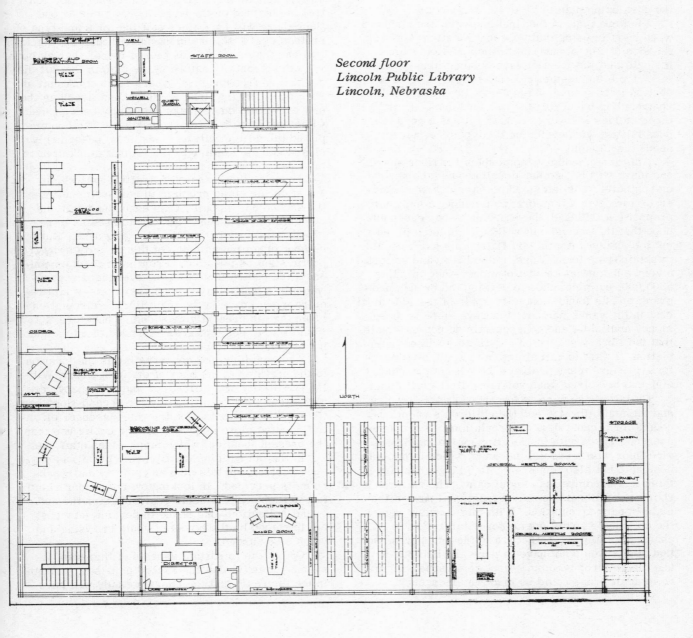

Second floor
Lincoln Public Library
Lincoln, Nebraska

Critique

MR. DAN WILLIAMS

I began on a very skeptical approach when I heard of this gift and wondered whether it ought not to be invested in securities for quite some time rather than used for building now. I was well aware of the total inadequacy of the present building.

Lincoln and Des Moines, where I am situated, are both state capitals, so I think I have a little understanding of some of the problems from a service angle—the related problems that one gains in a state capital. Although we have no state university, we do have a moderately sized university. Moving, then, from skepticism, I find that many of my questions are answered in terms of segment A or unit B of the developing plan.

I believe that, in the final analysis, the planners were right in using their present location, although the size of Lincoln and the transportation seem to indicate that the location leaves something to be desired from the aesthetic point of view. The first section is L-shaped. Completed, the library will be rectangular, occupying the full land area. It will be three stories instead of two, and it has a good many possibilities for developing the type of service needed in Lincoln.

This intermediate step doubles the floor space, and there will be another doubling when the second unit is built. The intermediate step can be considered more than a temporary interlude, a makeshift proposition, although there seems to be reasonable hope that the second unit will be completed in the not too distant future. Mr. Dalrymple has been able to obtain from foundations, individuals, and so forth a very substantial amount of money—not only this $300,000, but also funds to develop the branch program; and he found money for some of the additional cost in the same manner. I believe there is more money available, and consequently do not anticipate that the library will go on indefinitely without completion. I want to call attention to some minor factors, because many problems of this intermediate step can be solved when you move to the full plan.

Children's service is important in this library and the main library, and the children's room accounts for a great deal of circulation. As a consequence, I agree with the location on the main service floor with a special entrance, which is not only desirable but also important. In a larger library I think this becomes less significant. The children's room in my library is only a fractional part of the main library circulation. With this constant use of the children's room, one minor detail might be changed to allow some access to the adult areas so that adults would not have to leave the building to use the children's room. Also, some supervision from adult areas could be made in emergency.

Mr. Dalrymple mentioned that, with the variety of specialized libraries within Lincoln, there are no immediate plans for the development of subject departments staffed by specialists. Some of this service does exist in terms of book selection, but in terms of professional service to library users, each professional staff member works in the over-all adult areas. However, it seems that, in developing the second stage of the plan, departments such as music or art might be included. Within the framework of the modular plan they would seem to create no real problems in the expanded service areas on the second floor.

Immediately, however, I am concerned about the establishment of second-floor public areas without any immediate supervision. While good door control is obtained on the first floor, on the second floor there will have to be staffing for some type of professional desk, or during many hours the stacks will need to be treated as closed rather than as open.

An interesting feature of the plan is that all the stacks are freestanding. There is no stack unit as such on either the first or the second floors as they now exist, and these areas can easily be expanded with construction of the second unit. The contemplated third floor will be stack area, presumably closed stacks, similar to the limited stack area in the first unit as basement.

In noting those areas of the first unit which would create some problem in readjustment when the second unit is built, I am concerned with the circulation workroom. Its location seems to be proper—directly behind the charging desk. But I believe in getting as much of this activity away from public sight as possible. From my recent experience, the centralization of the overdue process—which is a possibility in such a system—would require more space in the main library circulation room than is presently provided. Therefore, I would like to see that area expanded, not to a double but at least to a larger area.

Another thing that concerns me is the location of the elevator at the back of the first floor. With the possibility of a third floor and with many service areas planned ultimately for second-floor use, the need is a combination freight-passenger elevator, located more strategically for public use than the present location, which emphasizes staff use.

In the old building the film collection was on open shelves. In this plan an audio-visual workroom is provided. In looking over the floor plan I fail to find any particular provisions for the audio-visual collection—one of the important services. I am intrigued by the layout of youth browsing and youth study areas.

One of the important aspects of this plan, it seems to me, is that the second unit is far enough in the future so that the users not only will have moved in but also will have a practical opportunity to see how well the arrangement functions, which will enhance planning of the second unit. Modular unit construction lends itself quite easily to this expansion, and without fixed stack areas almost anything can happen. I will not discuss the things I was not too happy about because, as I have said, almost every problem resolved itself in terms of its being easily changed in the second development. This plan seems to present a quite different opportunity from that of adding additional sections to additional libraries with the problems of floor articulation and other difficulties. Here is an opportunity in which the staff can take a step in the right direction, study it, evaluate it, see how the public reacts to it, and then develop the completed plan without a great deal of backtracking, additional expense, and compromise.

In summary, I believe that Mr. Dalrymple was right, and I was wrong, in thinking that the $300,000 should be spent immediately. It will provide a modern plant adequate for the next several years, as well as an opportunity to develop a service program for a growing city—some 40,000 population in the last three decades. In the second development, space will be available for extending the main office and service. We have here a plan which not only can be revised today and tomorrow, but can be substantially changed by adding not a second addition but the second half of a basically good plan for a public library in a city of the size of Lincoln, Nebraska.

Discussion

Question: I was interested in the elevator. Is there any particular reason for its location beyond the fact that it is adjacent to the shipping and receiving area?

MR. DALRYMPLE: Actually, we had not intended to emphasize the public service use of the elevator. I believe users can climb the stairs at the front corner about as quickly as they can catch an elevator, and the stairs will serve many more people. We really did not have in mind more than reserve use by the staff. The elevator is for people with heart conditions and so forth, but primarily for freight and staff. Also, 90 per cent of the public service facilities are on the first floor. Persons attending group meetings on the second floor can, of course, use the elevator.

Question: Are you utilizing a full basement now?

MR. DALRYMPLE: We have a third of a basement now. There was a proposal in the city council to fill in the complete basement.

Comment: I think you will meet one of the expenses of a full basement with your footings at the be-

ginning, especially if you are planning to go up to a third floor; and if you are planning your construction to handle bookstacks on the third floor, it would be much more economical and actually much more convenient to plan bookstacks in the basement. There would be less distance between your main-floor public areas and your basement stack areas than between your main floor and even your second floor, because there is quite a difference in the height of your floor levels. A stack area on your top level, your proposed third-floor level, would require a terrific amount of beams and columns to support the weight on your stacks.

Question: Your meeting rooms are on the second floor, but there are no rest rooms close by. Where are the public rest rooms?

MR. DALRYMPLE: They are at the opposite end of the building, and that may be a mistake. It is possible to put in toilet facilities on the second floor immediately adjacent. We have not drawn them in yet. I do not know how we will resolve that problem.

Question: I would like to suggest that your entrances will be difficult to find in this plan. I would like to see them expressed in a positive way. Also, when you go into a building, I think it is a comfortable feeling to know where you are going, to know where the different spaces are without a map or a guide. I wish there was more expression of circulation. I believe that you would be wending your way around tables and stacks to get to the various areas. I wish there was a clearer organization of the spaces, but I especially would like to see the entrance stated from the outside. Some buildings make you feel you have to run around them to find an entrance, and you do not know which is the main entrance. You might confuse the children's entrance for the main entrance here.

MR. WILLIAMS: I would be inclined to concur on the entrances. The pattern on the inside is a bit tight, and I would agree that, if the first development were to continue for twenty years, it would be a major handicap. But with a good possibility of building the rest of the structure within a few years, these patterns can be straightened out so that your stack areas will not predominate and your tables and low shelving will permit a better view. It is an L-shaped building now. It is my understanding that this will fill out so that you will have more of a vista than an alley effect. For that reason it seems that this criticism is valid at the moment but the problem can be adjusted in the ultimate building.

Question: If the second floor will be used to a limited extent by the public in the first phase and a great deal more in the completed phase, why are the director's office and board room located on the second floor in the prime public space, both in accessibility and in control?

MR. DALRYMPLE: I have no answer to that; the architect put them there.

Question: Observing the very beautiful sketch of the building, I notice that the lower floor at street level has a generous amount of glass. Of course, this is most attractive and most desirable as far as promoting the use of the library. My question is in the form of a consideration rather than a criticism. Realizing that this glass is most desirable but that a large amount of traffic circumvents this site, since the building is relatively close to the streets, I question would it not be disturbing to the people inside? If my observation is correct, the glass extends from nearly floor level to the ceiling in this first-floor area.

MR. DALRYMPLE: I do not suppose there is a complete answer, but there is an 11-foot sidewalk with a 4-foot setback of green planting 2-1/2 to 3 feet up from ground level outside the building. The overhang of the second floor will make this appear to be recessed window space. The problem of how traffic would distract patrons inside did occur to us, but we found that with high light intensity inside you do not notice things outside. We have a branch library with windows almost as tall on a main traffic intersection in South Lincoln, and inside you seldom notice anything happening outside.

Question: Where is the mechanical and heating equipment located?

MR. DALRYMPLE: There are units on both floors and in corners of the building. We are contracting to purchase steam from a steam supply company that serves the state capitol and state university. We will use individual zone air-conditioning units on each floor.

Comment: Last year at Montreal at the similar institute meeting, Keith Doms, the critic of the Rodman Public Library in Alliance, Ohio, said, "Mr. Bergerman has, I think, the exalted view that this building might be built for $14 a square foot. I would be very interested to hear about it when it is finally resolved." I admit it did not cost $14; it was $11.87, and that building has 65 tons of air conditioning and 76 foot-candles of lighting on all the reading services.

Question: In a building in a large downtown shopping district such as this, how many children come downtown themselves and will use a separate entrance?

MR. DALRYMPLE: Lincoln has quite a few activities for which families come downtown, and we plan to extend service to the entire family and have family nights. Families tend to make most frequent use of the branch libraries and, in many ways, our main library children's department will be the centralized, coordinating center for the library.

Question: I would like to go back to the entrance question. Philosophically, I question the idea of separate children's and adult entrances, particularly in view of what you have said about family usage. I would like to raise the question as to whether two entrances are desirable by grade level or age level. Children do grow up and become adults, and we like to have them continue to use the library. Secondly, while you may not be using the second floor right away for the public, it might be important to consider an escalator to open that space when you do need it. An escalator would make it more readily available than an elevator.

MR. DALRYMPLE: The entrance to the children's department also opens onto a stairway leading to the second floor, allowing entrance to the meeting rooms on the second floor.

Queens Borough Public Library

Jamaica, Queens Borough, New York City

Presentation of plans
HAROLD TUCKER
Chief Librarian

Critique
RAYMOND E. WILLIAMS
Minneapolis Public Library
Minneapolis, Minnesota

Building data
    Architect: Kiff, Colean, Voss & Souder,
           Office of York & Sawyer,
           New York City
    Type of library: Central building
    Population to be served: 1,809,578
    Area: 194,300 square feet
    Book capacity: 860,000 volumes
    Seating capacity: 1,000
    Cost
        Building: $4,993,300
        Equipment: $140,000
        Site: $275,000

MR. HAROLD TUCKER

The problem in our planning is to provide a central library building for service to the Borough of Queens. Although Queens is an integral part of New York City, it has many suburban characteristics and is separate from Manhattan. The population growth in Queens has been tremendous over the past twenty years. Between 1950 and 1960 an increase of almost a quarter million raised Queens from the fourth largest of the five boroughs of New York City to the second largest in terms of population. It is also the largest in terms of area, with 120 square miles.

The building is to serve not only as the central library but also as the service headquarters for a network of fifty branches as well as three bookmobiles serving the entire borough. The total area is 194,300 square feet.

The library system began in 1898 but had no central building until 1930. The present building was too small the day it was opened for service, and it was recognized for its inadequacy as far back as 1940 when there was a survey made of libraries in New York City. In this survey the Queens Borough library central building came out as priority for acquisition of land to expand the building. Between 1940 and 1955 many efforts were made to be-

gin the expansion, but nothing actually took place until 1955 when the architectural firm of York and Sawyer was authorized to make a survey of the library situation.

The firm made a thorough investigation, including studies of all existing standards for central library buildings, and brought this up to date by gathering data on recently constructed buildings. The firm analyzed our present organization and the future needs in this building, and determined the specific spaces required for each function and the development of the building.

The conclusions of this survey have served as a basis for the planning of the building on a new site. The total area of the site is 71,000 square feet and the site is completely used. There is no space left over. The present building consists of 75,000 square feet. Book collection capacity is 327,000. There are 271 reader seats. The new plan includes 194,300 square feet, 860,000 volumes, and 1,000 reader seats.

There is a major off-street bus terminal on one side of the street; the subway—expressway stop—is two blocks away; and the elevated line to Manhattan about two blocks away. The Jamaica Avenue shopping area is on the first street to the south.

The entrance to the building faces west; this is the major entrance and it is centered on the block front. At that point there is an auxiliary entrance for staff, which also serves as the entrance to the children's area. The garage and bookmobile area are in the back. The building is primarily a one-floor structure, with administrative offices on the second floor and a small mechanical area on the third floor.

The planning objective is to locate all major public services on the ground floor for maximum service and convenience to the public, to provide for smooth traffic and service flow, to provide flexibility for changes required in the future, and to locate on the first floor only those nonpublic activities which must be there for management purposes.

While compromises are necessary and we cannot always reach the ideal, these objectives have largely been achieved. The public services, except one minor unit, are located on the ground floor. The openness of the plan provides for a free traffic flow between the service areas and the book collection. At the main entrance are several service points which should be adjacent to the main entrance. We have had to compromise in setting these up.

The primary consideration was the location of a public catalog and public information desk so that the person coming in has guidance to the collection. There is a small checkroom at one side for leaving packages, brief cases, and what have you, and the return desk is located immediately to the right, so that these two functions which the individual needs on first coming in are relatively available.

In the adult service areas radiating out from the public catalog area, we have divided the book collection and services into subject areas—a complete division which exists only partially in our present building. We have carefully considered the number of books in each of these collections to the proportion of use in determining the reader seats and space. The placement is an effort to reflect interest relationships.

We have an art and music division which includes recordings as well as picture collections. Adjacent are the divisions of business, science, and technology; social sciences and education; language and literature; history and geography; local history and geography, and local history. These subdivisions run between 5,000 and 6,000 square feet. The collections vary depending on the subjects in the collection.

The service desk and workrooms are core arrangements, with each of the three serving two staffs but with those staffs separate. The only fixed items in these units are the stairways and the book-racks. The popular library, which is close to the entrance, is designed to serve the general reader-

Diagrammatic plans showing building organization
Queens Borough Public Library
Jamaica, Queens Borough, New York City

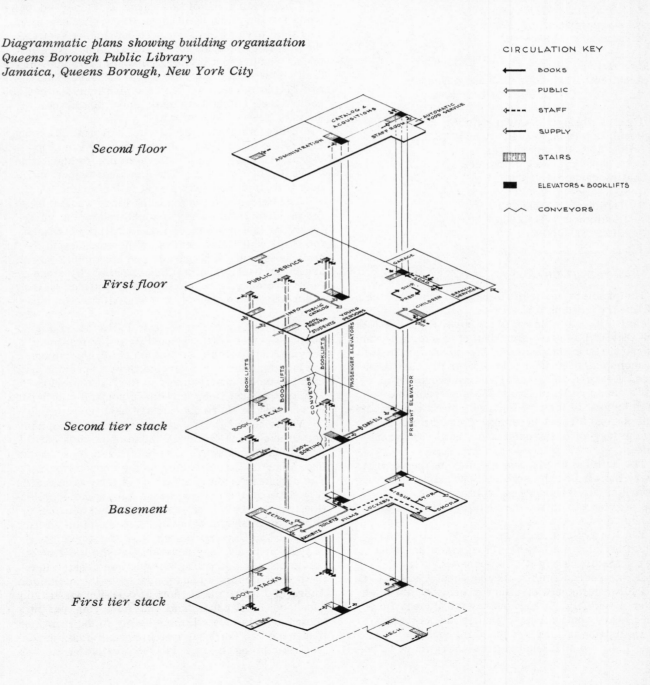

CIRCULATION KEY

◀—— BOOKS
⇐—— PUBLIC
◀- - - STAFF
◀—— SUPPLY
▨▨▨ STAIRS
■■■ ELEVATORS & BOOKLIFTS
〜〜 CONVEYORS

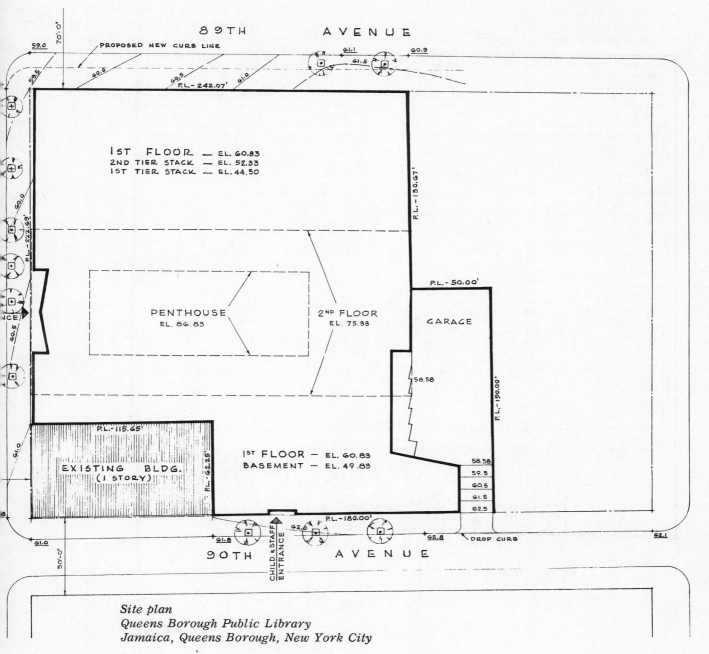

Site plan
Queens Borough Public Library
Jamaica, Queens Borough, New York City

ship through provision for fiction and popular non-fiction.

There is a slight change in our concept in the planning for children and young people, based on our experience since beginning this project and on the changes taking place in the immediate area of the central library. We have adjusted to set up a children's area to serve youngsters in Grades 1-6. These children are kept out of the traffic flow of the adult areas, although they have access if sent there. Charging and returning for children will be handled at that area. Adjacent to this is an area serving

children in Grades 7-9. The older group has considerably more access to the adult areas, which is necessary for their reference needs.

Because of the increasing use of periodicals by students, we have established a student area near the main entrance and young people's area. The student room will house approximately 100 periodical titles, with runs of about ten years and with microfilm on open shelves. This arrangement has the obvious advantages of immediately siphoning off heavy periodical use and of preventing running back and forth for the staff. This becomes almost a self-

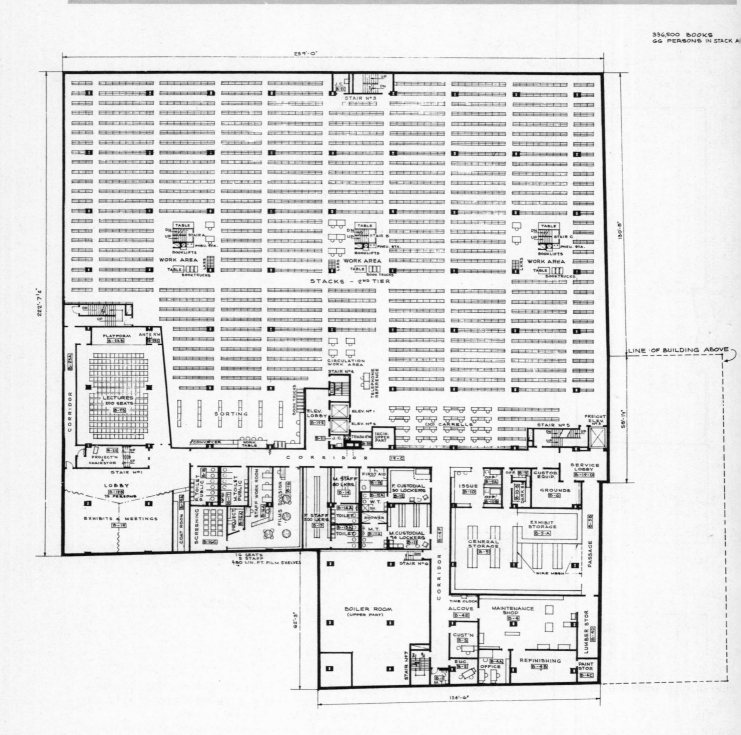

Basement
Queens Borough Public Library
Jamaica, Queens Borough, New York City

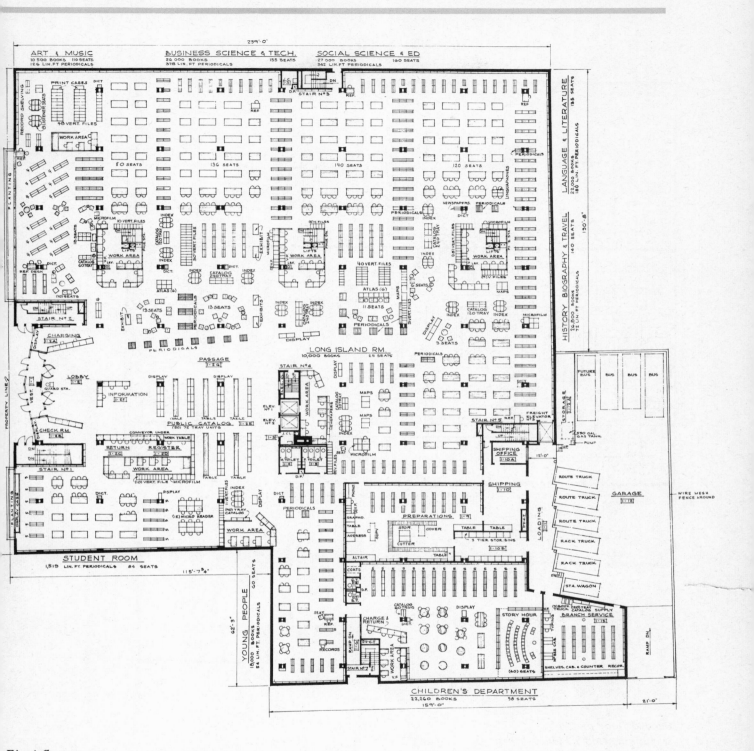

First floor
Queens Borough Public Library
Jamaica, Queens Borough, New York City

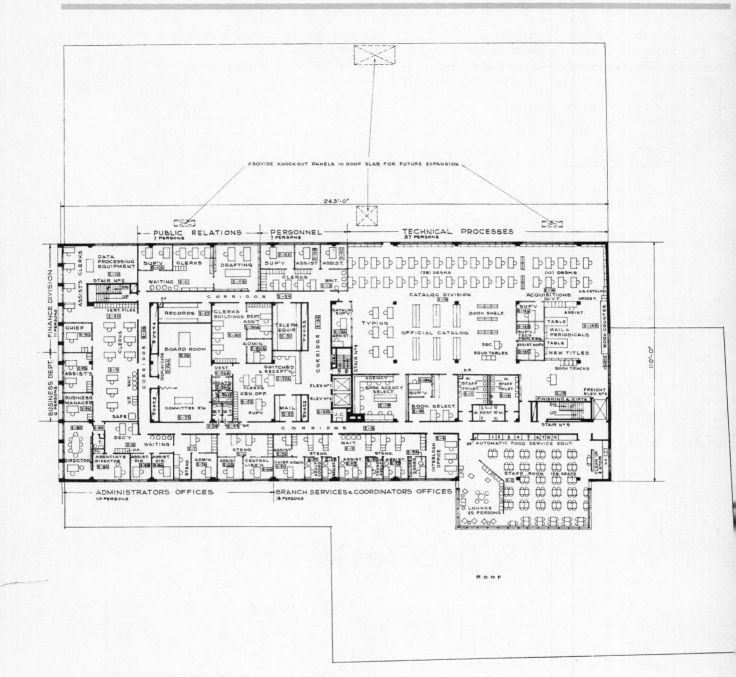

Second floor and roof
Queens Borough Public Library
Jamaica, Queens Borough, New York City

service area with minimum librarian involvement.

We have a minimum of nonpublic agencies on this floor. Shipping and receiving must be here because this is the ground level. We have been able to set up our loading facilities in such a fashion that all the route trucks which make trips out to the fifty branches can be loaded or unloaded simultaneously, in contrast to our present ability to handle only one truck at a time. There is a loading platform for bookmobiles and a small room for the bookmobile collections.

All supplies and other items that come into shipping can be immediately removed from this area by the freight elevator. The biggest volume of material coming in and going out is, of course, books. Therefore, the preparation unit is adjacent to the shipping area, and will include a mechanical conveyer system so that most books coming in here will be prepared and go right back out. With this arrangement, only one copy of any title goes to the cataloging unit on the second floor. The major part of the area below the main floor is stacks. Here are the service points for the collection from the stacks as well as stairways, book lists, telephones, and perhaps message tubes. We have a few places for chairs for private study for people who use typewriters and tape recorders.

The sorting area is below the return desk; books are sent to it on gravity conveyers as soon as they have been checked off at the main floor. After sorting, they go back out to the division areas on our regular dumb-waiter or our additional booklift.

From our 200-seat auditorium, exit can be made at the main entrance on the ground floor. Two smaller meeting rooms have folding partitions to open into exhibit areas in conjunction with any meetings here. The only public service unit not on the main floor is the film service, which includes a collection of about 1,000 films, a screening room, and a service point. We do not have a film service for literature at the present time.

There are areas for the custodian and staff lockers, and it is anticipated that each staff member will have a small purse locker as well as a coat locker. In the same area are the major supply storage and the maintenance shop, which does some carpentry and minor furniture refinishing. Access to all of these areas is by means of the freight elevator.

The second level is not a complete floor, as you can see. This level consists primarily of administrative offices. The acquisition and cataloging units are in close communication to the shipping area. We are not able to achieve the openness on this floor that we can on the main floor because of fire regulations. I had hoped it could be more open with simple partitions around the office areas, but these had to be regular plaster divisions, so that we do

not have full flexibility. With regular partitions we will have some interior offices.

The staff facility is not near what it should be. However, it has been greatly improved since the first plan. We have been able to double the amount of space, and I think it does become acceptable in size. The third floor houses simply the mechanical equipment for air conditioning. This, incidentally, was the building which broke the New York City policy on air conditioning in public buildings.

Cost data on the building are: demolition, $25,000; general construction, $3,800,300; plumbing, $150,000; heating, ventilating, and air conditioning, $500,000; electricity, $417,000; total development of the site, $10,000—a total of $4,993,300. The area is 194,300 square feet, 2,050,000 cubic feet.

Critique

MR. RAYMOND E. WILLIAMS

My questions are mostly internal, instead of structural, and concern the service area, use of collection, and relationship of certain collections to layout. I think Mr. Tucker did not give the building as much credit in some places as he should have; more architecture is here than was brought out, and I think that is important. Since the staff at Queens is capable of judging how much space it needs and where, I will not discuss that.

I would like to discuss the relationship of the service and the staff areas on the first floor as well as the philosophy of public service. For once, we are accepting a major library, a library serving areas of large population, where the public service area will be on the first floor, which many of us dream about and try to get in various ways. Here everything is on the first floor.

The plan includes a brick wall—a closed wall— with only a slight story above so that light is admitted. You have a single main entrance only, in addition to the children's entrance, and in a building with a floor of this area, somebody must have talked to the fire marshal about the space and the distances back to the corners. The principal advantage is having the control at the entrance in such a large plan.

Another advantage is the relation of the children's room to the rest of the building. With an entrance which has a validity of its own, the children will not feel left out. I did not like the statement made, "Keep them away from the rest," or something like that. It is an important entrance. It is the children's library and not a secondary place. It is another door, and I think the children will recognize that.

Now, where are the things that I wanted on the new plan? The places where the staff will be working with the public have low counter shelving, making an alcove with shelving around four sides; there is, however, access to the staff. There is no wall, nothing to hold back the public, but the department area is defined. I think the size of the workrooms should be reconsidered. The rooms appear to be small, but there are many good ways to operate libraries, and this may be the way they want to operate theirs.

The service desk for these areas is in front, and Mr. Tucker said this serves two departments. The staff work in pairs here to receive the public from two directions. In a building of this kind with this much public shelving, most staff reference work will be on the floor. The staff will help people at the shelves. They will be relating such materials as periodicals, clippings, and subject collections with the books. In the old Queens library—and I think I am correct—there is a closed stack and a tower stack. For much of the work the staff does not have enough space on the floor and must go back to the stack; thus, the staff and the philosophy of reference work have been related to a closed stack.

The staff members there want, as all staffs do, to get the collection out where they and the public can get their hands on it. They want to divide their reference work; and as you do reference work, you must relate all of your materials and resources to the question at hand. According to the planned arrangement, the staff will be working in the closed stack as well as with the public and will be a sizable distance from the back.

Each area has pneumatic tubes for calling the materials back into the closed portion of the work area. If the staff, working from the floor, needs to remove material quickly from the stack, it will be necessary to come back to pick up the message to receive materials. These are some of the many possibilities with the kind of construction you have.

This building is based on the column structure, and with a structural pattern like that, you normally would cut the holes down through the middle of the bay, or the building will be weakened. You will have these down in the middle, where they will not damage the structure. But I would like to suggest moving the reference or service desk around to the side. The periodicals and vertical file materials could be brought back further into this part to be near the service desk. Or they must be moved out to put the desk there.

This arrangement limits not only the travel distance from the service desk back to the book material but also the supervision. It would not require a change in plan or relocation of materials. No matter at what stage you are in the construction, you can arrange the partitions, which is undoubtedly what the planners had in mind. The partitions can

be arranged now or twenty years from now to accommodate a structural change.

The servicing of the collection and the accessibility of the stairs and lifts are well planned. With the penetration down into their storage area, the staff has easy access to materials. A service or work area could be built around elements of communication.

On the staff plan there are three places where pneumatic message tubes go down. It seems possible to gain some efficiency and economy by running the tubes together, perhaps at the center point, and do the paging from there. The tubes can go most anywhere. Bringing the tubes down to a central station and having the pages work from there may well reduce the number of people necessary at no major expense or change in plan. Having the return at these points is good; you need it there so that the messages can go to pages.

When libraries of this size plan their first-floor area, their services generally follow the outside of the building, and they have various solutions for the middle and larger service areas, which are major problems. If the library has a lounge area, keeps a cultural collection containing nonfiction as well as fiction, and has a student area with duplicate periodicals, there will be damage with much self-service. These areas must be clearly and carefully defined by signs and by traffic pattern of the furniture, which, of course, can be arranged so that the public will know what kind of service is available. The layout will require imagination by the architect and the staff to keep the public working its way from the main entrance through the books and into the proper areas, and to siphon off the proper groups to such areas or to the popular library, the youth library, and the children's library. However, it is far from impossible to do. These are some of the problems the planners have generated by having all public services on the first floor.

In considering the sizes of tables and so on, I think there is an overestimation of how many tables can go in—there is too much furniture. The space might be opened up by reducing the number of people who can actually sit down, not the number of people who can be handled. The relationship of the auxiliary parts of the library are fine, and I think Queens will be very happy with this library.

Discussion

Comment: You might tell them the size of those modules; they look very small in the plan.
MR. WILLIAMS: 27 feet.
MR. TUCKER: This is about the maximum you can get and still retain a reasonable floor thickness.
Comment: Mr. Williams' comment about the furniture is a good point. We are considering a suggestion to Mr. Tucker after we spend more time

studying the problem. Those racks of shelving are 9 feet long. I think they could be 12 feet long. Perhaps we could use two arrangements and gain a surprising amount of space. The table arrangement follows the accepted pattern of small tables, resembling salt-and-pepper shakers standing around. It may not look that way when you walk into the library, but I would like to experiment with an arrangement in which we violate one of the principles, and that is to return to some large tables.

I have thought for some time that we need more table space. We are often educated to 30 inches per reader and that sort of thing. If we had fewer and better aisles and more space, with readers using more and more books in their work, perhaps we would be gaining an advantage.

Question: How high are your ceilings?

MR. TUCKER: 12 feet.

Question: Did you deliberately refrain from telling why you had a space problem?

MR. TUCKER: You explain it.

Comment: I think Mr. Tucker and the architects have done a superlative job under the circumstances. New York City has a procedure that may be unique. You make all sorts of estimates of your needs. Then a commissioner of public works determines your square footage; in this case, he determined it and then stated that there could be no permission for expansion, which, of course, is ridiculous. It is almost unbelievable. The library people did manage, however, to obtain the privilege of expansion on the second floor; consequently, there will be additional space available later.

Question: Will the bookmobile be parked in an enclosed area?

MR. TUCKER: It will be parked in an enclosed area at the back. The area will be enclosed with a chain link fence. In the original planning this was a fully enclosed area, but we did not have enough money for it. We have had some difficulty in the allocation of certain amounts of space and now have approximately 200,000 square feet. We had to take the roof off the garage or compute that area in the square footage.

Question: Will you be able to accommodate the hordes of high school youngsters who are going to use a fine reference facility like this?

MR. TUCKER: We will be able to accommodate them much better than we have. There are 271 seats in the old building, 1,000 in the new.

Question: What I am referring to has been implicit in some of the questions on the use of periodicals—one of the popular materials in a metropolitan library.

MR. TUCKER: Not only in the high school but in the college as well. First, Queens College developed without a library; then it built one, but is still low on volumes. We handle a heavy student population there. St. John's University has moved out to Queens; since it has not yet built its library, we must service it for a long time. A new community college has been established, and with colleges around us, we service many students from outlying areas. While the colleges have some materials, we find students prefer our fuller services and collection.

Question: The amount of money budgeted for the furniture seems very small in relation to the new space and equipment.

MR. TUCKER: It is $140,000. This is another strange thing about our operations in New York. This figure can change upward as construction of the building progresses. In other words, our budget is primarily a program; the only funds authorized so far are for the architect's contract. As soon as he has finished his plans, the proposal must be approved again, at which time funds for construction will be appropriated. At that point, we will have completed our exact study of furniture needs and in a position to present a much closer figure. We have, incidentally, been requesting $250,000 for what we call initial book stock funds, to begin building up for $350,000.

Question: Is the steel stack part of the building?

Comment: I do not know how that problem has been settled but I am still hoping this will be considered equipment and not building, particularly from the standpoint of cubage.

MR. TUCKER: It must be equipment because that construction was based on $2.30 a cubic foot for construction.

MR. WILLIAMS: I was assuming that the stack and the furniture, including the desks and so on, would be part of the construction cost. If they are not, the equipment cost would be closer to $900,000 or $1,000,000 rather than $140,000. The steel stacks will cost $400,000 easily.

School Libraries

Lincoln Park
High School Library

1701 Champaign Road
Lincoln Park, Michigan

Presentation of plans
THEODOSIA CONKLIN
Librarian

Building data
    Architect: Eberle M. Smith Associates, Inc.
            Detroit, Michigan
    Staff: 2 trained librarians
            1 clerk
    Enrollment: 3,200
    Location: First floor, facing lobby
    School library quarters
        Reading room: 50 feet 9 inches by 83 feet
            6 inches
        Conference rooms: 2, each 11 feet 4 inches
            by 12 feet 3 inches
        Workroom: 18 feet 6 inches by 28 feet
        Storage room: 21 feet 6 inches by 28 feet
        Librarian's office: 16 feet by 22 feet 6
            inches
        Audio-visual facilities: 25 feet 1 inch by
            14 feet 9 inches
        Teachers' curriculum library: 13 feet 6
            inches by 22 feet 6 inches
    Type of school: Senior high, Grades 9-12
    Type of community: Residential
    Type of student: Average; 34 per cent college-
        bound
    Type of curriculum: Comprehensive (academic,
        commercial, industrial arts)
    School philosophy: Each student should be
        granted every opportunity to develop to
        the fullest extent of his abilities. Devel-
        opment should be through carefully
        guided experiences. Fostering of demo-
        cratic ideals and actions in every student
        should be the present as well as the ulti-
        mate goal.
    Relation of library to school program: Refer-
        ence center
    Community library resources: Wayne County
        Library

Critique
    Good features
    1. V-shaped shelving along one wall, allowing for
        traditional windows, but providing adequate
        shelving space.
    2. Faculty library.
    3. Library classroom (used continuously).
    4. Storage room used for magazine storage (in-
        valuable for work on term papers and classwork
        with *Readers' Guide*). Room for general storage
        also.
    5. Location, first floor on lobby. When collection
        is adequate, will remain open in the evenings.

    Suggestions for improvement
    1. Cooling system inadequate. Warm days (80° or
        over) very uncomfortable. All windows do not
        open.
    2. No storage available in workroom for 3 by 5
        cards and the like.
    3. No accession file available in office.

Reading room
Lincoln Park High School Library
Lincoln Park, Michigan

Lens—Art Photo ©

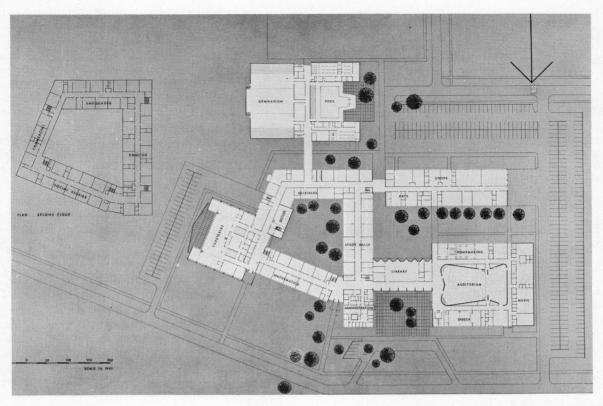

General layout
Lincoln Park High School
Lincoln Park, Michigan

The library area appears at lower right.

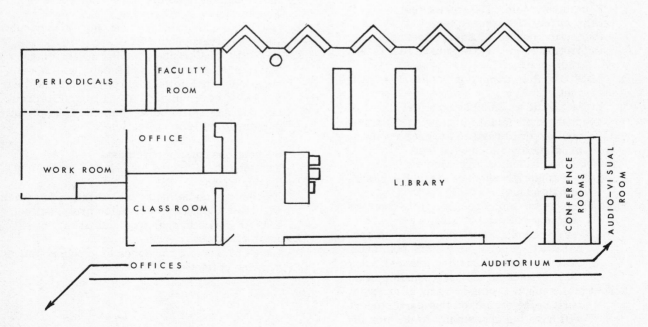

Enlargement of library area
Lincoln Park High School
Lincoln Park, Michigan

Proviso West High School Library

Wolf Road and Harrison Street
Hillside, Illinois

Presentation of plans
CHARLES D. De YOUNG
Director of Libraries

Building data
Architect: Perkins & Will
                    Chicago, Illinois
Staff: 3 trained librarians
            4 secretaries
            72 student pages
Enrollment: 2,600
Location: Centrally located on second floor be-
        tween academic wings
School library quarters
    Reading room: 5,040 square feet
    Conference room: 520 square feet; a folding
        wall easily divides this area into 2 rooms
    Workroom and storage room: Combined in
        390 square feet
    Librarian's office: 130 square feet
    Audio-visual facilities: Under library con-
        trol but located elsewhere in school
    Film storage room: 144 square feet
    Equipment room: 290 square feet
    Film office: 165 square feet
    Projection booth: 81 square feet
    Projection room: 1,514 square feet (seats
        190)
    Little Theater projection booth: 104 square
        feet
    Little Theater: 2,680 square feet (seats 250)
    Teachers' curriculum library: Located at
        one end of library conference room; ap-
        proximately 130 square feet
Type of school: Senior high, Grades 9-12
Type of community: Suburban (middle, upper-
        middle class)
Type of student: Good cross section; about 45
        per cent college preparatory
Type of curriculum: Four types—college pre-
        paratory; general (there are both accel-
        erated and slow learning groups); voca-
        tional; educable mentally handicapped.
School philosophy: Secondary school program
        must be so organized that each student
        will have the opportunity to develop his
        abilities, interests, and understandings,
        and to achieve the highest level of growth
        of which he is capable. All the educa-

tional experiences of each student—that
is, curricular, extracurricular, and out-
of-school—must be coordinated to assure
the attainment of his highest competence.
Relation of library to school program: Library
is planned to fill the role of a service
agency, a teaching agency, a book center,
and a reading center. Some of the main
objectives of the library program,
planned cooperatively with the teaching
and the administrative staff, are: to en-
rich the curriculum and supply reference
material; to provide for the worthy use
of leisure time; to train students in the
use of books and the library. Daily
hours are from 7:40 A.M. to 4:15 P.M.
Community library resources: The following
village library districts are located in
whole or in part in the district of Proviso West High School: Bellwood,
Berkeley, Hillside, Melrose Park, North-
lake, Stone Park, and Westchester. The
Chicago Public Library system as well
as the Oak Park Public Library system
are also accessible for more ambitious
students.

Critique

Good features
1. Central location in the school.
2. An appealing and pleasing atmosphere.
3. Individual study tables in reference section.
4. Adapts nicely to new uses.
5. Good wall-type display cases in corridor outside
    library entrance and exit.
6. Versatile conference room handy for classes
    and individual student and faculty use, housing
    such individual collections as special reading,
    teachers' curriculum library, microfilm read-
    ers and microfilm collection, and college and
    university bulletin collection.

Suggestions for improvement
1. Too long.
2. Too narrow.
3. Expansion can be made only at the ends, which
    will tend to create supervision problems.
4. Lack of space in charging desk area.
5. Lack of space in workroom area.
6. Lack of foresight for needs of growing staff and
    growing collection.

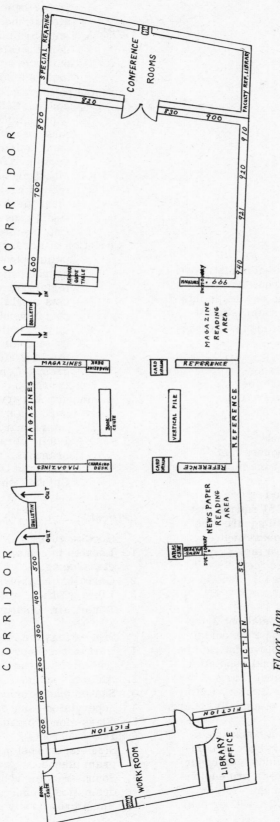

Floor plan
Proviso West High School Library
Hillside, Illinois

Loy Norrix
High School Library

Kalamazoo, Michigan

Presentation of plans
DOROTHY WERDEN
Librarian

Building data
Architect: Perkins & Will
                    Chicago, Illinois
Staff: 2 trained librarians
           1 clerk
Enrollment: 1,150
Location: Part of central unit—administrative
        and special services area. Surrounded
        by corridors. Possible expansion into
        speech and dramatics room, student
        center, meeting rooms (last two across
        corridor).
School library quarters
        Total space: 8,332 square feet
        Reading room: 3,600 square feet
        Conference room: 145 square feet
        Alcoves: 429 square feet
        Carrels: 120 square feet
        Classroom: 652 square feet
        Workroom-storage: 720 square feet
        Librarian's office: 150 square feet (included
            in above)
        Student center: 999 square feet
        Speech and dramatics: 1,151 square feet
        Audio-visual facilities: 516 square feet
        Storage-workroom: 300 square feet
        Preview rooms: 126 square feet
        Recording room: 90 square feet
        Teachers' curriculum library: None in
            building
Type of school: Senior high
Type of community: 80,000 population; 2 col-
        leges, 1 state university; 2 parochial
        high schools. High employment rate be-
        cause of large professional population
        and diversified industries. Largest in-
        dustries: paper and medicines. Cultur-
        ally minded, religious community. Large
        concentration of Dutch.
Type of student: No high school boundaries.
        Students come from anywhere in com-
        munity, mainly from middle- or upper-
        class families. Parents in professions
        or have steady employment. 76 per
        cent of students have I.Q. of 92 or over;

50 per cent of city's high school gradu-
        ates attend college.
Type of curriculum: Primary emphasis aca-
        demic. Offer commercial-cooperative,
        but little vocational emphasis. Industrial
        arts is a stepchild.
School philosophy: To develop each child ac-
        cording to his abilities to live usefully,
        happily, and successfully; education
        must provide unlimited opportunity for
        each individual to develop his maximum
        growth. To work with home and commu-
        nity agencies. Teacher stimulates intel-
        lectual curiosity, and provides environ-
        ment for discussion and resources for ˌ
        finding answers. Constant curriculum
        improvement.
Relation of library to school program: Basic
        philosophy—library a part of study re-
        source center. Wide resources and ma-
        terials for each student, whatever inter-
        ests or ability. Materials selected upon
        recommendations of faculty and guided
        by curriculum needs. Open to free use
        by students during study period, and be-
        fore and after school, as part of class
        group. Contains materials for all
        courses.
Community library resources: Since library is
        part of a system with a public library,
        interlibrary loans are easily obtained.
        Public library has bookmobile and 2
        branches. Additional libraries: Western
        Michigan University, Kalamazoo College,
        Upjohn Company.

Critique

Good features
1.   Located in center of school, close to office and
     classrooms.
2.   Carrels, conference room.
3.   Library office, workroom, storage.
4.   Decor, air conditioning.

Suggestions for improvement
1.   Part of resource center—has separate adminis-
     tration, few school-owned materials.
2.   Alcoves—subjects separated, hard to supervise.
3.   Sunken area—forms a retreat, hard to supervise.
4.   Supervision—sunken area, alcoves, stacks.
5.   Glass along corridor.
6.   Doors—9 exits.
7.   Size—no expansion, inadequate even for pro-
     gram planned.
8.   Sound—reading room, preview room, speech and
     dramatics room.
9.   Furniture—poorly planned.

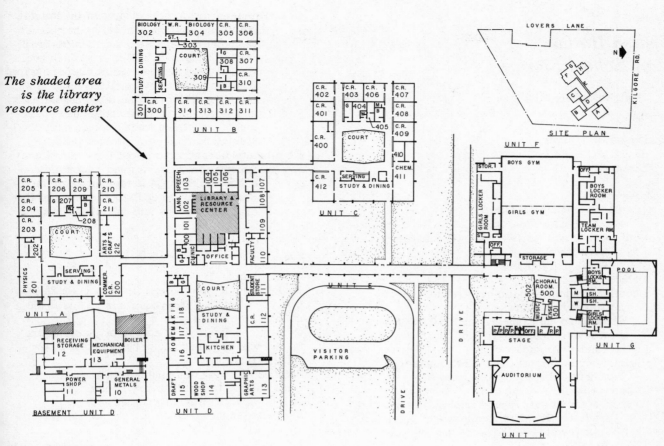

*The shaded area
is the library
resource center*

*General layout
Loy Norrix High School
Kalamazoo, Michigan*

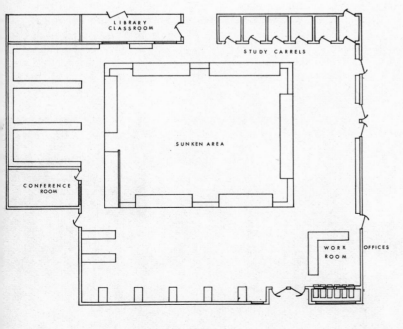

*Enlargement of library
and resource center area
Loy Norrix High School
Kalamazoo, Michigan*

Benton Harbor High School Library

Benton Harbor, Michigan

Presentation of plans
ELSIE SCHLEY
Librarian

Building data
Architect: Maurer & Maurer
South Bend, Indiana
Staff: 1-1/2 trained librarians (1 full time; 1 half time)
2 clerical helpers
Enrollment: 1,875
Location: Separate building, ground floor
School library quarters
Reading rooms, classroom: 120 by 68 feet
Workroom: 360 square feet
Storage: 180 square feet
Audio-visual facilities: 120 square feet
Teachers' library: 240 square feet
Type of school: Grades 9-12
Type of community: Fruit-farming, resort, and industrial. Most people work; many are comfortably well-to-do; few are very wealthy.
Type of student: 60-70 per cent say they want to go to college; some 40 per cent do.
Type of curriculum: Academic, general commercial, and some trade courses
School philosophy: To help each student find himself and develop to the fullest his own potential.

Relation of library to school program: Principal says, "Library should be the hub or the center so far as departmental teaching is concerned." This is still in evolution. Every department is clamoring for materials and service. Librarian is a member of the English department; asks and is permitted to attend other departmental meetings when textbooks and curricula are topics for consideration.
Community library resources: No elementary school libraries. A good junior high school library. A community college library of fairly good stock. A public library which is small and overcrowded.

Critique

Good features
1. Means rather than the end (library belongs to everyone because everyone feels he has made a contribution to it).
2. Quality construction, a good-looking structure. School will be proud of the building. Library Bureau furniture.
3. Small offices for staff members.
4. Card catalog to meet library needs.
5. Special shelving for encyclopedias.
6. Separate teachers' library.

Suggestions for improvement
1. Two-man exits to out-of-doors.
2. Doors between lobby and reading rooms should be stored rather than installed.
3. Door to magazine room should be nearer to main entry.
4. Doorway between two rooms should be wider.

Library addition
Benton Harbor High School
Benton Harbor, Michigan

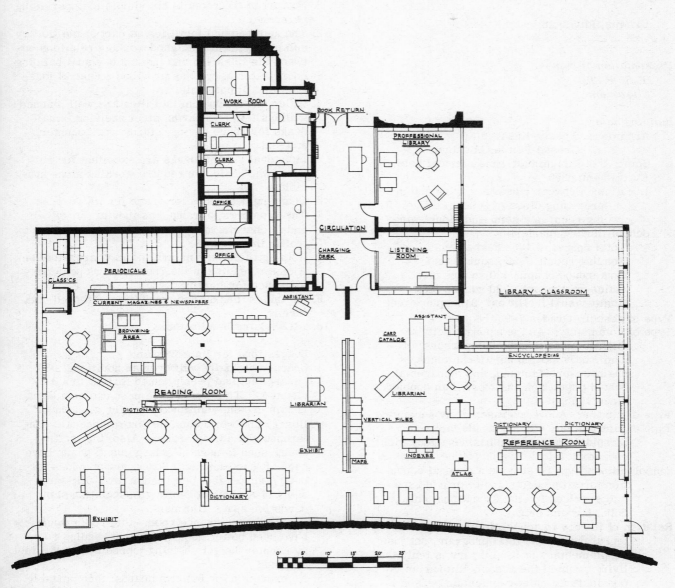

Floor plan
Benton Harbor High School Library
Benton Harbor, Michigan

Bryant Junior
High School Library

Livonia, Michigan

Presentation of plans
    B. K. PATE
    Librarian

Building data
    Architect: Wakely-Kushner
                Grosse Pointe, Michigan
    Staff: 1 librarian; half-time clerical help
    Enrollment: 850
    Location: Between classroom wing and special
        area wing close to general office. Read-
        ing room is a semi-individual wing.
    School library quarters
        Total space: 2,180 square feet
        Reading room: 1,588 square feet
        Conference room: 130 square feet
        Office-workroom: 220 square feet
        Audio-visual facilities: 242 square feet
Type of school: Grades 7-9
Type of community: An incorporated city of
    slightly more than 65,000 persons, pre-
    dominantly skilled auto technicians,
    business-professional, and managerial.
    School population has more than doubled
    since 1955.
Type of student: Above average; many superior
Type of curriculum: Chiefly academic; some
    technical training and business education
    courses.
School philosophy: To provide a general educa-
    tion for all students and to provide spe-
    cial services for the exceptional child,
    both slow and bright.
Relation of library to school program: An in-
    tegral part of the total program, not just
    supplementary to it. Library is truly the
    living room of the school. Librarian is
    considered a chief curriculum person to
    whom principal, counselors, and teachers
    turn for advice in curriculum making and
    execution. Librarian is on the general
    guidance committee, an ex officio mem-
    ber of each building curriculum, and on
    service committee.
Community library resources: Proper library
    resources are poor; however, all resi-
    dents of Wayne County are free to use
    any of the Wayne County Libraries of
    which there are several in the immedi-
    ate area.

Critique
    Good features
    1. Shape of reading room makes for a better flow
       of traffic and reduces traveling for the librarian.
    2. No part of the room is not visible to supervising
       personnel.
    3. The audio-visual facilities as part of the library
       unit have encouraged good working relations be-
       tween the librarian and the audio-visual building
       coordinator as well as provided a central loca-
       tion for all materials.
    4. Office and workroom facilities are well planned
       with built-in cupboards, steel shelving, small
       desks for space saving, sturdy work counter,
       and sink.
    5. Individual student desks are excellent for stu-
       dents who desire or require working alone at a
       table.
    6. Charging desk is tailor-made for its purpose.
    7. The two doors, arranged as they are at either
       end of charging desk, make for a smooth flow of
       traffic in and out.
    8. Both artificial and natural lighting are excellent.
       A meter reading of the rooms shows peak per-
       formance for lighting.
    9. All tables, desks, and counters are topped with
       formica.
    10. All shelving is adjustable.

    Suggestions for improvement
    1. Space—originally well over an additional 900
       square feet had been planned for the library
       quarters. This would have provided an adequate
       reading room, additional area for a teachers'
       library and workroom, and more adequate con-
       ference and storage room. Also, the traffic
       area, much in need of enlargement, would have
       been at least doubled. Space now provides for
       but 17 square feet per reader over-all—far
       short of American Library Association stan-
       dards for space allotment.
    2. Closed-in conference room—this room would
       have been better separated from reading room
       by counter-height shelving topped by about 3 feet
       of glass.
    3. No provision for bulletin boards; thus portable
       pegboards will have to be used.

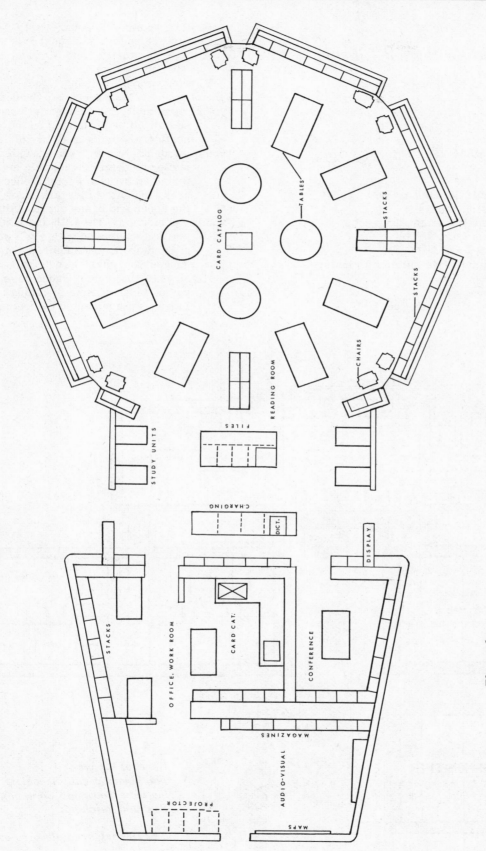

Floor plan
Bryant Junior High School Library
Livonia, Michigan

Mackinaw Middle School Library

Saginaw Township Community Schools
Saginaw, Michigan

Presentation of plans
LEONELLA JAMESON

Building data
    Architect: Caudill, Rowlett & Scott
           Houston, Texas
    Staff: 1 half-time librarian
        1 half-time clerk
    Enrollment: 650
    Location: Administrative suite of a cluster-
        type school
    School library quarters
        Total space: 970 square feet

Reading room: 970 square feet
Conference room: 513 square feet
Workroom, storage, and librarian's office:
    236 square feet
Viewing rooms: 84 square feet
Type of school: Middle school, Grades 5-8
Type of community: A residential area of 25.2
    square miles bordering on the west and
    north of the industrial city of Saginaw.
Type of student: Above average, with many su-
    perior students. Scholastic aptitude, de-
    termined by use of intelligence meas-
    ures, indicates they are skewed toward
    the upper end of the curve of distribution.
Type of curriculum: The fifth and sixth grades
    are self-contained with a full perimeter
    of handicraft, art, music, foreign lan-
    guages, and physical education. The
    seventh and eighth grades have a three-
    period block of time including foreign
    languages, augmented by special classes

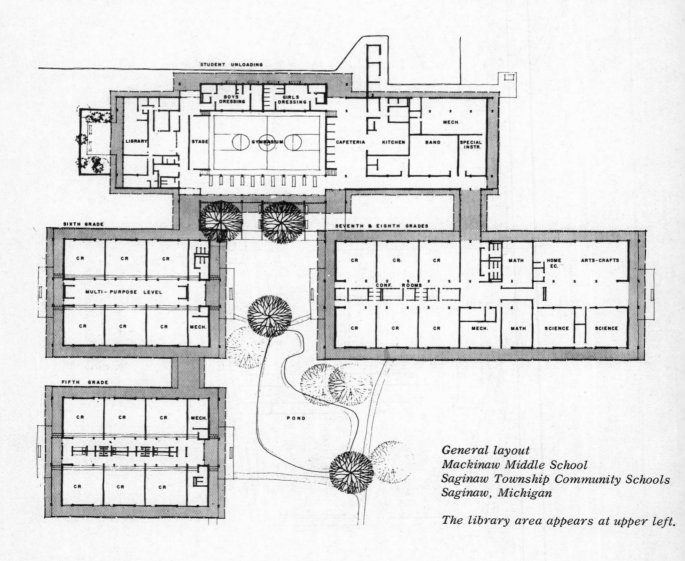

General layout
Mackinaw Middle School
Saginaw Township Community Schools
Saginaw, Michigan

The library area appears at upper left.

in science, music, mathematics, arts and crafts, and physical education.

School philosophy: "The middle schools seek to improve the transition between the self-contained classroom of the typical elementary school and the diverse environment with an emphasis upon individual responsibility which the student will encounter in the Saginaw Township High School."

Relation of library to school program: Library, as the instructional materials center of the school, brings together conveniently in one place all types of teaching and learning media. Materials are available freely to all faculty and students for use at home and anywhere in the building for varying lengths of time. Librarian, as instructional materials specialist, is primarily a consultant who helps to plan and carry through reading guidance and library instruction with teachers, integrating the library into classroom work.

Community library resources: No public library service in the township.

Critique

Good features
1. High ceiling is attractive. Ceiling lights are well placed.

2. Use of white in shelving, table tops, and trim gives a light, airy atmosphere.
3. Window-wall treatment gives vista of patio and the out-of-doors.
4. Use of Fiberglas shell chairs is in keeping with decor and color tones.
5. Vision panel between workroom and reading room provides a feeling of openness and allows for supervision.
6. Workroom counters provide an area where students or teachers may prepare tapes, charts, maps, and the like. Undercounter storage in the workroom is ample for the storage of smaller audio-visual equipment.
7. Vinyl wall covering provides adequate bulletin board space.
8. System-wide curriculum library is housed elsewhere in a centralized location for use by all teachers.

Suggestions for improvement
1. Instructional materials specialist should be scheduled full time for a school with an enrollment of this size.
2. Even with careful adaptation of library services to administrative and architectural concepts of the materials center, the reading room is too small. It is a definite possibility that an entire class (30 students) will need to use the center at one time.

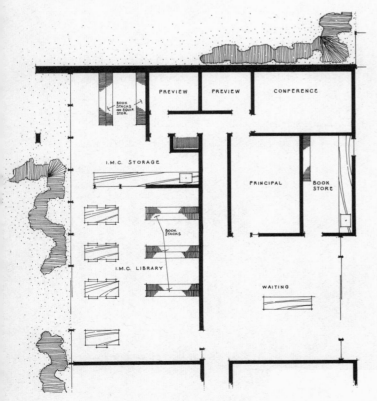

Enlargement of library area
Mackinaw Middle School
Saginaw Township Community Schools
Saginaw, Michigan

Published by the
American Library Association